ArtScroll Series®

THE LIPMAN EDITION

# מגילת אסתר
## עם תפילות ליל פורים

# THE MEGILLAH
## WITH THE COMPLETE PURIM EVENING SERVICES

### THE BOOK OF ESTHER
*Translation and anthologized commentary by*
Rabbi Meir Zlotowitz

### PURIM EVE PRAYERS
*Translation and anthologized commentary by*
Rabbi Nosson Scherman

*Published by*
Mesorah Publications, ltd

FIRST EDITION
First Impression . . . February 2003
Second Impression . . . February 2003
Third Impression . . . December 2003

Published and Distributed by
**MESORAH PUBLICATIONS, Ltd.**
4401 Second Avenue
Brooklyn, New York 11232

Distributed in Europe by
**LEHMANNS**
Unit E, Viking Industrial Park
Rolling Mill Road
Jarrow, Tyne & Wear NE32 3DP
England

Distributed in Australia & New Zealand by
**GOLDS WORLD OF JUDAICA**
3-13 William Street
Balaclava, Melbourne 3183
Victoria Australia

Distributed in Israel by
**SIFRIATI / A. GITLER — BOOKS**
6 Hayarkon Street
Bnei Brak 51127

Distributed in South Africa by
**KOLLEL BOOKSHOP**
Shop 8A Norwood Hypermarket
Norwood 2196, Johannesburg, South Africa

---

**THE ARTSCROLL SERIES® / LIPMAN EDITION**
**THE MEGILLAH WITH THE COMPLETE PURIM EVENING SERVICES**
© Copyright 2003, by MESORAH PUBLICATIONS, Ltd.
4401 Second Avenue / Brooklyn, N.Y. 11232 / (718) 921-9000 / www.artscroll.com

---

ISBN: 1-57819-717-1 (paperback)


Typography by Compuscribe at ArtScroll Studios, Ltd.

Printed in the United States of America by Noble Book Press
Bound by Sefercraft, Quality Bookbinders, Ltd. Brooklyn, N.Y.

# Dedication

In my view, the holiday of Purim represents a clear understanding of the hand of G-d in a special way. A queen is killed when the king becomes drunk, and, virtually overnight, a Jewish woman becomes queen in her place. Esther comes to serve as the protector of her people. The courageous acts of her cousin, Mordechai, and the vicious deeds of the king's advisor, Haman, occurred nearly 2400 years ago, but they represent character types that must be properly understood in this day and age. Purim to me represents a strong belief in Hashem and His deep caring for the Jewish people amid their trials, tribulations, and challenges.

The Lipman family has gained a better understanding of Purim through the guidance of our rabbis and teachers. This holiday evokes so many wonderful memories for us. RABBI SAMUEL FOX, formerly of Congregation Agudath Achim in Little Rock, Arkansas, first introduced me to the significance of the Purim story. Our learning continued with RABBI RAFAEL G. GROSSMAN, who served as the Senior Rabbi of Baron Hirsch Congregation in Memphis, Tennessee, for more than a quarter-century and as a president of the Rabbinical Council of America. His passion is contagious, and he instilled in us a great love of Torah. RABBI SOL ROTH of the Fifth Avenue Synagogue in New York, a former Rabbinical Council of America president, has inspired us to even further growth in our Jewish learning. His intellect, scholarship, and teaching are truly extraordinary and have made an indelible mark on our family. CANTOR JOSEPH MALOVANY'S passionate chanting has also helped us find new meaning in our sacred texts. Continuing the fight for equality for the Jewish people and all peoples is RABBI MARVIN HIER of the Simon Wiesenthal Center, whose friendship we cherish.

The end of the book of Esther obligates us to send gifts to the poor and to our friends, teaching us the importance of caring for all people. We are blessed with a beautiful family in which there is much caring for one another. My father, MR. MARK LIPMAN, of blessed memory, served as president of Congregation Agudath Achim in Little Rock, Arkansas, from 1948 through 1952. His memory continues to inspire us all. At age 93, my mother, MRS. BELLE ACKERMAN LIPMAN, reaffirms her passion for living with every adventurous step that she takes. Her energy and love of life can help us all achieve a newfound appreciation for the gift of life. I am thankful for the unwavering love and support of my sister, CAROL LIPMAN FRIEDMAN, and her husband, DR. HARRY FRIEDMAN.

When I think about our three sons, GUSTAVE, JOSHUA, and BENJAMIN, I can only think that "my cup runneth over" and that they are each such a blessing to more than just Barbara and me. Gus, and his wife, KAREN, constantly impress us with their drive for success and their sincere dedication to all that they hold dear. Josh's creativity and compassionate nature help us see the world through a clearer lens each and every day. We welcome into our family his wife, JOANNA GOLDMAN, whom he married in April 2003. Benjamin's thirst for learning and growth in Judaism inspire us to further pursue our own Jewish learning. We are so proud of Gus, Karen, Josh, Joanna, and Benjamin and all of their accomplishments.

Nothing could be complete without my wife, my *eishet chayil,* BARBARA K. LIPMAN. She has been the architect and superintendent of our family and of the development of our sons. Her courage in the face of adversity is an enormous source of encouragement for our entire family. As the book of Proverbs states, "many daughters have performed acts of valor, but you have surpassed them all."

May the Lipman edition of the book of Esther bring new and deeper meaning to your Purim celebration. *Chag Purim Sameach!*

Ira A. Lipman
*5764   December 2003*

# ❧ מנחה לחול לערב פורים ❧

**אַשְׁרֵי** יוֹשְׁבֵי בֵיתֶךָ, עוֹד יְהַלְלוּךָ סֶּלָה.[1] אַשְׁרֵי הָעָם שֶׁכָּכָה לּוֹ, אַשְׁרֵי הָעָם שֶׁיהוה אֱלֹהָיו.[2]

תהלים קמה

תְּהִלָּה לְדָוִד,

**אֲ**רוֹמִמְךָ* אֱלוֹהַי הַמֶּלֶךְ, וַאֲבָרְכָה שִׁמְךָ לְעוֹלָם וָעֶד.

**בְּ**כָל יוֹם אֲבָרְכֶךָּ,* וַאֲהַלְלָה שִׁמְךָ לְעוֹלָם וָעֶד.

**גָּ**דוֹל יהוה וּמְהֻלָּל מְאֹד, וְלִגְדֻלָּתוֹ אֵין חֵקֶר.*

**דּ**וֹר לְדוֹר יְשַׁבַּח מַעֲשֶׂיךָ, וּגְבוּרֹתֶיךָ יַגִּידוּ.

**הֲ**דַר כְּבוֹד הוֹדֶךָ, וְדִבְרֵי נִפְלְאֹתֶיךָ אָשִׂיחָה.

**וֶ**עֱזוּז נוֹרְאֹתֶיךָ יֹאמֵרוּ, וּגְדוּלָּתְךָ אֲסַפְּרֶנָּה.

**זֵ**כֶר רַב טוּבְךָ יַבִּיעוּ, וְצִדְקָתְךָ יְרַנֵּנוּ.

**חַ**נּוּן וְרַחוּם* יהוה, אֶרֶךְ אַפַּיִם וּגְדָל חָסֶד.

**טוֹ**ב יהוה לַכֹּל, וְרַחֲמָיו עַל כָּל מַעֲשָׂיו.

**יוֹ**דוּךָ יהוה כָּל מַעֲשֶׂיךָ, וַחֲסִידֶיךָ יְבָרְכוּכָה.

**כְּ**בוֹד מַלְכוּתְךָ יֹאמֵרוּ, וּגְבוּרָתְךָ יְדַבֵּרוּ.

---

## ❧ מִנְחָה לְחוֹל / WEEKDAY MINCHAH ❧

*Minchah* corresponds to the *tamid*, the daily afternoon offering in the Temple (*Berachos* 26b), so it is recited only when it was permissible to offer the *tamid*: from half an hour after midday until evening. The preferable time, however, is not before three and a half variable hours after midday (*Orach Chaim* 233:1). A variable hour is one twelfth of the time from sunrise to sunset.

### ❧ אַשְׁרֵי / Ashrei

The Talmud (*Berachos* 4b) teaches that the Sages assured a share in the World to Come to anyone who recites *Ashrei* properly three times a day. It has this special status because no other psalm possesses both of these virtues: (a) Beginning with the word אֲרוֹמִמְךָ (the first substantive word of the psalm), the initials of the psalm's respective verses follow the order of the *Aleph-Beis*; and (b) it contains the inspiring and reassuring testimony to God's mercy, פּוֹתֵחַ אֶת יָדֶךָ ..., *You open Your hand ...* As *Zohar*

teaches, the recitation of this verse is not a *request* that God open His hand for us; rather it is purely a recitation of praise.

Psalm 145 begins with the verse תְּהִלָּה לְדָוִד; the two preliminary verses, each beginning with the word אַשְׁרֵי, are affixed to תְּהִלָּה לְדָוִד for two reasons: (a) By expressing the idea that those who can dwell in God's house of prayer and service are praiseworthy, these verses set the stage for the succeeding psalms of praise, for we, the praiseworthy ones, are about to laud the God in Whose house we dwell; and (b) the word אַשְׁרֵי is found three times in these verses. This alludes to the Talmudic dictum that one who recites Psalm 145 three times a day is assured of a share in the World to Come; thus, those who do so are indeed אַשְׁרֵי, *praiseworthy*.

אֲרוֹמִמְךָ ... תְּהִלָּה — *A psalm ... I will exalt You.* Beginning with the word אֲרוֹמִמְךָ, the initials of the respective verses follow the

## ⚜ WEEKDAY MINCHAH FOR PURIM EVE ⚜

**אַשְׁרֵי** *Praiseworthy are those who dwell in Your house; may they always praise You, Selah!*[1] *Praiseworthy is the people for whom this is so, praiseworthy is the people whose God is HASHEM.*[2]

*Psalm 145*                    *A psalm of praise by David:*

**א** *I will exalt You,* * *my God the King,*
and I will bless Your Name forever and ever.

**ב** *Every day I will bless You,* *
and I will laud Your Name forever and ever.

**ג** *HASHEM is great and exceedingly lauded,*
and His greatness is beyond investigation.* *

**ד** *Each generation will praise Your deeds to the next*
and of Your mighty deeds they will tell;

**ה** *The splendrous glory of Your power*
and Your wondrous deeds I shall discuss.

**ו** *And of Your awesome power they will speak,*
and Your greatness I shall relate.

**ז** *A recollection of Your abundant goodness they will utter*
and of Your righteousness they will sing exultantly.

**ח** *Gracious and merciful* * *is HASHEM,*
slow to anger, and great in [bestowing] kindness.

**ט** *HASHEM is good to all; His mercies are on all His works.*

**י** *All Your works shall thank You, HASHEM,*
and Your devout ones will bless You.

**כ** *Of the glory of Your kingdom they will speak,*
and of Your power they will tell;

---

(1) *Psalms* 84:5. (2) 144:15.

---

order of the *Aleph-Beis.* According to Abudraham the *Aleph-Beis* structure symbolizes that we praise God with every sound available to the organs of speech. *Midrash Tadshei* records that the Psalmists and Sages used the *Aleph-Beis* formula in chapters that they wanted people to follow more easily or to memorize.

בְּכָל יוֹם אֲבָרְכֶךָ — *Every day I will bless You.* True, no mortal can pretend to know God's essence, but each of us *is* equipped to appreciate life, health, sustenance, sunshine, rainfall and so on. For these and their daily renewal, we give daily blessings (*Siach Yitzchak*).

וְלִגְדֻלָּתוֹ אֵין חֵקֶר — *And His greatness is beyond investigation.* Much though we may try, we can understand neither God's essence nor His ways through human analysis, for He is infinite. We *must* rely on the traditions that have come to us from earlier generations, as the next verse suggests (*Rama*).

חַנּוּן וְרַחוּם — *Gracious and Merciful.* Because God is *merciful,* He is אֶרֶךְ אַפַּיִם, *slow to anger,* so that punishment is delayed as long as possible to allow time for repentance. And because He is *gracious,* He is גְּדָל חָסֶד, *great in bestowing kindness* (*Siach Yitzchak*).

לְהוֹדִיעַ לִבְנֵי הָאָדָם גְּבוּרֹתָיו, וּכְבוֹד הֲדַר מַלְכוּתוֹ.

מַלְכוּתְךָ מַלְכוּת כָּל עֹלָמִים, וּמֶמְשַׁלְתְּךָ בְּכָל דּוֹר וָדֹר.

סוֹמֵךְ יהוה* לְכָל הַנֹּפְלִים, וְזוֹקֵף לְכָל הַכְּפוּפִים.

עֵינֵי כֹל אֵלֶיךָ יְשַׂבֵּרוּ,* וְאַתָּה נוֹתֵן לָהֶם אֶת אָכְלָם בְּעִתּוֹ.

פּוֹתֵחַ* אֶת יָדֶךָ,

Concentrate intently while reciting the verse, פּוֹתֵחַ.

וּמַשְׂבִּיעַ לְכָל חַי רָצוֹן.

צַדִּיק יהוה בְּכָל דְּרָכָיו, וְחָסִיד בְּכָל מַעֲשָׂיו.

קָרוֹב יהוה לְכָל קֹרְאָיו, לְכֹל אֲשֶׁר יִקְרָאֻהוּ בֶאֱמֶת.

רְצוֹן יְרֵאָיו יַעֲשֶׂה, וְאֶת שַׁוְעָתָם יִשְׁמַע וְיוֹשִׁיעֵם.

שׁוֹמֵר יהוה אֶת כָּל אֹהֲבָיו, וְאֵת כָּל הָרְשָׁעִים יַשְׁמִיד.

❖ תְּהִלַּת יהוה יְדַבֶּר פִּי,

וִיבָרֵךְ כָּל בָּשָׂר שֵׁם קָדְשׁוֹ לְעוֹלָם וָעֶד.

וַאֲנַחְנוּ נְבָרֵךְ יָהּ, מֵעַתָּה וְעַד עוֹלָם, הַלְלוּיָהּ.¹

The chazzan recites חֲצִי קַדִּישׁ:

יִתְגַּדַּל וְיִתְקַדַּשׁ שְׁמֵהּ רַבָּא. (.Cong – אָמֵן) בְּעָלְמָא דִּי בְרָא כִרְעוּתֵהּ. וְיַמְלִיךְ מַלְכוּתֵהּ, בְּחַיֵּיכוֹן וּבְיוֹמֵיכוֹן וּבְחַיֵּי דְכָל בֵּית יִשְׂרָאֵל, בַּעֲגָלָא וּבִזְמַן קָרִיב. וְאִמְרוּ: אָמֵן.

(.Cong – אָמֵן. יְהֵא שְׁמֵהּ רַבָּא מְבָרַךְ לְעָלַם וּלְעָלְמֵי עָלְמַיָּא.)

יְהֵא שְׁמֵהּ רַבָּא מְבָרַךְ לְעָלַם וּלְעָלְמֵי עָלְמַיָּא.

יִתְבָּרַךְ וְיִשְׁתַּבַּח וְיִתְפָּאַר וְיִתְרוֹמַם וְיִתְנַשֵּׂא וְיִתְהַדָּר וְיִתְעַלֶּה וְיִתְהַלָּל שְׁמֵהּ דְּקֻדְשָׁא בְּרִיךְ הוּא (.Cong – בְּרִיךְ הוּא) – לְעֵלָּא מִן כָּל בִּרְכָתָא וְשִׁירָתָא תֻּשְׁבְּחָתָא וְנֶחֱמָתָא, דַּאֲמִירָן בְּעָלְמָא. וְאִמְרוּ: אָמֵן. (.Cong – אָמֵן)

If less than seven members of the minyan are fasting, the Torah is not read and the service continues with Shemoneh Esrei (page 17).

סוֹמֵךְ ה' — HASHEM supports. No verse in Ashrei begins with a נ, because in the context of this verse that speaks of God supporting the fallen, the letter נ can be taken as an allusion to נְפִילָה, Israel's future downfall, ח"ו, and the Psalmist refused to use a letter that could suggest such tragedy. Nevertheless, knowing that downfalls would take place, the Psalmist comforted Israel by saying God supports all the fallen ones. This is an implied guarantee that even when a dreaded downfall happens, the people can look forward to His support (Berachos 4b). Maharsha comments that by omitting a direct mention of downfall, the Psalmist implies that even when Israel does suffer reverses, those reverses will never be complete. Rather, as the next verse declares, God will support the fallen.

עֵינֵי כֹל אֵלֶיךָ יְשַׂבֵּרוּ — The eyes of all look to You with hope. Even animals instinctively rely upon God for their sustenance [how

ל To inform human beings of His mighty deeds,
and the glorious splendor of His kingdom.

מ Your kingdom is a kingdom spanning all eternities,
and Your dominion is throughout every generation.

ס HASHEM supports* all the fallen ones
and straightens all the bent.

ע The eyes of all look to You with hope*
and You give them their food in its proper time;

פ You open* Your hand,                    Concentrate intently while reciting
and satisfy the desire of every living thing.       the verse "You open . . ."

צ Righteous is HASHEM in all His ways
and magnanimous in all His deeds.

ק HASHEM is close to all who call upon Him —
to all who call upon Him sincerely.

ר The will of those who fear Him He will do;
and their cry He will hear, and save them.

ש HASHEM protects all who love Him;
but all the wicked He will destroy.

ת ❖ May my mouth declare the praise of HASHEM
and may all flesh bless His Holy Name forever and ever.
We will bless God from this time and forever, Halleluyah![1]

The chazzan recites Half-Kaddish:

**יִתְגַּדַּל** May His great Name grow exalted and sanctified (Cong.– Amen.) in
the world that He created as He willed. May He give reign to His
kingship in your lifetimes and in your days, and in the lifetimes of the entire
Family of Israel, swiftly and soon. Now respond: Amen.

(Cong. – Amen. May His great Name be blessed forever and ever.)
May His great Name be blessed forever and ever.

Blessed, praised, glorified, exalted, extolled, mighty, upraised, and lauded
be the Name of the Holy One, Blessed is He (Cong.– Blessed is He) —
beyond any blessing and song, praise and consolation that are uttered in the
world. Now respond: Amen. (Cong.– Amen.)

If less than seven members of the minyan are fasting, the Torah is not read
and the service continues with Shemoneh Esrei (page 17).

---

(1) Psalms 115:18.

much more so should man recognize the beneficence of his Maker!] (Radak).

פּוֹתֵחַ — *[You] open. When reciting this verse, one must have in mind the translation of the words because this declaration of God's universal goodness is one of the two reasons the Sages required the thrice-daily recitation of this psalm. One who forgot to concentrate on the translation must recite the verse again (Tur and Shulchan Aruch 51:7). This verse should be recited with great joy at the knowledge that God cares for every creature (Yesod V'Shoresh HaAvodah).

**הוצאת ספר תורה**

From the moment the Ark is opened until the Torah is returned to it, one must conduct himself with the utmost respect, and avoid unnecessary conversation. It is commendable to kiss the Torah as it is carried to the *bimah* and back to the Ark.

THE ARK IS OPENED

All rise. Before the Torah is removed the congregation recites:

**וַיְהִי** בִּנְסֹעַ הָאָרֹן וַיֹּאמֶר מֹשֶׁה, קוּמָה יהוה וְיָפֻצוּ אֹיְבֶיךָ, וְיָנֻסוּ מְשַׂנְאֶיךָ מִפָּנֶיךָ.[1] כִּי מִצִּיּוֹן תֵּצֵא תוֹרָה, וּדְבַר יהוה מִירוּשָׁלָיִם.[2] בָּרוּךְ שֶׁנָּתַן תּוֹרָה לְעַמּוֹ יִשְׂרָאֵל בִּקְדֻשָּׁתוֹ.

**בְּרִיךְ** שְׁמֵהּ דְּמָרֵא עָלְמָא, בְּרִיךְ כִּתְרָךְ וְאַתְרָךְ. יְהֵא רְעוּתָךְ עִם עַמָּךְ יִשְׂרָאֵל לְעָלַם, וּפֻרְקַן יְמִינָךְ אַחֲזֵי לְעַמָּךְ בְּבֵית מַקְדְּשָׁךְ, וּלְאַמְטוּיֵי לָנָא מִטּוּב נְהוֹרָךְ, וּלְקַבֵּל צְלוֹתָנָא בְּרַחֲמִין. יְהֵא רַעֲוָא קֳדָמָךְ, דְּתוֹרִיךְ לָן חַיִּין בְּטִיבוּתָא, וְלֶהֱוֵי אֲנָא פְּקִידָא בְּגוֹ צַדִּיקַיָּא, לְמִרְחַם עֲלַי וּלְמִנְטַר יָתִי וְיָת כָּל דִּי לִי וְדִי לְעַמָּךְ יִשְׂרָאֵל. אַנְתְּ הוּא זָן לְכֹלָּא, וּמְפַרְנֵס לְכֹלָּא, אַנְתְּ הוּא שַׁלִּיט עַל כֹּלָּא. אַנְתְּ הוּא דְּשַׁלִּיט עַל מַלְכַיָּא, וּמַלְכוּתָא דִּילָךְ הִיא. אֲנָא עַבְדָּא דְּקֻדְשָׁא בְּרִיךְ הוּא, דְּסָגִידְנָא קַמֵּהּ וּמִקַּמָּא דִּיקַר אוֹרַיְתֵהּ בְּכָל עִדָּן וְעִדָּן. לָא עַל אֱנָשׁ רָחִיצְנָא, וְלָא עַל בַּר אֱלָהִין סָמִיכְנָא, אֶלָּא בֶּאֱלָהָא דִשְׁמַיָּא, דְּהוּא אֱלָהָא קְשׁוֹט, וְאוֹרַיְתֵהּ קְשׁוֹט, וּנְבִיאוֹהִי קְשׁוֹט, וּמַסְגֵּא לְמֶעְבַּד טַבְוָן וּקְשׁוֹט. בֵּהּ אֲנָא רָחִיץ, וְלִשְׁמֵהּ קַדִּישָׁא יַקִּירָא אֲנָא אֵמַר תֻּשְׁבְּחָן. יְהֵא רַעֲוָא קֳדָמָךְ, דְּתִפְתַּח לִבָּאִי בְּאוֹרַיְתָא, וְתַשְׁלִים מִשְׁאֲלִין דְּלִבָּאִי, וְלִבָּא דְכָל עַמָּךְ יִשְׂרָאֵל, לְטַב וּלְחַיִּין וְלִשְׁלָם. (אָמֵן.)

The *chazzan* accepts the Torah in his right arm.
He turns to the Ark and raises the Torah slightly as he bows and recites:

**גַּדְּלוּ לַיהוה אִתִּי וּנְרוֹמְמָה שְׁמוֹ יַחְדָּו.**[3]

Congregation responds:

**לְךָ** יהוה הַגְּדֻלָּה וְהַגְּבוּרָה וְהַתִּפְאֶרֶת וְהַנֵּצַח וְהַהוֹד, כִּי כֹל בַּשָּׁמַיִם וּבָאָרֶץ, לְךָ יהוה הַמַּמְלָכָה וְהַמִּתְנַשֵּׂא לְכֹל לְרֹאשׁ.[4] רוֹמְמוּ יהוה אֱלֹהֵינוּ, וְהִשְׁתַּחֲווּ לַהֲדֹם רַגְלָיו, קָדוֹשׁ הוּא. רוֹמְמוּ יהוה אֱלֹהֵינוּ, וְהִשְׁתַּחֲווּ לְהַר קָדְשׁוֹ, כִּי קָדוֹשׁ יהוה אֱלֹהֵינוּ.[5]

**אַב** הָרַחֲמִים, הוּא יְרַחֵם עַם עֲמוּסִים, וְיִזְכֹּר בְּרִית אֵיתָנִים, וְיַצִּיל נַפְשׁוֹתֵינוּ מִן הַשָּׁעוֹת הָרָעוֹת, וְיִגְעַר בְּיֵצֶר הָרָע מִן הַנְּשׂוּאִים, וְיָחֹן אוֹתָנוּ לִפְלֵיטַת עוֹלָמִים, וִימַלֵּא מִשְׁאֲלוֹתֵינוּ בְּמִדָּה טוֹבָה יְשׁוּעָה וְרַחֲמִים.

## REMOVAL OF THE TORAH FROM THE ARK

From the moment the Ark is opened until the Torah is returned to it, one must conduct himself with the utmost respect, and avoid unnecessary conversation. It is commendable to kiss the Torah as it is carried to the *bimah* and back to the Ark.

### THE ARK IS OPENED

All rise. Before the Torah is removed the congregation recites:

**וַיְהִי** *When the Ark would travel, Moses would say, "Arise, HASHEM, and let Your foes be scattered, let those who hate You flee from You."*[1] *For from Zion the Torah will come forth and the word of HASHEM from Jerusalem.*[2] *Blessed is He Who gave the Torah to His people Israel in His holiness.*

**בְּרִיךְ** *Blessed is the Name of the Master of the universe, blessed is Your crown and Your place. May Your favor remain with Your people Israel forever; may You display the salvation of Your right hand to Your people in Your Holy Temple, to benefit us with the goodness of Your luminescence and to accept our prayers with mercy. May it be Your will that You extend our lives with goodness and that I be numbered among the righteous; that You have mercy on me and protect me, all that is mine and that is Your people Israel's. It is You Who nourishes all and sustains all; You control everything. It is You Who controls kings, and kingship is Yours. I am a servant of the Holy One, Blessed is He, and I prostrate myself before Him and before the glory of His Torah at all times. Not in any man do I put trust, nor on any angel do I rely — only on the God of heaven Who is the God of truth, Whose Torah is truth and Whose prophets are true and Who acts liberally with kindness and truth. In Him do I trust, and to His glorious and holy Name do I declare praises. May it be Your will that You open my heart to the Torah and that You fulfill the wishes of my heart and the heart of Your entire people Israel for good, for life, and for peace. (Amen.)*

The *chazzan* accepts the Torah in his right arm.
He turns to the Ark and raises the Torah slightly as he bows and recites:

### Declare the greatness of HASHEM with me, and let us exalt His Name together.[3]

Congregation responds:

**לְךָ** *Yours, HASHEM, is the greatness, the strength, the splendor, the triumph, and the glory; even everything in heaven and earth; Yours, HASHEM, is the kingdom, and the sovereignty over every leader.*[4] *Exalt HASHEM, our God, and bow at His footstool; He is Holy! Exalt HASHEM, our God, and bow to His holy mountain; for holy is HASHEM, our God.*[5]

**אַב** *May the Father of compassion have mercy on the people that is borne by Him, and may He remember the covenant of the spiritually mighty. May He rescue our souls from the bad times, and upbraid the Evil Inclination to leave those borne by Him, graciously make us an eternal remnant, and fulfill our requests in good measure, for salvation and mercy.*

---

(1) *Numbers* 10:35. (2) *Isaiah* 2:3. (3) *Psalms* 34:4. (4) *I Chronicles* 29:11. (5) *Psalms* 99:5,9.

The *gabbai* uses the following formula to call a *Kohen* to the Torah:

**וְתִגָּלֶה** וְתֵרָאֶה מַלְכוּתוֹ עָלֵינוּ בִּזְמַן קָרוֹב, וְיָחֹן פְּלֵיטָתֵנוּ וּפְלֵיטַת עַמּוֹ בֵּית יִשְׂרָאֵל לְחֵן וּלְחֶסֶד וּלְרַחֲמִים וּלְרָצוֹן. וְנֹאמַר: אָמֵן. הַכֹּל הָבוּ גֹדֶל לֵאלֹהֵינוּ וּתְנוּ כָבוֹד לַתּוֹרָה. כֹּהֵן° קְרָב, יַעֲמֹד (name) בֶּן (father's name) הַכֹּהֵן.

°If no *Kohen* is present, the *gabbai* says:

„אֵין כָּאן כֹּהֵן, יַעֲמֹד (name) בֶּן (father's name) יִשְׂרָאֵל (לֵוִי) בִּמְקוֹם כֹּהֵן."

בָּרוּךְ שֶׁנָּתַן תּוֹרָה לְעַמּוֹ יִשְׂרָאֵל בִּקְדֻשָּׁתוֹ. (תּוֹרַת יהוה תְּמִימָה מְשִׁיבַת נָפֶשׁ, עֵדוּת יהוה נֶאֱמָנָה מַחְכִּימַת פֶּתִי. פִּקּוּדֵי יהוה יְשָׁרִים מְשַׂמְּחֵי לֵב, מִצְוַת יהוה בָּרָה מְאִירַת עֵינָיִם.¹ יהוה עֹז לְעַמּוֹ יִתֵּן, יהוה יְבָרֵךְ אֶת עַמּוֹ בַשָּׁלוֹם.² הָאֵל תָּמִים דַּרְכּוֹ, אִמְרַת יהוה צְרוּפָה, מָגֵן הוּא לְכֹל הַחוֹסִים בּוֹ.³)

Congregation, then *gabbai:*

**וְאַתֶּם הַדְּבֵקִים בַּיהוה אֱלֹהֵיכֶם, חַיִּים כֻּלְּכֶם הַיּוֹם.⁴**

### ברכות התורה

The reader shows the *oleh* (person called to the Torah) the place in the Torah. The *oleh* touches the Torah with a corner of his *tallis,* or the belt or mantle of the Torah, and kisses it. He then begins the blessing, bowing at בָּרְכוּ, and straightening up at ה'.

**בָּרְכוּ אֶת יהוה הַמְבֹרָךְ.**

Congregation, followed by *oleh,* responds, bowing at בָּרוּךְ, and straightening up at ה'.

**בָּרוּךְ יהוה הַמְבֹרָךְ לְעוֹלָם וָעֶד.**

*Oleh* continues:

**בָּרוּךְ** אַתָּה יהוה אֱלֹהֵינוּ מֶלֶךְ הָעוֹלָם, אֲשֶׁר בָּחַר בָּנוּ מִכָּל הָעַמִּים, וְנָתַן לָנוּ אֶת תּוֹרָתוֹ. בָּרוּךְ אַתָּה יהוה, נוֹתֵן הַתּוֹרָה. (.Cong– אָמֵן.)

After his Torah portion has been read, the *oleh* recites:

**בָּרוּךְ** אַתָּה יהוה אֱלֹהֵינוּ מֶלֶךְ הָעוֹלָם, אֲשֶׁר נָתַן לָנוּ תּוֹרַת אֱמֶת, וְחַיֵּי עוֹלָם נָטַע בְּתוֹכֵנוּ. בָּרוּךְ אַתָּה יהוה, נוֹתֵן הַתּוֹרָה. (.Cong– אָמֵן.)

### קריאת התורה

Upon reaching the words in bold type, the reader pauses.
The congregation recites these verses, which are then repeated by the reader.

שמות לב:יא-יד; לד:י-י

כהן – וַיְחַל מֹשֶׁה אֶת־פְּנֵי יהוה אֱלֹהָיו וַיֹּאמֶר לָמָה יהוה יֶחֱרֶה אַפְּךָ בְּעַמֶּךָ אֲשֶׁר הוֹצֵאתָ מֵאֶרֶץ מִצְרַיִם בְּכֹחַ גָּדוֹל וּבְיָד חֲזָקָה: לָמָה יֹאמְרוּ מִצְרַיִם לֵאמֹר בְּרָעָה הוֹצִיאָם לַהֲרֹג אֹתָם בֶּהָרִים וּלְכַלֹּתָם מֵעַל פְּנֵי הָאֲדָמָה שׁוּב מֵחֲרוֹן אַפֶּךָ וְהִנָּחֵם עַל־הָרָעָה לְעַמֶּךָ:

The *gabbai* uses the following formula to call a *Kohen* to the Torah:

**וְתִגָּלֶה** *And may His Kingship over us be revealed and become visible soon, and may He be gracious to our remnant and the remnant of His people the Family of Israel, for graciousness, kindness, mercy, and favor. And let us respond, Amen. All of you ascribe greatness to our God and give honor to the Torah. Kohen,* ° *approach. Stand* (name) *son of* (father's name) *the Kohen.*

---

°If no *Kohen* is present, the *gabbai* says:
*"There is no Kohen present, stand* (name) *son of* (father's name)
*an Israelite (Levite) in place of the Kohen."*

---

*Blessed is He Who gave the Torah to His people Israel in His holiness. (The Torah of* HASHEM *is perfect, restoring the soul; the testimony of* HASHEM *is trustworthy, making the simple one wise. The orders of* HASHEM *are upright, gladdening the heart; the command of* HASHEM *is clear, enlightening the eyes.* [1] HASHEM *will give might to His people;* HASHEM *will bless His people with peace.* [2] *The God Whose way is perfect, the promise of* HASHEM *is flawless, He is a shield for all who take refuge in Him.* [3])

Congregation, then *gabbai:*

**You who cling to HASHEM, your God, you are all alive today.** [4]

### BLESSINGS OF THE TORAH

The reader shows the *oleh* (person called to the Torah) the place in the Torah. The *oleh* touches the Torah with a corner of his *tallis,* or the belt or mantle of the Torah, and kisses it. He then begins the blessing, bowing at *"Bless,"* and straightening up at *"*HASHEM.*"*

### Bless HASHEM, the blessed One.

Congregation, followed by *oleh,* responds, bowing at "Blessed,"
and straightening up at "HASHEM."

*Blessed is* HASHEM, *the blessed One, for all eternity.*

Oleh continues:

**בָּרוּךְ** *Blessed are You,* HASHEM, *our God, King of the universe, Who selected us from all the peoples and gave us His Torah. Blessed are You,* HASHEM, *Giver of the Torah.*                    (Cong. – *Amen.*)

After his Torah portion has been read, the *oleh* recites:

**בָּרוּךְ** *Blessed are You,* HASHEM, *our God, King of the universe, Who gave us the Torah of truth and implanted eternal life within us. Blessed are You,* HASHEM, *Giver of the Torah.*                    (Cong. – *Amen.*)

### READING OF THE TORAH

Upon reaching the words in bold type, the reader pauses.
The congregation recites these verses, which are then repeated by the reader.

*Exodus 32:11-14; 34:1-10*

Kohen — *Moses pleaded before* HASHEM, *his God, and said, "Why,* HASHEM, *should Your anger flare up against Your people, whom You have taken out of the land of Egypt, with great power and a strong hand? Why should Egypt say the following: 'With evil intent did He take them out, to kill them in the mountains and to annihilate them from the face of the earth'?* **Relent from Your flaring anger and reconsider regarding the evil against Your people.**

---

(1) *Psalms* 19:8-9. (2) 29:11. (3) 18:31. (4) *Deuteronomy* 4:4.

זְכֹר לְאַבְרָהָם לְיִצְחָק וּלְיִשְׂרָאֵל עֲבָדֶיךָ אֲשֶׁר נִשְׁבַּעְתָּ לָהֶם בָּךְ וַתְּדַבֵּר אֲלֵהֶם אַרְבֶּה אֶת־זַרְעֲכֶם כְּכוֹכְבֵי הַשָּׁמָיִם וְכָל־הָאָרֶץ הַזֹּאת אֲשֶׁר אָמַרְתִּי אֶתֵּן לְזַרְעֲכֶם וְנָחֲלוּ לְעֹלָם: וַיִּנָּחֶם יהוה עַל־הָרָעָה אֲשֶׁר דִּבֶּר לַעֲשׂוֹת לְעַמּוֹ:

לוי – וַיֹּאמֶר יהוה אֶל־מֹשֶׁה פְּסָל־לְךָ שְׁנֵי־לֻחֹת אֲבָנִים כָּרִאשֹׁנִים וְכָתַבְתִּי עַל־הַלֻּחֹת אֶת־הַדְּבָרִים אֲשֶׁר הָיוּ עַל־הַלֻּחֹת הָרִאשֹׁנִים אֲשֶׁר שִׁבַּרְתָּ: וֶהְיֵה נָכוֹן לַבֹּקֶר וְעָלִיתָ בַבֹּקֶר אֶל־הַר סִינַי וְנִצַּבְתָּ לִי שָׁם עַל־רֹאשׁ הָהָר: וְאִישׁ לֹא־יַעֲלֶה עִמָּךְ וְגַם־אִישׁ אַל־יֵרָא בְּכָל־הָהָר גַּם־הַצֹּאן וְהַבָּקָר אַל־יִרְעוּ אֶל־מוּל הָהָר הַהוּא:

מפטיר – וַיִּפְסֹל שְׁנֵי־לֻחֹת אֲבָנִים כָּרִאשֹׁנִים וַיַּשְׁכֵּם מֹשֶׁה בַבֹּקֶר וַיַּעַל אֶל־הַר סִינַי כַּאֲשֶׁר צִוָּה יהוה אֹתוֹ וַיִּקַּח בְּיָדוֹ שְׁנֵי לֻחֹת אֲבָנִים: וַיֵּרֶד יהוה בֶּעָנָן וַיִּתְיַצֵּב עִמּוֹ שָׁם וַיִּקְרָא בְשֵׁם יהוה: וַיַּעֲבֹר יהוה עַל־פָּנָיו וַיִּקְרָא יהוה ׀ יהוה אֵל רַחוּם וְחַנּוּן אֶרֶךְ אַפַּיִם וְרַב־חֶסֶד וֶאֱמֶת: נֹצֵר חֶסֶד לָאֲלָפִים נֹשֵׂא עָוֺן וָפֶשַׁע וְחַטָּאָה וְנַקֵּה לֹא יְנַקֶּה פֹּקֵד ׀ עֲוֺן אָבוֹת עַל־בָּנִים וְעַל־בְּנֵי בָנִים עַל־שִׁלֵּשִׁים וְעַל־רִבֵּעִים: וַיְמַהֵר מֹשֶׁה וַיִּקֹּד אַרְצָה וַיִּשְׁתָּחוּ: וַיֹּאמֶר אִם־נָא מָצָאתִי חֵן בְּעֵינֶיךָ אֲדֹנָי יֵלֶךְ־נָא אֲדֹנָי בְּקִרְבֵּנוּ כִּי עַם־קְשֵׁה־עֹרֶף הוּא וְסָלַחְתָּ לַעֲוֺנֵנוּ וּלְחַטָּאתֵנוּ וּנְחַלְתָּנוּ: וַיֹּאמֶר הִנֵּה אָנֹכִי כֹּרֵת בְּרִית נֶגֶד כָּל־עַמְּךָ אֶעֱשֶׂה נִפְלָאֹת אֲשֶׁר לֹא־נִבְרְאוּ בְכָל־הָאָרֶץ וּבְכָל־הַגּוֹיִם וְרָאָה כָל־הָעָם אֲשֶׁר־אַתָּה בְקִרְבּוֹ אֶת־מַעֲשֵׂה יהוה כִּי־נוֹרָא הוּא אֲשֶׁר אֲנִי עֹשֶׂה עִמָּךְ:

**הגבהה וגלילה**

The Torah is raised for all to see.
Each person looks at the Torah and recites aloud:

וְזֹאת הַתּוֹרָה אֲשֶׁר שָׂם מֹשֶׁה לִפְנֵי בְּנֵי יִשְׂרָאֵל,¹ עַל פִּי יהוה בְּיַד מֹשֶׁה.²

Some add:

עֵץ חַיִּים הִיא לַמַּחֲזִיקִים בָּהּ, וְתֹמְכֶיהָ מְאֻשָּׁר.³ דְּרָכֶיהָ דַרְכֵי נֹעַם, וְכָל נְתִיבוֹתֶיהָ שָׁלוֹם.⁴ אֹרֶךְ יָמִים בִּימִינָהּ, בִּשְׂמֹאלָהּ עֹשֶׁר וְכָבוֹד.⁵ יהוה חָפֵץ לְמַעַן צִדְקוֹ, יַגְדִּיל תּוֹרָה וְיַאְדִּיר.⁶

Remember for the sake of Abraham, Isaac, and Israel, Your servants, to whom You swore by Yourself, and You told them, 'I shall increase your offspring like the stars of heaven, and this entire land of which I spoke, I shall give to your offspring and it shall be their heritage forever.'" HASHEM reconsidered regarding the evil that He declared He would do to His people.

Levi — HASHEM said to Moses, "Carve for yourself two stone Tablets like the first ones, and I shall inscribe on the Tablets the words that were on the first Tablets, which you shattered. Be prepared in the morning; ascend Mount Sinai in the morning and stand by Me there on the mountaintop. No man may ascend with you nor may anyone be seen on the entire mountain. Even the flock and the cattle may not graze facing that mountain."

Maftir — So he carved out two stone Tablets like the first ones. Moses arose early in the morning and ascended to Mount Sinai, as HASHEM had commanded him, and he took two stone Tablets in his hand. HASHEM descended in a cloud and stood with him there, and He called out with the Name HASHEM. HASHEM passed before him and proclaimed: **HASHEM, HASHEM, God, Compassionate and Gracious, Slow to Anger, and Abundant in Kindness and Truth; Preserver of Kindness for thousands of generations, Forgiver of Iniquity, Willful Sin, and Error, and Who Cleanses** — but does not cleanse completely, recalling the iniquity of parents upon children and grandchildren, to the third and fourth generations. Moses hastened to bow his head toward the ground and prostrate himself. He said, "If I have now found favor in Your eyes, my Lord, let my Lord go among us — for it is a stiff-necked people, **and You shall forgive our iniquity and error, and make us Your heritage."** He said, "Behold! I seal a covenant: Before your entire people I shall make distinctions such as have never been created in the entire world and among all the nations; and the entire people among whom you are will see the work of HASHEM — which is awesome — that I am about to do with you."

### HAGBAHAH AND GELILAH

The Torah is raised for all to see.
Each person looks at the Torah and recites aloud:

**This is the Torah that Moses placed before the Children of Israel,**[1] **upon the command of HASHEM, through Moses' hand.**[2]

Some add:

עֵץ It is a tree of life for those who grasp it, and its supporters are praiseworthy.[3] Its ways are ways of pleasantness and all its paths are peace.[4] Lengthy days are at its right; at its left are wealth and honor.[5] HASHEM desired, for the sake of its [Israel's] righteousness, that the Torah be made great and glorious.[6]

---

(1) *Deuteronomy* 4:44. (2) *Numbers* 9:23.
(3) *Proverbs* 3:18. (4) 3:17. (5) 3:16. (6) *Isaiah* 42:21.

## ברכה קודם ההפטרה

After the Torah Scroll has been wound, tied, and covered,
the *oleh* for *Maftir* recites the blessing before the *Haftarah*.

**בָּרוּךְ** אַתָּה יהוה אֱלֹהֵינוּ מֶלֶךְ הָעוֹלָם, אֲשֶׁר בָּחַר בִּנְבִיאִים
טוֹבִים, וְרָצָה בְדִבְרֵיהֶם הַנֶּאֱמָרִים בֶּאֱמֶת, בָּרוּךְ אַתָּה
יהוה, הַבּוֹחֵר בַּתּוֹרָה וּבְמֹשֶׁה עַבְדּוֹ, וּבְיִשְׂרָאֵל עַמּוֹ, וּבִנְבִיאֵי
הָאֱמֶת וָצֶדֶק: (אָמֵן. – Cong.)

ישעיה נה:ו-נו:ח

**דִּרְשׁוּ** יהוה בְּהִמָּצְאוֹ קְרָאֻהוּ בִּהְיוֹתוֹ קָרוֹב: יַעֲזֹב רָשָׁע דַּרְכּוֹ
וְאִישׁ אָוֶן מַחְשְׁבֹתָיו וְיָשֹׁב אֶל־יהוה וִירַחֲמֵהוּ וְאֶל־
אֱלֹהֵינוּ כִּי־יַרְבֶּה לִסְלוֹחַ: כִּי לֹא מַחְשְׁבוֹתַי מַחְשְׁבוֹתֵיכֶם וְלֹא
דַרְכֵיכֶם דְּרָכָי נְאֻם יהוה: כִּי־גָבְהוּ שָׁמַיִם מֵאָרֶץ כֵּן גָּבְהוּ דְרָכַי
מִדַּרְכֵיכֶם וּמַחְשְׁבֹתַי מִמַּחְשְׁבֹתֵיכֶם: כִּי כַּאֲשֶׁר יֵרֵד הַגֶּשֶׁם וְהַשֶּׁלֶג
מִן־הַשָּׁמַיִם וְשָׁמָּה לֹא יָשׁוּב כִּי אִם־הִרְוָה אֶת־הָאָרֶץ וְהוֹלִידָהּ
וְהִצְמִיחָהּ וְנָתַן זֶרַע לַזֹּרֵעַ וְלֶחֶם לָאֹכֵל: כֵּן יִהְיֶה דְבָרִי אֲשֶׁר יֵצֵא
מִפִּי לֹא־יָשׁוּב אֵלַי רֵיקָם כִּי אִם־עָשָׂה אֶת־אֲשֶׁר חָפַצְתִּי וְהִצְלִיחַ
אֲשֶׁר שְׁלַחְתִּיו: כִּי־בְשִׂמְחָה תֵצֵאוּ וּבְשָׁלוֹם תּוּבָלוּן הֶהָרִים
וְהַגְּבָעוֹת יִפְצְחוּ לִפְנֵיכֶם רִנָּה וְכָל־עֲצֵי הַשָּׂדֶה יִמְחֲאוּ־כָף: תַּחַת
הַנַּעֲצוּץ יַעֲלֶה בְרוֹשׁ וְתַחַת הַסִּרְפַּד יַעֲלֶה הֲדַס וְהָיָה לַיהוה לְשֵׁם
לְאוֹת עוֹלָם לֹא יִכָּרֵת: כֹּה אָמַר יהוה שִׁמְרוּ מִשְׁפָּט וַעֲשׂוּ צְדָקָה
כִּי־קְרוֹבָה יְשׁוּעָתִי לָבוֹא וְצִדְקָתִי לְהִגָּלוֹת: אַשְׁרֵי אֱנוֹשׁ יַעֲשֶׂה־
זֹּאת וּבֶן־אָדָם יַחֲזִיק בָּהּ שֹׁמֵר שַׁבָּת מֵחַלְּלוֹ וְשֹׁמֵר יָדוֹ מֵעֲשׂוֹת כָּל־
רָע: וְאַל־יֹאמַר בֶּן־הַנֵּכָר הַנִּלְוָה אֶל־יהוה לֵאמֹר הַבְדֵּל יַבְדִּילַנִי
יהוה מֵעַל עַמּוֹ וְאַל־יֹאמַר הַסָּרִיס הֵן אֲנִי עֵץ יָבֵשׁ: כִּי־כֹה | אָמַר
יהוה לַסָּרִיסִים אֲשֶׁר יִשְׁמְרוּ אֶת־שַׁבְּתוֹתַי וּבָחֲרוּ בַּאֲשֶׁר חָפָצְתִּי
וּמַחֲזִיקִים בִּבְרִיתִי: וְנָתַתִּי לָהֶם בְּבֵיתִי וּבְחוֹמֹתַי יָד וָשֵׁם טוֹב מִבָּנִים
וּמִבָּנוֹת שֵׁם עוֹלָם אֶתֶּן־לוֹ אֲשֶׁר לֹא יִכָּרֵת: וּבְנֵי הַנֵּכָר הַנִּלְוִים עַל־
יהוה לְשָׁרְתוֹ וּלְאַהֲבָה אֶת־שֵׁם יהוה לִהְיוֹת לוֹ לַעֲבָדִים כָּל־שֹׁמֵר
שַׁבָּת מֵחַלְּלוֹ וּמַחֲזִיקִים בִּבְרִיתִי: וַהֲבִיאוֹתִים אֶל־הַר קָדְשִׁי
וְשִׂמַּחְתִּים בְּבֵית תְּפִלָּתִי עוֹלֹתֵיהֶם וְזִבְחֵיהֶם לְרָצוֹן עַל־מִזְבְּחִי כִּי
בֵיתִי בֵּית־תְּפִלָּה יִקָּרֵא לְכָל־הָעַמִּים: נְאֻם אֲדֹנָי יֱהֹוִה מְקַבֵּץ נִדְחֵי
יִשְׂרָאֵל עוֹד אֲקַבֵּץ עָלָיו לְנִקְבָּצָיו:

## BLESSING BEFORE THE HAFTARAH

After the Torah Scroll has been wound, tied, and covered,
the *oleh* for *Maftir* recites the blessing before the *Haftarah*.

בָּרוּךְ *Blessed are You, HASHEM, our God, King of the universe, Who has chosen good prophets and was pleased with their words that were uttered with truth. Blessed are You, HASHEM, Who chooses the Torah; Moses, His servant; Israel, His people; and the prophets of truth and righteousness.* (Cong.— Amen.)

Isaiah 55:6-56:8

דִּרְשׁוּ *Seek HASHEM when He can be found; call upon Him when He is near.*

*Let the wicked one forsake his way and the iniquitous man his thoughts; let him return to HASHEM and He will show him mercy; to our God, for He is abundantly forgiving. For My thoughts are not your thoughts and your ways are not My ways — the word of HASHEM. As high as the heavens over the earth, so are My ways higher than your ways, and My thoughts than your thoughts. For just as the rain and snow descend from heaven and will not return there, rather it waters the earth and causes it to produce and sprout, and gives seed to the sower and food to the eater, so shall be My word that emanates from My mouth, it will not return to Me unfulfilled unless it will have accomplished what I desired and brought success where I sent it. For in gladness shall you go out and in peace shall you arrive, the mountains and hills will break out in glad song before you, and all the trees of the field will clap hands. In place of the thornbush, a cypress will rise; and in place of the nettle, a myrtle will rise. This will be a monument to HASHEM, an eternal sign never to be cut down.*

*Thus said HASHEM: Observe justice and perform righteousness, for My salvation is soon to come and My righteousness to be revealed. Praiseworthy is the man who does this and the person who grasps it tightly: who guards the Sabbath against desecrating it and guards his hand against doing any evil.*

*Let not the foreigner, who has joined himself to HASHEM, speak, saying, "HASHEM will utterly separate me from His people"; and let not the barren one say, "Behold I am a shriveled tree." For thus said HASHEM to the barren ones who observe My Sabbaths and choose what I desire, and grasp My covenant tightly: In My house and within My walls I will give them a place of honor and renown, which is better than sons and daughters; eternal renown will I give them, which will never be terminated. And the foreigners who join themselves to HASHEM to serve Him and to love the Name of HASHEM to become servants unto Him, all who guard the Sabbath against desecration, and grasp My covenant tightly — I will bring them to My holy mountain, and I will gladden them in My house of prayer; their elevation-offerings and their feast-offerings will find favor on My Altar, for My House will be called a house of prayer for all the peoples. The word of my Lord, HASHEM/ELOHIM, Who gathers in the dispersed of Israel: I shall gather to him even more than those already gathered to him.*

After the *Haftarah* is read, the *oleh* recites the following blessings:

**בָּרוּךְ** אַתָּה יהוה אֱלֹהֵינוּ מֶלֶךְ הָעוֹלָם, צוּר כָּל הָעוֹלָמִים, צַדִּיק בְּכָל הַדּוֹרוֹת, הָאֵל הַנֶּאֱמָן הָאוֹמֵר וְעֹשֶׂה, הַמְדַבֵּר וּמְקַיֵּם, שֶׁכָּל דְּבָרָיו אֱמֶת וָצֶדֶק. נֶאֱמָן אַתָּה הוּא יהוה אֱלֹהֵינוּ, וְנֶאֱמָנִים דְּבָרֶיךָ, וְדָבָר אֶחָד מִדְּבָרֶיךָ אָחוֹר לֹא יָשׁוּב רֵיקָם, כִּי אֵל מֶלֶךְ נֶאֱמָן (וְרַחֲמָן) אָתָּה. בָּרוּךְ אַתָּה יהוה, הָאֵל הַנֶּאֱמָן בְּכָל דְּבָרָיו. (.אָמֵן —Cong.)

**רַחֵם** עַל צִיּוֹן כִּי הִיא בֵּית חַיֵּינוּ, וְלַעֲלוּבַת נֶפֶשׁ תּוֹשִׁיעַ בִּמְהֵרָה בְיָמֵינוּ. בָּרוּךְ אַתָּה יהוה, מְשַׂמֵּחַ צִיּוֹן בְּבָנֶיהָ. (.אָמֵן —Cong.)

**שַׂמְּחֵנוּ** יהוה אֱלֹהֵינוּ בְּאֵלִיָּהוּ הַנָּבִיא עַבְדֶּךָ, וּבְמַלְכוּת בֵּית דָּוִד מְשִׁיחֶךָ, בִּמְהֵרָה יָבֹא וְיָגֵל לִבֵּנוּ, עַל כִּסְאוֹ לֹא יֵשֵׁב זָר וְלֹא יִנְחֲלוּ עוֹד אֲחֵרִים אֶת כְּבוֹדוֹ, כִּי בְשֵׁם קָדְשְׁךָ נִשְׁבַּעְתָּ לּוֹ, שֶׁלֹּא יִכְבֶּה נֵרוֹ לְעוֹלָם וָעֶד. בָּרוּךְ אַתָּה יהוה, מָגֵן דָּוִד. (.אָמֵן —Cong.)

*Chazzan* takes the Torah in his right arm and recites:

**יְהַלְלוּ אֶת שֵׁם יהוה, כִּי נִשְׂגָּב שְׁמוֹ לְבַדּוֹ —**

Congregation responds:

**— הוֹדוֹ עַל אֶרֶץ וְשָׁמָיִם. וַיָּרֶם קֶרֶן לְעַמּוֹ, תְּהִלָּה לְכָל חֲסִידָיו, לִבְנֵי יִשְׂרָאֵל עַם קְרֹבוֹ, הַלְלוּיָהּ.**[1]

As the Torah is carried to the Ark, congregation recites Psalm 24.

**לְדָוִד** מִזְמוֹר, לַיהוה הָאָרֶץ וּמְלוֹאָהּ, תֵּבֵל וְיֹשְׁבֵי בָהּ. כִּי הוּא עַל יַמִּים יְסָדָהּ, וְעַל נְהָרוֹת יְכוֹנְנֶהָ. מִי יַעֲלֶה בְהַר יהוה, וּמִי יָקוּם בִּמְקוֹם קָדְשׁוֹ. נְקִי כַפַּיִם וּבַר לֵבָב, אֲשֶׁר לֹא נָשָׂא לַשָּׁוְא נַפְשִׁי וְלֹא נִשְׁבַּע לְמִרְמָה. יִשָּׂא בְרָכָה מֵאֵת יהוה, וּצְדָקָה מֵאֱלֹהֵי יִשְׁעוֹ. זֶה דּוֹר דֹּרְשָׁיו, מְבַקְשֵׁי פָנֶיךָ, יַעֲקֹב, סֶלָה. שְׂאוּ שְׁעָרִים רָאשֵׁיכֶם, וְהִנָּשְׂאוּ פִּתְחֵי עוֹלָם, וְיָבוֹא מֶלֶךְ הַכָּבוֹד. מִי זֶה מֶלֶךְ הַכָּבוֹד, יהוה עִזּוּז וְגִבּוֹר, יהוה גִּבּוֹר מִלְחָמָה. שְׂאוּ שְׁעָרִים רָאשֵׁיכֶם, וּשְׂאוּ פִּתְחֵי עוֹלָם, וְיָבֹא מֶלֶךְ הַכָּבוֹד. מִי הוּא זֶה מֶלֶךְ הַכָּבוֹד, יהוה צְבָאוֹת הוּא מֶלֶךְ הַכָּבוֹד, סֶלָה.

As the Torah is placed into the Ark, the congregation recites:

**וּבְנֻחֹה** יֹאמַר, שׁוּבָה יהוה רִבְבוֹת אַלְפֵי יִשְׂרָאֵל.[2] קוּמָה יהוה לִמְנוּחָתֶךָ, אַתָּה וַאֲרוֹן עֻזֶּךָ. כֹּהֲנֶיךָ יִלְבְּשׁוּ צֶדֶק,

After the *Haftarah* is read, the *oleh* recites the following blessings:

בָּרוּךְ *Blessed are You, HASHEM, our God, King of the universe, Rock of all eternities, Righteous in all generations, the trustworthy God, Who says and does, Who speaks and fulfills, all of Whose words are true and righteous. Trustworthy are You HASHEM, our God, and trustworthy are Your words, not one of Your words is turned back to its origin unfulfilled, for You are God, trustworthy (and compassionate) King. Blessed are You, HASHEM, the God Who is trustworthy in all His words.*                    (Cong. — *Amen.*)

רַחֵם *Have mercy on Zion for it is the source of our life; to the one who is deeply humiliated bring salvation speedily, in our days. Blessed are You, HASHEM, Who gladdens Zion through her children.*                    (Cong. — *Amen.*)

שַׂמְּחֵנוּ *Gladden us, HASHEM, our God, with Elijah the prophet, Your servant, and with the kingdom of the House of David, Your anointed, may he come speedily and cause our heart to exult. On his throne let no stranger sit nor let others continue to inherit his honor, for by Your holy Name You swore to him that his lamp will not be extinguished forever and ever. Blessed are You, HASHEM, Shield of David.*                    (Cong. — *Amen.*)

Chazzan takes the Torah in his right arm and recites:

**Let them praise the Name of HASHEM,**
**for His Name alone will have been exalted —**

Congregation responds:

*— His glory is above earth and heaven. And He will have exalted the pride of His people, causing praise for all His devout ones, for the Children of Israel, His intimate people. Halleluyah!*[1]

As the Torah is carried to the Ark, congregation recites Psalm 24.

לְדָוִד *Of David a psalm. HASHEM's is the earth and its fullness, the inhabited land and those who dwell in it. For He founded it upon seas, and established it upon rivers. Who may ascend the mountain of HASHEM, and who may stand in the place of His sanctity? One with clean hands and pure heart, who has not sworn in vain by My soul and has not sworn deceitfully. He will receive a blessing from HASHEM and just kindness from the God of his salvation. This is the generation of those who seek Him, those who strive for Your Presence — Jacob, Selah. Raise up your heads, O gates, and be uplifted, you everlasting entrances, so that the King of Glory may enter. Who is this King of Glory? — HASHEM, the mighty and strong, HASHEM, the strong in battle. Raise up your heads, O gates, and raise up, you everlasting entrances, so that the King of Glory may enter. Who then is the King of Glory? HASHEM, Master of Legions, He is the King of Glory. Selah!*

As the Torah is placed into the Ark, the congregation recites:

וּבְנֻחֹה *And when it rested he would say, "Return, HASHEM, to the myriad thousands of Israel."*[2] *Arise, HASHEM, to Your resting place, You and the Ark of Your strength. Let Your priests be clothed in righteousness,*

---

(1) *Psalms* 148:13-14. (2) *Numbers* 10:36.

וַחֲסִידֶיךָ יְרַנֵּנוּ. בַּעֲבוּר דָּוִד עַבְדֶּךָ אַל תָּשֵׁב פְּנֵי מְשִׁיחֶךָ.[1] כִּי לֶקַח טוֹב נָתַתִּי לָכֶם, תּוֹרָתִי אַל תַּעֲזְבוּ.[2] ❖ עֵץ חַיִּים הִיא לַמַּחֲזִיקִים בָּהּ, וְתֹמְכֶיהָ מְאֻשָּׁר.[3] דְּרָכֶיהָ דַרְכֵי נֹעַם, וְכָל נְתִיבוֹתֶיהָ שָׁלוֹם.[4] הֲשִׁיבֵנוּ יהוה אֵלֶיךָ וְנָשׁוּבָה, חַדֵּשׁ יָמֵינוּ כְּקֶדֶם.[5]

The chazzan recites חֲצִי קַדִּישׁ:

**יִתְגַּדַּל** וְיִתְקַדַּשׁ שְׁמֵהּ רַבָּא. (.Cong – אָמֵן.) בְּעָלְמָא דִּי בְרָא כִרְעוּתֵהּ. וְיַמְלִיךְ מַלְכוּתֵהּ, בְּחַיֵּיכוֹן וּבְיוֹמֵיכוֹן וּבְחַיֵּי דְכָל בֵּית יִשְׂרָאֵל, בַּעֲגָלָא וּבִזְמַן קָרִיב. וְאִמְרוּ: אָמֵן.

(.Cong – אָמֵן. יְהֵא שְׁמֵהּ רַבָּא מְבָרַךְ לְעָלַם וּלְעָלְמֵי עָלְמַיָּא.)

יְהֵא שְׁמֵהּ רַבָּא מְבָרַךְ לְעָלַם וּלְעָלְמֵי עָלְמַיָּא.

יִתְבָּרַךְ וְיִשְׁתַּבַּח וְיִתְפָּאַר וְיִתְרוֹמַם וְיִתְנַשֵּׂא וְיִתְהַדָּר וְיִתְעַלֶּה וְיִתְהַלָּל שְׁמֵהּ דְּקֻדְשָׁא בְּרִיךְ הוּא (.Cong – בְּרִיךְ הוּא) – לְעֵלָּא מִן כָּל בִּרְכָתָא וְשִׁירָתָא תֻּשְׁבְּחָתָא וְנֶחֱמָתָא, דַּאֲמִירָן בְּעָלְמָא. וְאִמְרוּ: אָמֵן. (.Cong – אָמֵן.)

## ‹‹ שמונה עשרה – עמידה ››

Take three steps backward, then three steps forward. Remain standing with feet together while reciting *Shemoneh Esrei*. Recite it with quiet devotion and without any interruption. Although it should not be audible to others, one must pray loudly enough to hear himself.

כִּי שֵׁם יהוה אֶקְרָא, הָבוּ גֹדֶל לֵאלֹהֵינוּ.[6]

אֲדֹנָי שְׂפָתַי תִּפְתָּח, וּפִי יַגִּיד תְּהִלָּתֶךָ.[7]

### אבות

Bend the knees at בָּרוּךְ; bow at אַתָּה; straighten up at ה'.

**בָּרוּךְ** אַתָּה* יהוה אֱלֹהֵינוּ וֵאלֹהֵי אֲבוֹתֵינוּ,* אֱלֹהֵי אַבְרָהָם, אֱלֹהֵי יִצְחָק, וֵאלֹהֵי יַעֲקֹב, הָאֵל הַגָּדוֹל הַגִּבּוֹר וְהַנּוֹרָא, אֵל עֶלְיוֹן, גּוֹמֵל חֲסָדִים טוֹבִים, וְקוֹנֵה הַכֹּל, וְזוֹכֵר חַסְדֵי אָבוֹת, וּמֵבִיא גוֹאֵל* לִבְנֵי בְנֵיהֶם, לְמַעַן שְׁמוֹ בְּאַהֲבָה. מֶלֶךְ עוֹזֵר וּמוֹשִׁיעַ וּמָגֵן.

---

‹‹ שְׁמוֹנֶה עֶשְׂרֵה / SHEMONEH ESREI ››

*Shemoneh Esrei* has three sections: (a) In the first three blessings, the supplicant pays homage to God, like a slave praising his master before he dares make a request; (b) the middle section of thirteen blessings contains the supplicant's requests; (c) in the last three blessings, he takes leave, expressing gratitude and confidence in his Master's graciousness (*Berachos* 34a).

Even the middle section is not merely a catalogue of selfish requests. In each blessing, we acknowledge God's mastery before making the request. Thus, each blessing is an affirmation of God's power (*Vilna Gaon*).

◆§ **אָבוֹת / Patriarchs**

The first blessing, אָבוֹת, *Patriarchs*, recalls the greatness of our forefathers in whose merit God pledged to help Israel throughout history, even if we are unworthy.

בָּרוּךְ אַתָּה — *Blessed are You.* [Since God is perfect by definition, what benefit can

*and Your devout ones will sing joyously. For the sake of David, Your servant, turn not away the face of Your anointed.* [1] *For I have given you a good teaching, do not forsake My Torah.* [2] Chazzan — *It is a tree of life for those who grasp it, and its supporters are praiseworthy.* [3] *Its ways are ways of pleasantness and all its paths are peace.* [4] *Bring us back to You,* HASHEM, *and we shall return, renew our days as of old.* [5]

The chazzan recites Half-Kaddish:

**יִתְגַּדַּל** *May His great Name grow exalted and sanctified* (Cong.— Amen.) *in the world that He created as He willed. May He give reign to His kingship in your lifetimes and in your days, and in the lifetimes of the entire Family of Israel, swiftly and soon. Now respond: Amen.*

(Cong. — Amen. *May His great Name be blessed forever and ever.*)

*May His great Name be blessed forever and ever.*

*Blessed, praised, glorified, exalted, extolled, mighty, upraised, and lauded be the Name of the Holy One, Blessed is He* (Cong.— *Blessed is He*) — *beyond any blessing and song, praise and consolation that are uttered in the world. Now respond: Amen.* (Cong.— Amen.)

## ⊰ SHEMONEH ESREI — AMIDAH ⊱

Take three steps backward, then three steps forward. Remain standing with feet together while reciting *Shemoneh Esrei*. Recite it with quiet devotion and without any interruption. Although it should not be audible to others, one must pray loudly enough to hear himself.

*When I call out the Name of* HASHEM, *ascribe greatness to our God.* [6]

*My Lord, open my lips, that my mouth may declare Your praise.* [7]

### PATRIARCHS
Bend the knees at "Blessed"; bow at "You"; straighten up at "HASHEM."

**בָּרוּךְ** *Blessed are You,* * HASHEM, *our God and the God of our fore- fathers,* * *God of Abraham, God of Isaac, and God of Jacob; the great, mighty, and awesome God, the supreme God, Who bestows beneficial kindnesses and creates everything, Who recalls the kind- nesses of the Patriarchs and brings a Redeemer* * *to their children's chil- dren, for His Name's sake, with love. O King, Helper, Savior, and Shield.*

---

(1) *Psalms* 132:8-10. (2) *Proverbs* 4:2. (3) 3:18. (4) 3:17.
(5) *Lamentations* 5:21. (6) *Deuteronomy* 32:3. (7) *Psalms* 51:17.

---

man's blessing confer upon Him?]
❏ This is a declaration of fact: God *is* blessed in the sense that He is perfect and complete (*Sefer HaChinuch* 430).
❏ God is the *Source* of inexhaustible bless- ing, and He has created the world in order to do good to His creatures. Since this is His will, we pray for the Redemption, when man will be worthy of His utmost blessing (*Rashba; R' Bachya*).

אֱלֹהֵינוּ וֵאלֹהֵי אֲבוֹתֵינוּ — *Our God and the God of our forefathers.* First we call Him *our God*

because we are obligated to serve Him and know Him to the limit of *our* capacity. But there is much about His ways that we cannot understand. In response to such doubts we proclaim that He is *the God of our fore- fathers,* and we have faith in the tradition they transmitted (*Dover Shalom*).

וּמֵבִיא גוֹאֵל — *And brings a Redeemer.* The phrase is in present tense. Every event, no matter how terrible it may seem, is a step toward the ultimate redemption by the Mes- siah (*Siach Yitzchak*).

Bend the knees at בָּרוּךְ; bow at אַתָּה; straighten up at ה'.

## בָּרוּךְ אַתָּה יהוה, מָגֵן אַבְרָהָם.

### גבורות

**אַתָּה** גִּבּוֹר לְעוֹלָם אֲדֹנָי, מְחַיֵּה מֵתִים* אַתָּה, רַב לְהוֹשִׁיעַ.
מַשִּׁיב הָרוּחַ וּמוֹרִיד הַגֶּשֶׁם [נ"א הַגָּשֶׁם]. מְכַלְכֵּל חַיִּים
בְּחֶסֶד, מְחַיֵּה מֵתִים בְּרַחֲמִים רַבִּים, סוֹמֵךְ נוֹפְלִים, וְרוֹפֵא חוֹלִים,
וּמַתִּיר אֲסוּרִים, וּמְקַיֵּם אֱמוּנָתוֹ לִישֵׁנֵי עָפָר. מִי כָמְוֹךָ בַּעַל גְּבוּרוֹת,
וּמִי דְוֹמֶה לָּךְ, מֶלֶךְ מֵמִית וּמְחַיֶּה וּמַצְמִיחַ יְשׁוּעָה. וְנֶאֱמָן אַתָּה
לְהַחֲיוֹת מֵתִים. בָּרוּךְ אַתָּה יהוה, מְחַיֵּה הַמֵּתִים.

During the *chazzan's* repetition, *Kedushah* (below) is recited here.

### קדושת השם

**אַתָּה** קָדוֹשׁ וְשִׁמְךָ קָדוֹשׁ, וּקְדוֹשִׁים בְּכָל יוֹם יְהַלְלְוּךָ סֶּלָה.
בָּרוּךְ אַתָּה יהוה, הָאֵל הַקָּדוֹשׁ.

### בינה

**אַתָּה** חוֹנֵן לְאָדָם דַּעַת, וּמְלַמֵּד לֶאֱנוֹשׁ בִּינָה. חָנֵּנוּ מֵאִתְּךָ דֵּעָה
בִּינָה וְהַשְׂכֵּל. בָּרוּךְ אַתָּה יהוה, חוֹנֵן הַדָּעַת.

---

### קדושה

Stand with feet together and avoid any interruptions.
Rise on toes when saying קָדוֹשׁ, קָדוֹשׁ, קָדוֹשׁ; בָּרוּךְ (of בְּרוּךְ כְּבוֹד); and יִמְלֹךְ.

**נְקַדֵּשׁ** אֶת שִׁמְךָ בָּעוֹלָם, כְּשֵׁם שֶׁמַּקְדִּישִׁים אוֹתוֹ בִּשְׁמֵי — Cong.
מָרוֹם, כַּכָּתוּב עַל יַד נְבִיאֶךָ, וְקָרָא זֶה אֶל זֶה וְאָמַר:¹ then chazzan

קָדוֹשׁ קָדוֹשׁ קָדוֹשׁ יהוה צְבָאוֹת, מְלֹא כָל הָאָרֶץ כְּבוֹדוֹ.¹ — All

לְעֻמָּתָם בָּרוּךְ יֹאמֵרוּ: — Chazzan

בָּרוּךְ כְּבוֹד יהוה, מִמְּקוֹמוֹ.² — All

וּבְדִבְרֵי קָדְשְׁךָ כָּתוּב לֵאמֹר: — Chazzan

יִמְלֹךְ יהוה לְעוֹלָם, אֱלֹהַיִךְ צִיּוֹן לְדֹר וָדֹר, הַלְלוּיָהּ.³ — All

— Chazzan only concludes לְדוֹר וָדוֹר נַגִּיד גָּדְלֶךָ וּלְנֵצַח נְצָחִים קְדֻשָּׁתְךָ
נַקְדִּישׁ, וְשִׁבְחֲךָ אֱלֹהֵינוּ מִפִּינוּ לֹא יָמוּשׁ לְעוֹלָם וָעֶד, כִּי אֵל מֶלֶךְ גָּדוֹל
וְקָדוֹשׁ אָתָּה. בָּרוּךְ אַתָּה יהוה, הָאֵל הַקָּדוֹשׁ.

*Chazzan* continues . . . אַתָּה חוֹנֵן (above).

---

**גבורות / God's Might**

מְחַיֵּה מֵתִים — *The Resuscitator of the dead.*
The concept that God restores life is found
three times in this section, alluding to the
three kinds of resuscitation: man's awaken-
ing every morning after deathlike slumber;
the rain that has the life-sustaining quality
of making vegetation grow; and the literal
resuscitation of the dead that will take place
in the Messianic age (*Abudraham*).

Bend the knees at *"Blessed"*; bow at *"You"*; straighten up at *"HASHEM."*
*Blessed are You, HASHEM, Shield of Abraham.*

### GOD'S MIGHT

**אַתָּה** *You are eternally mighty, my Lord, the Resuscitator of the dead\* are You; abundantly able to save, Who makes the wind blow and makes the rain descend; Who sustains the living with kindness, resuscitates the dead with abundant mercy, supports the fallen, heals the sick, releases the confined, and maintains His faith to those asleep in the dust. Who is like You, O Master of mighty deeds, and who is comparable to You, O King Who causes death and restores life and makes salvation sprout! And You are faithful to resuscitate the dead. Blessed are You, HASHEM, Who resuscitates the dead.*

During the *chazzan's* repetition, *Kedushah* (below) is recited here.

### HOLINESS OF GOD'S NAME

**אַתָּה** *You are holy and Your Name is holy, and holy ones praise You every day, forever. Blessed are You, HASHEM, the holy God.*

### INSIGHT

**אַתָּה** *You graciously endow man with wisdom and teach insight to a frail mortal. Endow us graciously from Yourself with wisdom, insight, and discernment. Blessed are You, HASHEM, gracious Giver of wisdom.*

---

### KEDUSHAH
Stand with feet together and avoid any interruptions.
Rise on toes when saying *Holy, holy, holy; Blessed is;* and *HASHEM shall reign.*

Cong. then chazzan — **נְקַדֵּשׁ** *We shall sanctify Your Name in this world, just as they sanctify it in heaven above, as it is written by Your prophet,* "And one [angel] will call another and say:

All — 'Holy, holy, holy is HASHEM, Master of Legions, the whole world is filled with His glory.'"[1]

Chazzan — *Those facing them say: "Blessed":*

All — "Blessed is the glory of HASHEM from His place."[2]

Chazzan — *And in Your holy Writings the following is written:*

All — "HASHEM shall reign forever — your God, O Zion — from generation to generation, Halleluyah!"[3]

*Chazzan only concludes: From generation to generation we shall relate Your greatness and for infinite eternities we shall proclaim Your holiness. Your praise, our God, shall not leave our mouth forever and ever, for You, O God, are a great and holy King. Blessed are You, HASHEM, the holy God.*

*Chazzan continues* אַתָּה חוֹנֵן, *You graciously endow . . .* (above).

---

(1) *Isaiah* 6:3. (2) *Ezekiel* 3:12. (3) *Psalms* 146:10.

קְדוּשָׁה / **Kedushah**

*Kedushah*, Sanctification, expresses the concept that God is exalted above and separated from the limitations of material existence. When a *minyan* (quorum of ten) is present, it becomes the representative of the nation and echoes the angels who sing God's praises by proclaiming His holiness and glory. We do this by reciting *Kedushah*, a prayer based on that of the angels themselves, and with feet together, in the manner of the angels (*Ezekiel* 1:7).

### תשובה

**הֲשִׁיבֵנוּ** אָבִינוּ לְתוֹרָתֶךָ, וְקָרְבֵנוּ מַלְכֵּנוּ לַעֲבוֹדָתֶךָ, וְהַחֲזִירֵנוּ בִּתְשׁוּבָה שְׁלֵמָה לְפָנֶיךָ. בָּרוּךְ אַתָּה יהוה, הָרוֹצֶה בִּתְשׁוּבָה.

### סליחה

Strike the left side of the chest with the right fist
while reciting the words פָּשָׁעְנוּ and חָטָאנוּ.

**סְלַח** לָנוּ אָבִינוּ כִּי חָטָאנוּ, מְחַל לָנוּ מַלְכֵּנוּ כִּי פָשָׁעְנוּ, כִּי מוֹחֵל וְסוֹלֵחַ אָתָּה. בָּרוּךְ אַתָּה יהוה, חַנּוּן הַמַּרְבֶּה לִסְלוֹחַ.

### גאולה

**רְאֵה** בְעָנְיֵנוּ,* וְרִיבָה רִיבֵנוּ, וּגְאָלֵנוּ[1] מְהֵרָה לְמַעַן שְׁמֶךָ, כִּי גּוֹאֵל חָזָק אָתָּה. בָּרוּךְ אַתָּה יהוה, גּוֹאֵל יִשְׂרָאֵל.

The *chazzan* recites עֲנֵנוּ at this point in his repetition.

**עֲנֵנוּ** יהוה עֲנֵנוּ, בְּיוֹם צוֹם תַּעֲנִיתֵנוּ, כִּי בְצָרָה גְדוֹלָה אֲנָחְנוּ. אַל תֵּפֶן אֶל רִשְׁעֵנוּ, וְאַל תַּסְתֵּר פָּנֶיךָ מִמֶּנּוּ, וְאַל תִּתְעַלַּם מִתְּחִנָּתֵנוּ. הֱיֵה נָא קָרוֹב לְשַׁוְעָתֵנוּ, יְהִי נָא חַסְדְּךָ לְנַחֲמֵנוּ, טֶרֶם נִקְרָא אֵלֶיךָ עֲנֵנוּ, כַּדָּבָר שֶׁנֶּאֱמַר: וְהָיָה טֶרֶם יִקְרָאוּ וַאֲנִי אֶעֱנֶה, עוֹד הֵם מְדַבְּרִים וַאֲנִי אֶשְׁמָע.[2] כִּי אַתָּה יהוה הָעוֹנֶה בְּעֵת צָרָה, פּוֹדֶה וּמַצִּיל בְּכָל עֵת צָרָה וְצוּקָה. בָּרוּךְ אַתָּה יהוה, הָעוֹנֶה בְּעֵת צָרָה.

### רפואה

**רְפָאֵנוּ** יהוה וְנֵרָפֵא,* הוֹשִׁיעֵנוּ וְנִוָּשֵׁעָה, כִּי תְהִלָּתֵנוּ אָתָּה,[3] וְהַעֲלֵה רְפוּאָה שְׁלֵמָה לְכָל מַכּוֹתֵינוּ,°° כִּי אֵל מֶלֶךְ רוֹפֵא נֶאֱמָן וְרַחֲמָן אָתָּה. בָּרוּךְ אַתָּה יהוה, רוֹפֵא חוֹלֵי עַמּוֹ יִשְׂרָאֵל.

°°At this point one may interject a prayer for one who is ill:
יְהִי רָצוֹן מִלְּפָנֶיךָ, יהוה אֱלֹהַי וֵאלֹהֵי אֲבוֹתַי,
שֶׁתִּשְׁלַח מְהֵרָה רְפוּאָה שְׁלֵמָה מִן הַשָּׁמַיִם, רְפוּאַת הַנֶּפֶשׁ וּרְפוּאַת הַגּוּף
for a male—לַחוֹלֶה (patient's name) בֶּן (mother's name) בְּתוֹךְ שְׁאָר חוֹלֵי יִשְׂרָאֵל.
for a female—לַחוֹלָה (patient's name) בַּת (mother's name) בְּתוֹךְ שְׁאָר חוֹלֵי יִשְׂרָאֵל.
Continue—כִּי אֵל ...

סְלִיחָה / Forgiveness

סְלִיחָה, *forgiveness,* means not even harboring resentment or ill-will, but מְחִילָה, *pardon,* means giving up the right to punish a wrong (*Abudraham*).

גְּאוּלָה / Redemption

רְאֵה בְעָנְיֵנוּ — *Behold our affliction.* Though Israel suffers because of its own sins, our enemies have no right to claim that they are merely doing God's work, because they

## REPENTANCE

**הֲשִׁיבֵנוּ** *Bring us back, our Father, to Your Torah, and bring us near, our King, to Your service, and influence us to return in perfect repentance before You. Blessed are You, H*ASHEM*, Who desires repentance.*

## FORGIVENESS

Strike the left side of the chest with the right fist
while reciting the words *"erred"* and *"sinned."*

**סְלַח** *Forgive us, our Father, for we have erred; pardon us, our King, for we have willfully sinned; for You pardon and forgive. Blessed are You, H*ASHEM*, the gracious One Who pardons abundantly.*

## REDEMPTION

**רְאֵה** *Behold our affliction,* take up our grievance, and redeem us[1] speedily for Your Name's sake, for You are a powerful Redeemer. Blessed are You, H*ASHEM*, Redeemer of Israel.*

---

The chazzan recites *"Answer us"* at this point in his repetition.

**עֲנֵנוּ** *Answer us, H*ASHEM*, answer us, on this day of our fast, for we are in great distress. Do not pay attention to our wickedness; do not hide Your Face from us, and do not ignore our supplication. Please be near to our outcry; please let Your kindness comfort us — before we call to You answer us, as it is said: "And it will be that before they call, I will answer; while they yet speak, I will hear."[2] For You, H*ASHEM*, are the One Who responds in time of distress, Who redeems and rescues in every time of distress and woe. Blessed are You, H*ASHEM*, Who responds in time of distress.*

---

### HEALTH AND HEALING

**רְפָאֵנוּ** *Heal us, H*ASHEM* — then we will be healed;* save us — then we will be saved, for You are our praise.[3] Bring complete recovery for all our ailments,* ° ° for You are God, King, the faithful and compassionate Healer. Blessed are You, H*ASHEM*, Who heals the sick of His people Israel.*

---

°°At this point one may interject a prayer for one who is ill:

*May it be Your will, H*ASHEM*, my God, and the God of my forefathers, that You quickly send a complete recovery from heaven, spiritual healing and physical healing to the patient (name) son/daughter of (mother's name) among the other patients of Israel.*
                                                           Continue: *for You are God . . .*

---

(1) Cf. *Psalms* 119:153-154. (2) *Isaiah* 65:24. (3) Cf. *Jeremiah* 17:14.

cause Israel to suffer much more than necessary (*Etz Yosef*).

**רְפוּאה** §⊷ / **Health and Healing**

רְפָאֵנוּ ה' וְנֵרָפֵא — *Heal us, H*ASHEM* — then we will be healed.* Sometimes human beings or angels are God's agents to heal illness, but in that case, the cure may be only par-

tial or temporary. [Or the pain or other symptoms may be relieved, while the illness itself remains uncured (*Siach Yitzchak*). But if God *Himself* undertakes to cure the patient, we are confident that it will not be a temporary nor a partial measure: *then we will be healed* (*Etz Yosef* from *Zohar*).]

### ברכת השנים

**בָּרֵךְ** עָלֵינוּ יהוה אֱלֹהֵינוּ אֶת הַשָּׁנָה הַזֹּאת וְאֶת כָּל מִינֵי תְבוּאָתָהּ לְטוֹבָה, וְתֵן טַל וּמָטָר לִבְרָכָה עַל פְּנֵי הָאֲדָמָה, וְשַׂבְּעֵנוּ מִטּוּבֶךָ, וּבָרֵךְ שְׁנָתֵנוּ כַּשָּׁנִים הַטּוֹבוֹת. בָּרוּךְ אַתָּה יהוה, מְבָרֵךְ הַשָּׁנִים.

### קיבוץ גליות

**תְּקַע** בְּשׁוֹפָר גָּדוֹל לְחֵרוּתֵנוּ, וְשָׂא נֵס לְקַבֵּץ גָּלֻיּוֹתֵינוּ, וְקַבְּצֵנוּ יַחַד מֵאַרְבַּע כַּנְפוֹת הָאָרֶץ.[1] בָּרוּךְ אַתָּה יהוה, מְקַבֵּץ נִדְחֵי עַמּוֹ יִשְׂרָאֵל.

### דין

**הָשִׁיבָה** שׁוֹפְטֵינוּ כְּבָרִאשׁוֹנָה, וְיוֹעֲצֵינוּ כְּבַתְּחִלָּה,[2] וְהָסֵר מִמֶּנּוּ יָגוֹן וַאֲנָחָה, וּמְלוֹךְ עָלֵינוּ אַתָּה יהוה לְבַדְּךָ בְּחֶסֶד וּבְרַחֲמִים, וְצַדְּקֵנוּ בַּמִּשְׁפָּט. בָּרוּךְ אַתָּה יהוה, מֶלֶךְ אוֹהֵב צְדָקָה וּמִשְׁפָּט.

### ברכת המינים

**וְלַמַּלְשִׁינִים** אַל תְּהִי תִקְוָה, וְכָל הָרִשְׁעָה כְּרֶגַע תֹּאבֵד, וְכָל אֹיְבֶיךָ מְהֵרָה יִכָּרֵתוּ, וְהַזֵּדִים מְהֵרָה תְעַקֵּר וּתְשַׁבֵּר וּתְמַגֵּר וְתַכְנִיעַ בִּמְהֵרָה בְיָמֵינוּ. בָּרוּךְ אַתָּה יהוה, שׁוֹבֵר אֹיְבִים וּמַכְנִיעַ זֵדִים.

### צדיקים

**עַל הַצַּדִּיקִים** וְעַל הַחֲסִידִים, וְעַל זִקְנֵי עַמְּךָ בֵּית יִשְׂרָאֵל, וְעַל פְּלֵיטַת סוֹפְרֵיהֶם, וְעַל גֵּרֵי הַצֶּדֶק וְעָלֵינוּ, יֶהֱמוּ רַחֲמֶיךָ יהוה אֱלֹהֵינוּ, וְתֵן שָׂכָר טוֹב לְכָל הַבּוֹטְחִים בְּשִׁמְךָ בֶּאֱמֶת, וְשִׂים חֶלְקֵנוּ עִמָּהֶם לְעוֹלָם, וְלֹא נֵבוֹשׁ כִּי בְךָ בָּטָחְנוּ. בָּרוּךְ אַתָּה יהוה, מִשְׁעָן וּמִבְטָח לַצַּדִּיקִים.

### בנין ירושלים

**וְלִירוּשָׁלַיִם** עִירְךָ בְּרַחֲמִים תָּשׁוּב, וְתִשְׁכּוֹן בְּתוֹכָהּ כַּאֲשֶׁר דִּבַּרְתָּ, וּבְנֵה אוֹתָהּ בְּקָרוֹב בְּיָמֵינוּ בִּנְיַן עוֹלָם, וְכִסֵּא דָוִד מְהֵרָה לְתוֹכָהּ תָּכִין. בָּרוּךְ אַתָּה יהוה, בּוֹנֵה יְרוּשָׁלָיִם.

---

•⊰ בִּרְכַּת הַשָּׁנִים / **Year of Prosperity**

We request a blessing on our general business activities and then go on to ask for abundant crops. Even in bad times some people prosper, and even in good times

some farms and businesses fail. We ask not only for general prosperity, but that we be enabled to share in it (R' S.R. Hirsch).

•⊰ בִּרְכַּת הַמִּינִים / **Against Heretics**

Chronologically, this is the *nineteenth*

### YEAR OF PROSPERITY

בָּרֵךְ Bless on our behalf — O HASHEM, our God — this year and all its kinds of crops for the best, and give dew and rain for a blessing on the face of the earth, and satisfy us from Your bounty, and bless our year like the best years. Blessed are You, HASHEM, Who blesses the years.

### INGATHERING OF EXILES

תְּקַע Sound the great shofar for our freedom, raise the banner to gather our exiles and gather us together from the four corners of the earth.[1] Blessed are You, HASHEM, Who gathers in the dispersed of His people Israel.

### RESTORATION OF JUSTICE

הָשִׁיבָה Restore our judges as in earliest times and our counselors as at first;[2] remove from us sorrow and groan; and reign over us — You, HASHEM, alone — with kindness and compassion, and justify us through judgment. Blessed are You, HASHEM, the King Who loves righteousness and judgment.

### AGAINST HERETICS

וְלַמַּלְשִׁינִים And for slanderers let there be no hope; and may all wickedness perish in an instant; and may all Your enemies be cut down speedily. May You speedily uproot, smash, cast down, and humble the wanton sinners — speedily in our days. Blessed are You, HASHEM, Who breaks enemies and humbles wanton sinners.

### THE RIGHTEOUS

עַל הַצַּדִּיקִים On the righteous, on the devout, on the elders of Your people the Family of Israel, on the remnant of their scholars, on the righteous converts and on ourselves — may Your compassion be aroused, HASHEM, our God, and give goodly reward to all who sincerely believe in Your Name. Put our lot with them forever, and we will not feel ashamed, for we trust in You. Blessed are You, HASHEM, Mainstay and Assurance of the righteous.

### REBUILDING JERUSALEM

וְלִירוּשָׁלַיִם And to Jerusalem, Your city, may You return in compassion, and may You rest within it, as You have spoken. May You rebuild it soon in our days as an eternal structure, and may You speedily establish the throne of David within it. Blessed are You, HASHEM, the Builder of Jerusalem.

---

(1) Cf. *Isaiah* 11:12. (2) Cf. 1:26.

---

blessing of *Shemoneh Esrei*; it was instituted in Yavneh, during the tenure of Rabban Gamliel II as *Nassi* of Israel, some time after the destruction of the Second Temple. It was composed in response to the threats of heretical Jewish sects who tried to lead Jews astray through example and persuasion, and who used their political power to oppress observant Jews and to slander them to the anti-Semitic Roman government.

Despite the disappearance from within Israel of the particular sects against whom it was directed, this blessing is always rele-vant, because there are still nonbelievers and heretics who endanger the spiritual continuity of Israel (*Yaaros D'vash*).

#### ◆§ צַדִּיקִים / The Righteous

These four categories of people — righteous, devout, elders, scholars — are the leaders of the nation. Because the nation needs them, the Sages instituted a special prayer for their welfare (*R' Yehudah ben Yakar*).

#### ◆§ בִּנְיַן יְרוּשָׁלַיִם / Rebuilding Jerusalem

After having sought God's blessing on Israel's leaders and righteous people, we seek

### מלכות בית דוד

**אֶת צֶמַח** דָּוִד עַבְדְּךָ מְהֵרָה תַצְמִיחַ, וְקַרְנוֹ תָּרוּם בִּישׁוּעָתֶךָ, כִּי לִישׁוּעָתְךָ קִוִּינוּ כָּל הַיּוֹם. בָּרוּךְ אַתָּה יהוה, מַצְמִיחַ קֶרֶן יְשׁוּעָה.

### קבלת תפלה

**שְׁמַע** קוֹלֵנוּ יהוה אֱלֹהֵינוּ, חוּס וְרַחֵם עָלֵינוּ, וְקַבֵּל בְּרַחֲמִים וּבְרָצוֹן אֶת תְּפִלָּתֵנוּ, כִּי אֵל שׁוֹמֵעַ תְּפִלּוֹת וְתַחֲנוּנִים אָתָּה. וּמִלְּפָנֶיךָ מַלְכֵּנוּ, רֵיקָם אַל תְּשִׁיבֵנוּ,°° כִּי אַתָּה שׁוֹמֵעַ תְּפִלַּת עַמְּךָ יִשְׂרָאֵל בְּרַחֲמִים. בָּרוּךְ אַתָּה יהוה, שׁוֹמֵעַ תְּפִלָּה.

---

°°One who is fasting adds the following during the silent *Shemoneh Esrei.*
[If forgotten, do not repeat *Shemoneh Esrei.*]

**עֲנֵנוּ** יהוה עֲנֵנוּ, בְּיוֹם צוֹם תַּעֲנִיתֵנוּ, כִּי בְצָרָה גְדוֹלָה אֲנָחְנוּ. אַל תֵּפֶן אֶל רִשְׁעֵנוּ, וְאַל תַּסְתֵּר פָּנֶיךָ מִמֶּנּוּ, וְאַל תִּתְעַלַּם מִתְּחִנָּתֵנוּ. הֱיֵה נָא קָרוֹב לְשַׁוְעָתֵנוּ, יְהִי נָא חַסְדְּךָ לְנַחֲמֵנוּ, טֶרֶם נִקְרָא אֵלֶיךָ עֲנֵנוּ, כַּדָּבָר שֶׁנֶּאֱמַר: וְהָיָה טֶרֶם יִקְרָאוּ וַאֲנִי אֶעֱנֶה, עוֹד הֵם מְדַבְּרִים וַאֲנִי אֶשְׁמָע.[1] כִּי אַתָּה יהוה הָעוֹנֶה בְּעֵת צָרָה, פּוֹדֶה וּמַצִּיל בְּכָל עֵת צָרָה וְצוּקָה.
— Continue כִּי אַתָּה שׁוֹמֵעַ תְּפִלַּת . . . (above)

---

°°During the silent *Shemoneh Esrei* one may insert
either or both of these personal prayers.

For livelihood:

**אַתָּה** הוּא יהוה הָאֱלֹהִים, הַזָּן וּמְפַרְנֵס וּמְכַלְכֵּל מִקַּרְנֵי רְאֵמִים עַד בֵּיצֵי כִנִּים. הַטְרִיפֵנִי לֶחֶם חֻקִּי, וְהַמְצֵא לִי וּלְכָל בְּנֵי בֵיתִי מְזוֹנוֹתַי קֹדֶם שֶׁאֶצְטָרֵךְ לָהֶם, בְּנַחַת וְלֹא בְצַעַר, בְּהֶתֵּר וְלֹא בְאִסּוּר, בְּכָבוֹד וְלֹא בְבִזָּיוֹן, לְחַיִּים וּלְשָׁלוֹם, מִשֶּׁפַע בְּרָכָה וְהַצְלָחָה, וּמִשֶּׁפַע בְּרָכָה עֶלְיוֹנָה, כְּדֵי שֶׁאוּכַל לַעֲשׂוֹת רְצוֹנֶךָ, וְלַעֲסוֹק בְּתוֹרָתֶךָ וּלְקַיֵּם מִצְוֹתֶיךָ. וְאַל תַּצְרִיכֵנִי לִידֵי מַתְּנַת בָּשָׂר וָדָם. וִיקֻיַּם בִּי מִקְרָא שֶׁכָּתוּב: פּוֹתֵחַ אֶת יָדֶךָ, וּמַשְׂבִּיעַ לְכָל חַי רָצוֹן.[2] וְכָתוּב: הַשְׁלֵךְ עַל יהוה יְהָבְךָ, וְהוּא יְכַלְכְּלֶךָ.[3]
— Continue כִּי אַתָּה שׁוֹמֵעַ תְּפִלַּת . . . (above)

For forgiveness:

**אָנָּא** יהוה, חָטָאתִי עָוִיתִי וּפָשַׁעְתִּי לְפָנֶיךָ, מִיּוֹם הֱיוֹתִי עַל הָאֲדָמָה עַד הַיּוֹם הַזֶּה (וּבִפְרָט בַּחֵטְא.........). אָנָּא יהוה, עֲשֵׂה לְמַעַן שִׁמְךָ הַגָּדוֹל, וּתְכַפֶּר לִי עַל עֲוֹנִי וַחֲטָאַי וּפְשָׁעַי שֶׁחָטָאתִי וְשֶׁעָוִיתִי וְשֶׁפָּשַׁעְתִּי לְפָנֶיךָ, מִנְּעוּרַי עַד הַיּוֹם הַזֶּה. וּתְמַלֵּא כָּל הַשֵּׁמוֹת שֶׁפָּגַמְתִּי בְּשִׁמְךָ הַגָּדוֹל.

---

**⊷ מַלְכוּת בֵּית דָּוִד / Davidic Reign**

In this blessing we are taught that the ultimate salvation of the Jewish people is possible only through the Davidic Messiah.

His blessing for the Holy City. No blessing is complete until the seat of holiness, Jerusalem, is rebuilt in all its grandeur (*Iyun Tefillah*).

### DAVIDIC REIGN

אֶת צֶמַח *The offspring of Your servant David may You speedily cause to flourish, and enhance his pride through Your salvation, for we hope for Your salvation all day long. Blessed are You, HASHEM, Who causes the pride of salvation to flourish.*

### ACCEPTANCE OF PRAYER

שְׁמַע *Hear our voice, HASHEM, our God, pity and be compassionate to us, and accept — with compassion and favor — our prayer, for God Who hears prayers and supplications are You. From before Yourself, our King, turn us not away empty-handed,°° for You hear the prayer of Your people Israel with compassion. Blessed are You, HASHEM, Who hears prayer.*

°°One who is fasting adds the following during the silent *Shemoneh Esrei.*
[If forgotten, do not repeat *Shemoneh Esrei.*]

עֲנֵנוּ *Answer us, HASHEM, answer us, on this day of our fast, for we are in great distress. Do not pay attention to our wickedness; do not hide Your Face from us, and do not ignore our supplication. Please be near to our outcry; please let Your kindness comfort us — before we call to You answer us, as it is said: "And it will be that before they call, I will answer; while they yet speak, I will hear."[1] For You, HASHEM, are the One Who responds in time of distress, Who redeems and rescues in every time of distress and woe.*

Continue: *for You hear the prayer . . .* (above).

°°During the silent *Shemoneh Esrei* one may insert either or both of these personal prayers.

For forgiveness:

אָנָּא *Please, O HASHEM, I have erred, been iniquitous, and willfully sinned before You, from the day I have existed on earth until this very day (and especially with the sin of . . .). Please, HASHEM, act for the sake of Your Great Name and grant me atonement for my iniquities, my errors, and my willful sins through which I have erred, been iniquitous, and willfully sinned before You, from my youth until this day. And make whole all the Names that I have blemished in Your Great Name.*

For livelihood:

אַתָּה *It is You, HASHEM, the God Who nourishes, sustains, and supports, from the horns of re'eimim to the eggs of lice. Provide me with my allotment of bread; and bring forth for me and all members of my household, my food, before I have need for it; in contentment but not in pain, in a permissible but not a forbidden manner, in honor but not in disgrace, for life and for peace; from the flow of blessing and success and from the flow of the Heavenly spring, so that I be enabled to do Your will and engage in Your Torah and fulfill Your commandments. Make me not needful of people's largesse; and may there be fulfilled in me the verse that states, "You open Your hand and satisfy the desire of every living thing,"[2] and that states, "Cast your burden upon HASHEM and He will support you."[3]*

Continue: *for You hear the prayer . . .* (above).

(1) *Isaiah* 65:24. (2) *Psalms* 145:16. (3) 55:23.

קַבָּלַת תְּפִלָּה / Acceptance of Prayer

[In the middle section of *Shemoneh Esrei* we have asked God to grant our specific needs. We now close the section with a general plea that He take note of our call and grant our requests.]

Personal Prayers

In this blessing, one may add specific, personal requests for any private or general need in any language or style, for the feelings and devotion of the supplicant are more important than the form of the prayer.

**עבודה**

רְצֵה יהוה אֱלֹהֵינוּ בְּעַמְּךָ יִשְׂרָאֵל וּבִתְפִלָּתָם, וְהָשֵׁב אֶת הָעֲבוֹדָה לִדְבִיר בֵּיתֶךָ. וְאִשֵּׁי יִשְׂרָאֵל וּתְפִלָּתָם בְּאַהֲבָה תְקַבֵּל בְּרָצוֹן, וּתְהִי לְרָצוֹן תָּמִיד עֲבוֹדַת יִשְׂרָאֵל עַמֶּךָ.

וְתֶחֱזֶינָה עֵינֵינוּ בְּשׁוּבְךָ לְצִיּוֹן בְּרַחֲמִים. בָּרוּךְ אַתָּה יהוה, הַמַּחֲזִיר שְׁכִינָתוֹ לְצִיּוֹן.

**הודאה**

Bow at מוֹדִים; straighten up at ה׳. In his repetition the *chazzan* recites the entire מוֹדִים aloud, while the congregation recites מוֹדִים דְּרַבָּנָן softly.

מוֹדִים אֲנַחְנוּ לָךְ, שָׁאַתָּה הוּא יהוה אֱלֹהֵינוּ וֵאלֹהֵי אֲבוֹתֵינוּ לְעוֹלָם וָעֶד. צוּר חַיֵּינוּ, מָגֵן יִשְׁעֵנוּ אַתָּה הוּא לְדוֹר וָדוֹר. נוֹדֶה לְּךָ* וּנְסַפֵּר תְּהִלָּתֶךָ[1] עַל חַיֵּינוּ הַמְּסוּרִים בְּיָדֶךָ, וְעַל נִשְׁמוֹתֵינוּ הַפְּקוּדוֹת לָךְ, וְעַל נִסֶּיךָ שֶׁבְּכָל יוֹם עִמָּנוּ, וְעַל נִפְלְאוֹתֶיךָ* וְטוֹבוֹתֶיךָ שֶׁבְּכָל עֵת, עֶרֶב וָבֹקֶר וְצָהֳרָיִם. הַטּוֹב כִּי לֹא כָלוּ רַחֲמֶיךָ, וְהַמְרַחֵם כִּי לֹא תַמּוּ חֲסָדֶיךָ,[2] מֵעוֹלָם קִוִּינוּ לָךְ.

**מוֹדִים דְּרַבָּנָן**

מוֹדִים אֲנַחְנוּ לָךְ, שָׁאַתָּה הוּא יהוה אֱלֹהֵינוּ וֵאלֹהֵי אֲבוֹתֵינוּ, אֱלֹהֵי כָל בָּשָׂר, יוֹצְרֵנוּ, יוֹצֵר בְּרֵאשִׁית. בְּרָכוֹת וְהוֹדָאוֹת לְשִׁמְךָ הַגָּדוֹל וְהַקָּדוֹשׁ, עַל שֶׁהֶחֱיִיתָנוּ וְקִיַּמְתָּנוּ. כֵּן תְּחַיֵּנוּ וּתְקַיְּמֵנוּ, וְתֶאֱסוֹף גָּלֻיּוֹתֵינוּ לְחַצְרוֹת קָדְשֶׁךָ, לִשְׁמוֹר חֻקֶּיךָ וְלַעֲשׂוֹת רְצוֹנֶךָ, וּלְעָבְדְּךָ בְּלֵבָב שָׁלֵם, עַל שֶׁאֲנַחְנוּ מוֹדִים לָךְ. בָּרוּךְ אֵל הַהוֹדָאוֹת.

וְעַל כֻּלָּם יִתְבָּרַךְ וְיִתְרוֹמַם שִׁמְךָ מַלְכֵּנוּ תָּמִיד לְעוֹלָם וָעֶד.

Bend the knees at בָּרוּךְ; bow at אַתָּה; straighten up at ה׳.

וְכֹל הַחַיִּים יוֹדוּךָ סֶּלָה, וִיהַלְלוּ אֶת שִׁמְךָ בֶּאֱמֶת, הָאֵל יְשׁוּעָתֵנוּ וְעֶזְרָתֵנוּ סֶלָה. בָּרוּךְ אַתָּה יהוה, הַטּוֹב שִׁמְךָ וּלְךָ נָאֶה לְהוֹדוֹת.

The *chazzan* recites בִּרְכַּת כֹּהֲנִים during his repetition. He faces right at וְיִשְׁמְרֶךָ; faces left at וִיחֻנֶּךָּ פָּנָיו אֵלֶיךָ; faces the Ark for the rest of the blessings.

אֱלֹהֵינוּ וֵאלֹהֵי אֲבוֹתֵינוּ, בָּרְכֵנוּ בַבְּרָכָה הַמְשֻׁלֶּשֶׁת בַּתּוֹרָה הַכְּתוּבָה עַל יְדֵי מֹשֶׁה עַבְדֶּךָ, הָאֲמוּרָה מִפִּי אַהֲרֹן וּבָנָיו, כֹּהֲנִים עַם קְדוֹשֶׁךָ,

כָּאָמוּר: יְבָרֶכְךָ יהוה, וְיִשְׁמְרֶךָ.    (.Cong – כֵּן יְהִי רָצוֹן)

יָאֵר יהוה פָּנָיו אֵלֶיךָ, וִיחֻנֶּךָּ.    (.Cong – כֵּן יְהִי רָצוֹן)

יִשָּׂא יהוה פָּנָיו אֵלֶיךָ, וְיָשֵׂם לְךָ שָׁלוֹם.[3]    (.Cong – כֵּן יְהִי רָצוֹן)

━━━━━━

**עֲבוֹדָה / Temple Service**

This begins the final section of *Shemoneh Esrei*. Like a servant who is grateful for having had the opportunity to express himself

before his master, we thank God for hearing us out.

**הוֹדָאָה / Thanksgiving [Modim]**

נוֹדֶה לְּךָ — *We shall thank You.* Having begun

### TEMPLE SERVICE

**רְצֵה** Be favorable, HASHEM, our God, toward Your people Israel and their prayer and restore the service to the Holy of Holies of Your Temple. The fire-offerings of Israel and their prayer accept with love and favor, and may the service of Your people Israel always be favorable to You.

**וְתֶחֱזֶינָה** May our eyes behold Your return to Zion in compassion. Blessed are You, HASHEM, Who restores His Presence to Zion.

### THANKSGIVING [MODIM]

Bow at "We gratefully thank You"; straighten up at "HASHEM." In his repetition the chazzan recites the entire Modim aloud, while the congregation recites Modim of the Rabbis softly.

**מוֹדִים** We gratefully thank You, for it is You Who are HASHEM, our God and the God of our forefathers for all eternity; Rock of our lives, Shield of our salvation are You from generation to generation. We shall thank You\* and relate Your praise[1] — for our lives, which are committed to Your power and for our souls that are entrusted to You; for Your miracles that are with us every day; and for Your wonders\* and favors in every season — evening, morning, and afternoon. The Beneficent One, for Your compassions were never exhausted, and the Compassionate One, for Your kindnesses never ended[2] — always have we put our hope in You.

> **MODIM OF THE RABBIS**
>
> **מוֹדִים** We gratefully thank You, for it is You Who are HASHEM, our God and the God of our forefathers, the God of all flesh, our Molder, the Molder of the universe. Blessings and thanks are due Your great and holy Name for You have given us life and sustained us. So may You continue to give us life and sustain us and gather our exiles to the Courtyards of Your Sanctuary, to observe Your decrees, to do Your will and to serve You wholeheartedly. [We thank You] for inspiring us to thank You. Blessed is the God of thanksgivings.

For all these, may Your Name be blessed and exalted, our King, continually forever and ever.

Bend the knees at "Blessed"; bow at "You"; straighten up at "HASHEM."

Everything alive will gratefully acknowledge You, Selah! and praise Your Name sincerely, O God of our salvation and help, Selah! Blessed are You, HASHEM, Your Name is "The Beneficent One" and to You it is fitting to give thanks.

The chazzan recites the Priestly Blessing during his repetition.

**אֱלֹהֵינוּ** Our God and the God of our forefathers, bless us with the three-verse blessing in the Torah that was written by the hand of Moses, Your servant, that was said by Aaron and his sons, the Kohanim, Your holy people, as it is said:

May HASHEM bless you and safeguard you.          (Cong.— So may it be.)

May HASHEM illuminate His countenance for you and be gracious to you.
                                                   (Cong.— So may it be.)

May HASHEM turn His countenance to you and establish peace for you.[3]
                                                   (Cong.— So may it be.)

---

(1) Cf. Psalms 79:13. (2) Cf. Lamentations 3:22. (3) Numbers 6:24-26.

---

the blessing by describing God's greatness and our relationship to Him, we now specify what we thank Him for.

נִסֶּיךָ ... נִפְלְאוֹתֶיךָ — Your miracles ... Your wonders. We thank God for both miracles, the extraordinary events everyone recog-

**שלום**

**שִׂים שָׁלוֹם,** טוֹבָה, וּבְרָכָה, חֵן, וָחֶסֶד וְרַחֲמִים, עָלֵינוּ וְעַל כָּל יִשְׂרָאֵל עַמֶּךָ. בָּרְכֵנוּ אָבִינוּ, כֻּלָּנוּ כְּאֶחָד בְּאוֹר פָּנֶיךָ, כִּי בְאוֹר פָּנֶיךָ נָתַתָּ לָּנוּ, יהוה אֱלֹהֵינוּ, תּוֹרַת חַיִּים וְאַהֲבַת חֶסֶד, וּצְדָקָה, וּבְרָכָה, וְרַחֲמִים, וְחַיִּים, וְשָׁלוֹם. וְטוֹב בְּעֵינֶיךָ לְבָרֵךְ אֶת עַמְּךָ יִשְׂרָאֵל, בְּכָל עֵת וּבְכָל שָׁעָה בִּשְׁלוֹמֶךָ. בָּרוּךְ אַתָּה יהוה, הַמְבָרֵךְ אֶת עַמּוֹ יִשְׂרָאֵל בַּשָּׁלוֹם.

THE *CHAZZAN'S* REPETITION ENDS HERE. INDIVIDUALS CONTINUE BELOW:

יִהְיוּ לְרָצוֹן* אִמְרֵי פִי וְהֶגְיוֹן לִבִּי לְפָנֶיךָ, יהוה צוּרִי וְגֹאֲלִי.[1]

**אֱלֹהַי,** נְצוֹר לְשׁוֹנִי מֵרָע, וּשְׂפָתַי מִדַּבֵּר מִרְמָה,[2] וְלִמְקַלְלַי נַפְשִׁי תִדּוֹם, וְנַפְשִׁי כֶּעָפָר לַכֹּל תִּהְיֶה. פְּתַח לִבִּי בְּתוֹרָתֶךָ, וּבְמִצְוֹתֶיךָ תִּרְדּוֹף נַפְשִׁי. וְכָל הַחוֹשְׁבִים עָלַי רָעָה, מְהֵרָה הָפֵר עֲצָתָם וְקַלְקֵל מַחֲשַׁבְתָּם. עֲשֵׂה לְמַעַן שְׁמֶךָ, עֲשֵׂה לְמַעַן יְמִינֶךָ, עֲשֵׂה לְמַעַן קְדֻשָּׁתֶךָ, עֲשֵׂה לְמַעַן תּוֹרָתֶךָ. לְמַעַן יֵחָלְצוּן יְדִידֶיךָ, הוֹשִׁיעָה יְמִינְךָ וַעֲנֵנִי.[3] Some recite verses pertaining to their names at this point.

יִהְיוּ לְרָצוֹן אִמְרֵי פִי וְהֶגְיוֹן לִבִּי לְפָנֶיךָ, יהוה צוּרִי וְגֹאֲלִי. עֹשֶׂה שָׁלוֹם בִּמְרוֹמָיו, הוּא יַעֲשֶׂה שָׁלוֹם עָלֵינוּ, וְעַל כָּל יִשְׂרָאֵל. וְאִמְרוּ: אָמֵן.

Bow. Take three steps back. Bow left and say ... עֹשֶׂה; bow right and say ... הוּא; bow forward and say ... וְעַל כָּל.

**יְהִי רָצוֹן** מִלְּפָנֶיךָ, יהוה אֱלֹהֵינוּ וֵאלֹהֵי אֲבוֹתֵינוּ, שֶׁיִּבָּנֶה בֵּית הַמִּקְדָּשׁ בִּמְהֵרָה בְיָמֵינוּ, וְתֵן חֶלְקֵנוּ בְּתוֹרָתֶךָ. וְשָׁם נַעֲבָדְךָ בְּיִרְאָה, כִּימֵי עוֹלָם וּכְשָׁנִים קַדְמוֹנִיּוֹת. וְעָרְבָה לַיהוה מִנְחַת יְהוּדָה וִירוּשָׁלָיִם, כִּימֵי עוֹלָם וּכְשָׁנִים קַדְמוֹנִיּוֹת.[4]

THE INDIVIDUAL'S RECITATION OF *SHEMONEH ESREI* ENDS HERE.

Remain standing in place until the chazzan reaches Kedushah — or at least until the chazzan begins his repetition — then take three steps forward. The chazzan himself, or one praying alone, should remain in place for a few moments before taking three steps forward.

nizes as the results of God's intervention, and *wonders,* the familiar things that we have grown accustomed to, such as breathing, raining, and growing (*Etz Yosef*).

◆§ שָׁלוֹם / **Peace**

The consensus of commentators is that שִׂים שָׁלוֹם, *Establish peace,* is recited only at times when the Priestly Blessings are recited, because it alludes to those blessings.

◆§ יִהְיוּ לְרָצוֹן — *May . . . find favor.* We conclude *Shemoneh Esrei* with this brief prayer that our prayers find favor before God. Kabbalistic literature stresses that due to its great sanctity it be recited slowly and fervently.

◆§ אֱלֹהַי, נְצוֹר / **Concluding Prayers**

Many Talmudic Sages composed supplications that they would recite at the conclusion of *Shemoneh Esrei*, some of which are

### PEACE

**שִׂים שָׁלוֹם** Establish peace, goodness, blessing, graciousness, kindness, and compassion upon us and upon all of Your people Israel. Bless us, our Father, all of us as one, with the light of Your countenance, for with the light of Your countenance You gave us, HASHEM, our God, the Torah of life and a love of kindness, righteousness, blessing, compassion, life, and peace. And may it be good in Your eyes to bless Your people Israel, at every time and at every hour, with Your peace. Blessed are You, HASHEM, Who blesses His people Israel with peace.

THE *CHAZZAN'S* REPETITION ENDS HERE. INDIVIDUALS CONTINUE:

May the expressions of my mouth and the thoughts of my heart find favor* before You, HASHEM, my Rock and my Redeemer. [1]

**אֱלֹהַי** My God, guard my tongue from evil and my lips from speaking deceitfully. [2] To those who curse me, let my soul be silent; and let my soul be like dust to everyone. Open my heart to Your Torah, then my soul will pursue Your commandments. As for all those who design evil against me, speedily nullify their counsel and disrupt their design. Act for Your Name's sake; act for Your right hand's sake; act for Your sanctity's sake; act for Your Torah's sake. That Your beloved ones may be given rest; let Your right hand save, and respond to me. [3]

Some recite verses pertaining to their names at this point.

May the expressions of my mouth and the thoughts of my heart find favor be-

Bow. Take three steps back. fore You, HASHEM, my Rock and my Redeemer. He
Bow left and say, "He Who Who makes peace in His heights, may He make
. . ."; bow right and say, "may He . . ."; bow forward peace upon us, and upon all Israel. Now respond:
and say, "and upon all . . ." Amen.

**יְהִי רָצוֹן** May it be Your will, HASHEM, our God and the God of our forefathers, that the Holy Temple be rebuilt, speedily in our days. Grant us our share in Your Torah, and may we serve You there with reverence, as in days of old and in former years. Then the offering of Judah and Jerusalem will be pleasing to HASHEM, as in days of old and in former years. [4]

THE INDIVIDUAL'S RECITATION OF *SHEMONEH ESREI* ENDS HERE.

Remain standing in place until the *chazzan* reaches *Kedushah* — or at least until the *chazzan* begins his repetition — then take three steps forward. The *chazzan* himself, or one praying alone, should remain in place for a few moments before taking three steps forward.

---

(1) *Psalms* 19:15. (2) Cf. 34:14. (3) 60:7; 108:7. (4) *Malachi* 3:4.

---

cited in *Berachos* 16b-17a. The prayer now in universal use is based on that of Mar, son of Rabina (ibid. 18a).

While one is reciting נְצוֹר ,אֱלֹהַי, he may not respond to blessings and the like except for the exceptions given below. In the case of those exceptions, it is preferable to recite יְהִיוּ לְרָצוֹן before responding, but if there is

not enough time to do so, the responses should be said anyway. The responses are: *Borchu*, the amen after הָאֵל הַקָּדוֹשׁ and שׁוֹמֵעַ אָמֵן יְהֵא שְׁמֵהּ רַבָּא ;תְּפִלָּה and the last amen of the Half-*Kaddish;* and in *Kedushah* the two verses בָּרוּךְ כְּבוֹד and קָדוֹשׁ; and the three words מוֹדִים אֲנַחְנוּ לָךְ. (See *Orach Chaim* Ch. 122.)

קדיש שלם

The *chazzan* recites קַדִּישׁ שָׁלֵם.

**יִתְגַּדַּל** וְיִתְקַדַּשׁ שְׁמֵהּ רַבָּא. (.Cong – אָמֵן) בְּעָלְמָא דִּי בְרָא
כִרְעוּתֵהּ. וְיַמְלִיךְ מַלְכוּתֵהּ, בְּחַיֵּיכוֹן וּבְיוֹמֵיכוֹן וּבְחַיֵּי דְּכָל
בֵּית יִשְׂרָאֵל, בַּעֲגָלָא וּבִזְמַן קָרִיב. וְאִמְרוּ: אָמֵן.

(.Cong – אָמֵן. יְהֵא שְׁמֵהּ רַבָּא מְבָרַךְ לְעָלַם וּלְעָלְמֵי עָלְמַיָּא.)
יְהֵא שְׁמֵהּ רַבָּא מְבָרַךְ לְעָלַם וּלְעָלְמֵי עָלְמַיָּא.

יִתְבָּרַךְ וְיִשְׁתַּבַּח וְיִתְפָּאַר וְיִתְרוֹמַם וְיִתְנַשֵּׂא וְיִתְהַדָּר וְיִתְעַלֶּה
וְיִתְהַלָּל שְׁמֵהּ דְּקֻדְשָׁא בְּרִיךְ הוּא (.Cong – בְּרִיךְ הוּא) – לְעֵלָּא מִן כָּל
בִּרְכָתָא וְשִׁירָתָא תֻּשְׁבְּחָתָא וְנֶחֱמָתָא, דַּאֲמִירָן בְּעָלְמָא. וְאִמְרוּ: אָמֵן.
(.Cong – אָמֵן)

(.Cong– קַבֵּל בְּרַחֲמִים וּבְרָצוֹן אֶת תְּפִלָּתֵנוּ.)
תִּתְקַבֵּל צְלוֹתְהוֹן וּבָעוּתְהוֹן דְּכָל (בֵּית) יִשְׂרָאֵל קֳדָם אֲבוּהוֹן דִּי
בִשְׁמַיָּא. וְאִמְרוּ: אָמֵן. (.Cong – אָמֵן.)

(.Cong – יְהִי שֵׁם יהוה מְבֹרָךְ, מֵעַתָּה וְעַד עוֹלָם.[1])
יְהֵא שְׁלָמָא רַבָּא מִן שְׁמַיָּא, וְחַיִּים עָלֵינוּ וְעַל כָּל יִשְׂרָאֵל. וְאִמְרוּ:
אָמֵן. (.Cong – אָמֵן.)

(.Cong – עֶזְרִי מֵעִם יהוה, עֹשֵׂה שָׁמַיִם וָאָרֶץ.[2])

Bow. Take three steps back.
Bow left and say . . . עֹשֶׂה; bow right and say . . . הוּא; bow forward and say . . . וְעַל כָּל.
Remain in place for a few moments, then take three steps forward.

עֹשֶׂה שָׁלוֹם בִּמְרוֹמָיו, הוּא יַעֲשֶׂה שָׁלוֹם עָלֵינוּ, וְעַל כָּל יִשְׂרָאֵל.
וְאִמְרוּ: אָמֵן. (.Cong– אָמֵן.)

Stand while reciting עָלֵינוּ.

**עָלֵינוּ** לְשַׁבֵּחַ לַאֲדוֹן הַכֹּל, לָתֵת גְּדֻלָּה לְיוֹצֵר בְּרֵאשִׁית,
שֶׁלֹּא עָשָׂנוּ כְּגוֹיֵי הָאֲרָצוֹת, וְלֹא שָׂמָנוּ כְּמִשְׁפְּחוֹת
הָאֲדָמָה. שֶׁלֹּא שָׂם חֶלְקֵנוּ כָּהֶם, וְגוֹרָלֵנוּ כְּכָל הֲמוֹנָם. (שֶׁהֵם
מִשְׁתַּחֲוִים לְהֶבֶל וָרִיק, וּמִתְפַּלְלִים אֶל אֵל לֹא יוֹשִׁיעַ.[3])

Bow while reciting
וַאֲנַחְנוּ כּוֹרְעִים
וּמִשְׁתַּחֲוִים

וַאֲנַחְנוּ כּוֹרְעִים וּמִשְׁתַּחֲוִים וּמוֹדִים, לִפְנֵי מֶלֶךְ
מַלְכֵי הַמְּלָכִים הַקָּדוֹשׁ בָּרוּךְ הוּא. שֶׁהוּא נוֹטֶה
שָׁמַיִם וְיֹסֵד אָרֶץ,[4] וּמוֹשַׁב יְקָרוֹ בַּשָּׁמַיִם מִמַּעַל, וּשְׁכִינַת עֻזּוֹ בְּגָבְהֵי
מְרוֹמִים. הוּא אֱלֹהֵינוּ, אֵין עוֹד. אֱמֶת מַלְכֵּנוּ, אֶפֶס זוּלָתוֹ, כַּכָּתוּב
בְּתוֹרָתוֹ: וְיָדַעְתָּ הַיּוֹם וַהֲשֵׁבֹתָ אֶל לְבָבֶךָ, כִּי יהוה הוּא הָאֱלֹהִים
בַּשָּׁמַיִם מִמַּעַל וְעַל הָאָרֶץ מִתָּחַת, אֵין עוֹד.[5]

### FULL KADDISH

The chazzan recites Full Kaddish:

**יִתְגַּדַּל** May His great Name grow exalted and sanctified (Cong.— Amen.) in the world that He created as He willed. May He give reign to His kingship in your lifetimes and in your days, and in the lifetimes of the entire Family of Israel, swiftly and soon. Now respond: Amen.

(Cong. — Amen. May His great Name be blessed forever and ever.)

May His great Name be blessed forever and ever.

Blessed, praised, glorified, exalted, extolled, mighty, upraised, and lauded be the Name of the Holy One, Blessed is He (Cong.— Blessed is He) — beyond any blessing and song, praise and consolation that are uttered in the world. Now respond: Amen. (Cong.— Amen.)

(Cong.— Accept our prayers with mercy and favor.)

May the prayers and supplications of the entire Family of Israel be accepted before their Father Who is in Heaven. Now respond: Amen. (Cong.— Amen.)

(Cong.— Blessed be the Name of HASHEM, from this time and forever.[1])

May there be abundant peace from Heaven, and life, upon us and upon all Israel. Now respond: Amen. (Cong.— Amen.)

(Cong.— My help is from HASHEM, Maker of heaven and earth.[2])

Bow. Take three steps back. Bow left and say, "He Who makes . . ."; bow right and say, "may He . . ."; bow forward and say, "and upon all . . ." Remain in place for a few moments, then take three steps forward.

He Who makes peace in His heights, may He make peace upon us, and upon all Israel. Now respond: Amen. (Cong.— Amen.)

Stand while reciting עָלֵינוּ, "It is our duty . . ."

**עָלֵינוּ** It is our duty to praise the Master of all, to ascribe greatness to the Molder of primeval creation, for He has not made us like the nations of the lands and has not emplaced us like the families of the earth; for He has not assigned our portion like theirs nor our lot like all their multitudes. (For they bow to vanity and emptiness and pray to a god which helps not.[3])

Bow while reciting "But we bend our knees." But we bend our knees, bow, and acknowledge our thanks before the King Who reigns over kings, the Holy One, Blessed is He. He stretches out heaven and establishes earth's foundation,[4] the seat of His homage is in the heavens above and His powerful Presence is in the loftiest heights. He is our God and there is none other. True is our King, there is nothing beside Him, as it is written in His Torah: "You are to know this day and take to your heart that HASHEM is the only God — in heaven above and on the earth below — there is none other."[5]

---

(1) Psalms 113:2. (2) 121:2. (3) Isaiah 45:20. (4) 51:13. (5) Deuteronomy 4:39.

◆§ עָלֵינוּ / **Aleinu**

According to many early sources, this declaration of faith and dedication was composed by Joshua after he led Israel across the Jordan. During the Talmudic era it was part of the Rosh Hashanah Mussaf service, and at some point during medieval times it began to find its way into the daily service.

**עַל כֵּן** נְקַוֶּה לְּךָ, יהוה אֱלֹהֵינוּ, לִרְאוֹת מְהֵרָה בְּתִפְאֶרֶת
עֻזֶּךָ, לְהַעֲבִיר גִּלּוּלִים מִן הָאָרֶץ, וְהָאֱלִילִים כָּרוֹת
יִכָּרֵתוּן, לְתַקֵּן עוֹלָם בְּמַלְכוּת שַׁדַּי. וְכָל בְּנֵי בָשָׂר יִקְרְאוּ בִשְׁמֶךָ,
לְהַפְנוֹת אֵלֶיךָ כָּל רִשְׁעֵי אָרֶץ. יַכִּירוּ וְיֵדְעוּ כָּל יוֹשְׁבֵי תֵבֵל, כִּי לְךָ
תִּכְרַע כָּל בֶּרֶךְ, תִּשָּׁבַע כָּל לָשׁוֹן.¹ לְפָנֶיךָ יהוה אֱלֹהֵינוּ יִכְרְעוּ וְיִפֹּלוּ,
וְלִכְבוֹד שִׁמְךָ יְקָר יִתֵּנוּ. וִיקַבְּלוּ כֻלָּם אֶת עוֹל מַלְכוּתֶךָ, וְתִמְלֹךְ
עֲלֵיהֶם מְהֵרָה לְעוֹלָם וָעֶד. כִּי הַמַּלְכוּת שֶׁלְּךָ הִיא וּלְעוֹלְמֵי עַד
תִּמְלוֹךְ בְּכָבוֹד, כַּכָּתוּב בְּתוֹרָתֶךָ: יהוה יִמְלֹךְ לְעֹלָם וָעֶד.² ❖ וְנֶאֱמַר:
וְהָיָה יהוה לְמֶלֶךְ עַל כָּל הָאָרֶץ, בַּיּוֹם הַהוּא יִהְיֶה יהוה אֶחָד וּשְׁמוֹ
אֶחָד.³

**אַל תִּירָא** מִפַּחַד פִּתְאֹם, וּמִשֹּׁאַת רְשָׁעִים כִּי תָבֹא.⁴ עֻצוּ עֵצָה
וְתֻפָר, דַּבְּרוּ דָבָר וְלֹא יָקוּם, כִּי עִמָּנוּ אֵל.⁵ וְעַד זִקְנָה אֲנִי
הוּא, וְעַד שֵׂיבָה אֲנִי אֶסְבֹּל, אֲנִי עָשִׂיתִי וַאֲנִי אֶשָּׂא, וַאֲנִי אֶסְבֹּל
וַאֲמַלֵּט.⁶

### קדיש יתום

In the presence of a *minyan,* mourners recite קַדִּישׁ יָתוֹם, the Mourner's *Kaddish.*

**יִתְגַּדַּל** וְיִתְקַדַּשׁ שְׁמֵהּ רַבָּא. (.Cong – אָמֵן) בְּעָלְמָא דִּי בְרָא כִרְעוּתֵהּ.
וְיַמְלִיךְ מַלְכוּתֵהּ, בְּחַיֵּיכוֹן וּבְיוֹמֵיכוֹן וּבְחַיֵּי דְכָל בֵּית יִשְׂרָאֵל,
בַּעֲגָלָא וּבִזְמַן קָרִיב. וְאִמְרוּ: אָמֵן.
(.Cong – אָמֵן. יְהֵא שְׁמֵהּ רַבָּא מְבָרַךְ לְעָלַם וּלְעָלְמֵי עָלְמַיָּא.)
יְהֵא שְׁמֵהּ רַבָּא מְבָרַךְ לְעָלַם וּלְעָלְמֵי עָלְמַיָּא.
יִתְבָּרַךְ וְיִשְׁתַּבַּח וְיִתְפָּאַר וְיִתְרוֹמַם וְיִתְנַשֵּׂא וְיִתְהַדָּר וְיִתְעַלֶּה
וְיִתְהַלָּל שְׁמֵהּ דְּקֻדְשָׁא בְּרִיךְ הוּא (.Cong – בְּרִיךְ הוּא) – לְעֵלָּא מִן
כָּל בִּרְכָתָא וְשִׁירָתָא תֻּשְׁבְּחָתָא וְנֶחֱמָתָא, דַּאֲמִירָן בְּעָלְמָא. וְאִמְרוּ: אָמֵן.
(.Cong – אָמֵן)
יְהֵא שְׁלָמָא רַבָּא מִן שְׁמַיָּא, וְחַיִּים עָלֵינוּ וְעַל כָּל יִשְׂרָאֵל. וְאִמְרוּ: אָמֵן.
(.Cong – אָמֵן)

Bow. Take three steps back.
Bow left and say . . . עֹשֶׂה; bow right and say . . . הוּא; bow forward and say . . . וְעַל כָּל.
Remain in place for a few moments, then take three steps forward.

עֹשֶׂה שָׁלוֹם בִּמְרוֹמָיו, הוּא יַעֲשֶׂה שָׁלוֹם עָלֵינוּ, וְעַל כָּל יִשְׂרָאֵל.
וְאִמְרוּ: אָמֵן. (.Cong – אָמֵן)

**עַל כֵּן** *Therefore we put our hope in You, HASHEM, our God, that we may soon see Your mighty splendor, to remove detestable idolatry from the earth, and false gods will be utterly cut off, to perfect the universe through the Almighty's sovereignty. Then all humanity will call upon Your Name, to turn all the earth's wicked toward You. All the world's inhabitants will recognize and know that to You every knee should bend, every tongue should swear.* [1] *Before You, HASHEM, our God, they will bend every knee and cast themselves down, and to the glory of Your Name they will render homage, and they will all accept upon themselves the yoke of Your kingship that You may reign over them soon and eternally. For the kingdom is Yours and You will reign for all eternity in glory, as it is written in Your Torah: HASHEM shall reign for all eternity.* [2] Chazzan— *And it is said: HASHEM will be King over all the world — on that day HASHEM will be One and His Name will be One.* [3]

**אַל תִּירָא** *Do not fear sudden terror, or the holocaust of the wicked when it comes.* [4] *Plan a conspiracy and it will be annulled; speak your piece and it shall not stand, for God is with us.* [5] *Even till your seniority, I remain unchanged; and even till your ripe old age, I shall endure. I created you and I shall bear you; I shall endure and rescue.* [6]

MOURNER'S KADDISH

In the presence of a *minyan*, mourners recite the Mourner's *Kaddish*.

**יִתְגַּדַּל** *May His great Name grow exalted and sanctified* (Cong.— *Amen.*) *in the world that He created as He willed. May He give reign to His kingship in your lifetimes and in your days, and in the lifetimes of the entire Family of Israel, swiftly and soon. Now respond: Amen.*

(Cong. — *Amen. May His great Name be blessed forever and ever.*)
*May His great Name be blessed forever and ever.*

*Blessed, praised, glorified, exalted, extolled, mighty, upraised, and lauded be the Name of the Holy One, Blessed is He* (Cong.— *Blessed is He*) — *beyond any blessing and song, praise and consolation that are uttered in the world. Now respond: Amen.* (Cong.— *Amen.*)

*May there be abundant peace from Heaven, and life, upon us and upon all Israel. Now respond: Amen.* (Cong.— *Amen.*)

Bow. Take three steps back. Bow left and say, "He Who makes . . ."; bow right and say, "may He . . ."; bow forward and say, "and upon all . . ." Remain in place for a few moments, then take three steps forward.

*He Who makes peace in His heights, may He make peace upon us, and upon all Israel. Now respond: Amen.* (Cong.— *Amen.*)

---

(1) Cf. *Isaiah* 45:23. (2) *Exodus* 15:18. (3) *Zechariah* 14:9.
(4) *Proverbs* 3:25. (5) *Isaiah* 8:10. (6) 46:4.

# מעריב לפורים ﷼

Congregation, then *chazzan:*

**וְהוּא** רַחוּם יְכַפֵּר עָוֹן וְלֹא יַשְׁחִית, וְהִרְבָּה לְהָשִׁיב אַפּוֹ, וְלֹא יָעִיר כָּל חֲמָתוֹ.¹ ❖ יהוה הוֹשִׁיעָה, הַמֶּלֶךְ יַעֲנֵנוּ בְיוֹם קָרְאֵנוּ.²

*Chazzan bows at* בָּרְכוּ *and straightens up at* ה'.

## בָּרְכוּ אֶת יהוה הַמְבֹרָךְ.

Congregation, followed by *chazzan,* responds, bowing at בָּרוּךְ *and straightening up at* ה'.

## בָּרוּךְ יהוה הַמְבֹרָךְ לְעוֹלָם וָעֶד.

### ברכות קריאת שמע

**בָּרוּךְ** אַתָּה יהוה אֱלֹהֵינוּ מֶלֶךְ הָעוֹלָם, אֲשֶׁר בִּדְבָרוֹ* מַעֲרִיב עֲרָבִים, בְּחָכְמָה פּוֹתֵחַ שְׁעָרִים, וּבִתְבוּנָה מְשַׁנֶּה עִתִּים, וּמַחֲלִיף אֶת הַזְּמַנִּים, וּמְסַדֵּר אֶת הַכּוֹכָבִים בְּמִשְׁמְרוֹתֵיהֶם בָּרָקִיעַ כִּרְצוֹנוֹ. בּוֹרֵא יוֹם וָלַיְלָה, גּוֹלֵל אוֹר מִפְּנֵי חֹשֶׁךְ וְחֹשֶׁךְ מִפְּנֵי אוֹר. וּמַעֲבִיר יוֹם וּמֵבִיא לָיְלָה, וּמַבְדִּיל בֵּין יוֹם וּבֵין לָיְלָה, יהוה צְבָאוֹת שְׁמוֹ. ❖ אֵל חַי וְקַיָּם, תָּמִיד יִמְלוֹךְ עָלֵינוּ, לְעוֹלָם וָעֶד. בָּרוּךְ אַתָּה יהוה, הַמַּעֲרִיב עֲרָבִים. (אָמֵן. – Cong.)

**אַהֲבַת** עוֹלָם* בֵּית יִשְׂרָאֵל עַמְּךָ אָהָבְתָּ. תּוֹרָה וּמִצְוֹת, חֻקִּים וּמִשְׁפָּטִים, אוֹתָנוּ לִמַּדְתָּ. עַל כֵּן יהוה אֱלֹהֵינוּ, בְּשָׁכְבֵנוּ וּבְקוּמֵנוּ נָשִׂיחַ בְּחֻקֶּיךָ, וְנִשְׂמַח בְּדִבְרֵי תוֹרָתֶךָ, וּבְמִצְוֹתֶיךָ לְעוֹלָם וָעֶד. ❖ כִּי הֵם חַיֵּינוּ, וְאֹרֶךְ יָמֵינוּ, וּבָהֶם נֶהְגֶּה יוֹמָם וָלָיְלָה. וְאַהֲבָתְךָ, אַל תָּסִיר מִמֶּנּוּ לְעוֹלָמִים. בָּרוּךְ אַתָּה יהוה, אוֹהֵב עַמּוֹ יִשְׂרָאֵל. (אָמֵן. – Cong.)

---

**WEEKDAY MAARIV / מַעֲרִיב לְחוֹל** ﷼

As a general rule, no אָמֵן, *Amen,* or other prayer response may be recited between *Borchu* and *Shemoneh Esrei,* but there are exceptions. The main exception is "between chapters" [בֵּין הַפְּרָקִים] of the *Shema* blessings — i.e., after each of the blessings, and between the three chapters of *Shema.* At those points, every אָמֵן (but not בָּרוּךְ הוּא וּבָרוּךְ שְׁמוֹ) may be said.

Some responses are permitted at any point in the *Shema* blessings. They are: (a) In *Kaddish,* אָמֵן יְהֵא שְׁמֵהּ רַבָּא ... עָלְמַיָּא and the אָמֵן after דַּאֲמִירָן בְּעָלְמָא; and (b) the

response to בָּרְכוּ.

No interruptions whatever are permitted during the two verses of שְׁמַע and בָּרוּךְ שֵׁם.

**ברכות קריאת שמע / Blessings of the Shema** ﷼

The nighttime Blessings of the *Shema* are similar in theme to those of the morning, except that there are three in the morning and four in the evening. The total of seven is based on the verse (*Psalms* 119:164): *Seven times a day I praise You* (*Berachos* 11a, *Rashi*). The first of the evening blessings describes God's control over nature, seasons, and the cycles of light. The second

### ⊰§ MAARIV FOR PURIM §⊱

Congregation, then *chazzan:*

**וְהוּא** *He, the Merciful One, is forgiving of iniquity and does not destroy.
Frequently He withdraws His anger, not arousing His entire rage.* [1]
*Chazzan —* HASHEM, *save! May the King answer us on the day we call.* [2]

Chazzan bows at "Bless" and straightens up at "HASHEM."

## Bless HASHEM, the blessed One.

Congregation, followed by chazzan, responds,
bowing at "Blessed" and straightening up at "HASHEM."

### Blessed is HASHEM, the blessed One, for all eternity.

#### BLESSINGS OF THE SHEMA

**בָּרוּךְ** *Blessed are You,* HASHEM, *our God, King of the universe, Who by His
word\* brings on evenings, with wisdom opens gates, with understanding alters periods, changes the seasons, and orders the stars in their heavenly
constellations as He wills. He creates day and night, removing light before
darkness and darkness before light. He causes day to pass and brings night,
and separates between day and night —* HASHEM, *Master of Legions, is His
Name.* Chazzan— *May the living and enduring God continuously reign over us,
for all eternity. Blessed are You,* HASHEM, *Who brings on evenings.*

(Cong.— Amen.)

**אַהֲבַת** *[With] an eternal love\* have You loved the House of Israel,Your
nation. Torah and commandments, decrees and ordinances have You
taught us. Therefore* HASHEM, *our God, upon our retiring and arising, we will
discuss Your decrees and we will rejoice with the words of Your Torah and with
Your commandments for all eternity.* Chazzan— *For they are our life and the
length of our days and about them we will meditate day and night. May You
not remove Your love from us forever. Blessed are You,* HASHEM, *Who loves His
people Israel.* (Cong. — Amen.)

---

(1) *Psalms* 78:38. (2) 20:10.

speaks of God's gift of the Torah, the very essence of Israel's survival. The third refers to the Exodus, but with emphasis on the future redemption. The fourth stresses God's protection of His people from the terrors and dangers of night and slumber.

**בָּרוּךְ אַתָּה ... אֲשֶׁר בִּדְבָרוֹ** §⊱ — *Blessed are You ... Who by His word.* The command of God created day just as it created night, for every moment of the day and night has a purpose in God's plan. This recognition of God's everpresent will is especially important at night, which represents the period of fear, failure, and exile (R' Hirsch).

⊰§ **אַהֲבַת עוֹלָם** — *[With] an eternal love.* This blessing is an ecstatic expression of gratitude to God for the gift of Torah. Only after acknowledging our dependence on, and love for, the Torah, can we go on to express our undivided loyalty and dedication to ה' אֶחָד, HASHEM, the One and Only God, Who gave us this most precious gift.

The blessing begins with an expression of an axiom of Jewish existence: God loves us. The fact that He chose to give us His Torah proves that it is the vehicle for our national fulfillment. Therefore we dedicate ourselves to study it — constantly, joyously, and devotedly (Siach Yitzchak).

**שמע**

Immediately before its recitation concentrate on fulfilling the positive commandment of reciting the *Shema* twice daily. It is important to enunciate each word clearly and not to run words together. For this reason, vertical lines have been placed between two words that are prone to be slurred into one and are not separated by a comma or a hyphen.

When praying without a *minyan,* begin with the following three-word formula:

אֵל מֶלֶךְ נֶאֱמָן.*

Recite the first verse aloud, with the right hand covering the eyes,
and concentrate intensely upon accepting God's absolute sovereignty.

שְׁמַע ׀ יִשְׂרָאֵל,* יהוה ׀ אֱלֹהֵינוּ, יהוה ׀ אֶחָד:*¹

In an undertone – בָּרוּךְ שֵׁם* כְּבוֹד מַלְכוּתוֹ לְעוֹלָם וָעֶד.

While reciting the first paragraph (דברים ו:ה-ט), concentrate
on accepting the commandment to love God.

וְאָהַבְתָּ* אֵת ׀ יהוה ׀ אֱלֹהֶיךָ, בְּכָל־לְבָבְךָ, וּבְכָל־נַפְשְׁךָ, וּבְכָל־
מְאֹדֶךָ: וְהָיוּ הַדְּבָרִים הָאֵלֶּה, אֲשֶׁר ׀ אָנֹכִי מְצַוְּךָ הַיּוֹם,
עַל־לְבָבֶךָ: וְשִׁנַּנְתָּם לְבָנֶיךָ, וְדִבַּרְתָּ בָּם, בְּשִׁבְתְּךָ בְּבֵיתֶךָ, וּבְלֶכְתְּךָ
בַדֶּרֶךְ, וּבְשָׁכְבְּךָ וּבְקוּמֶךָ: וּקְשַׁרְתָּם לְאוֹת ׀ עַל־יָדֶךָ, וְהָיוּ לְטֹטָפֹת
בֵּין ׀ עֵינֶיךָ: וּכְתַבְתָּם ׀ עַל־מְזֻזוֹת בֵּיתֶךָ, וּבִשְׁעָרֶיךָ:

While reciting the second paragraph (דברים יא:יג-כא), concentrate on
accepting all the commandments and the concept of reward and punishment.

וְהָיָה,* אִם־שָׁמֹעַ תִּשְׁמְעוּ אֶל־מִצְוֹתַי, אֲשֶׁר ׀ אָנֹכִי מְצַוֶּה ׀
אֶתְכֶם הַיּוֹם, לְאַהֲבָה אֶת־יהוה ׀ אֱלֹהֵיכֶם ׀ וּלְעָבְדוֹ,

---

❊ שְׁמַע / THE SHEMA ❊

The recitation of the three paragraphs of *Shema* is required by the Torah, and one must have in mind that he is about to fulfill this commandment. Although one should try to concentrate on the meaning of all three paragraphs, one must concentrate at least on the meaning of the first verse (שְׁמַע) and the second verse (בָּרוּךְ שֵׁם) because the recitation of *Shema* represents fulfillment of the paramount commandment of acceptance of God's absolute sovereignty (קַבָּלַת עוֹל מַלְכוּת שָׁמַיִם). By declaring that God is One, Unique, and Indivisible, we subordinate every facet of our personalities, possessions — our very lives — to His will.

◗ אֵל מֶלֶךְ נֶאֱמָן ❧ — *God, trustworthy King.* He is אֵל, *God,* the All-powerful source of all mercy; He is the מֶלֶךְ, *King,* Who rules, leads, and exercises supervision over all; and He is

נֶאֱמָן, *trustworthy,* i.e., fair, apportioning no more suffering nor less good than one deserves (*Anaf Yosef*).

◗ שְׁמַע יִשְׂרָאֵל ❧ — *Hear, O Israel.* Although the commentators find many layers of profound meaning in this seminal verse, one should have at least the following points in mind during its recitation:

☐ At this point in history, HASHEM is only אֱלֹהֵינוּ, *our God,* for He is not acknowledged universally. Ultimately, however, all will recognize Him as אֶחָד ,ה׳, *the One and Only God* (*Rashi; Aruch HaShulchan* 61:4).

☐ ה׳ — *HASHEM.* God is the Eternal One, Who was, is, and always will be [הָיָה הֹוֶה וְיִהְיֶה], and He is אָדוֹן, *Master,* of all.

☐ אֱלֹהֵינוּ — *Our God.* He is all-Powerful (*Orach Chaim* 5).

אֶחָד — *The One [and Only].* The word has two connotations: (a) There is no God other

### THE SHEMA

Immediately before its recitation concentrate on fulfilling the positive commandment of reciting the *Shema* twice daily. It is important to enunciate each word clearly and not to run words together.

When praying without a *minyan,* begin with the following three-word formula:

*God, trustworthy King.* *

Recite the first verse aloud, with the right hand covering the eyes,
and concentrate intensely upon accepting God's absolute sovereignty.

# Hear, O Israel:* HASHEM is our God, HASHEM, the One and Only. *¹

In an undertone: *Blessed is the Name* of His glorious kingdom for all eternity.*

While reciting the first paragraph (*Deuteronomy 6:5-9*),
concentrate on accepting the commandment to love God.

וְאָהַבְתָּ *You shall love*\* HASHEM, your God, with all your heart, with all your soul and with all your resources. Let these matters that I command you today be upon your heart. Teach them thoroughly to your children and speak of them while you sit in your home, while you walk on the way, when you retire and when you arise. Bind them as a sign upon your arm and let them be tefillin between your eyes. And write them on the doorposts of your house and upon your gates.*

While reciting the second paragraph (*Deuteronomy 11:13-21*), concentrate on accepting all the commandments and the concept of reward and punishment.

וְהָיָה *And it will come to pass*\* that if you continually hearken to My commandments that I command you today, to love HASHEM, your God, and*

---

(1) *Deuteronomy* 6:4.

than HASHEM (*Rashbam*); and, (b) though we perceive God in many roles — kind, angry, merciful, wise, judging, and so on — these different attitudes are not contradictory, even though human intelligence does not comprehend their harmony. *Harav Gedaliah Schorr* likened this concept to a ray of light seen through a prism. Though one sees a myriad of different colors, they are all a single ray of light. So, too, God's many manifestations are truly one.

In saying the word אֶחָד, *the One and Only,* draw out the second syllable (חָ) a bit and emphasize the final consonant (ד). While drawing out the ח — a letter with the numerical value of eight — bear in mind that God is Master of the earth and the seven heavens. While clearly enunciating the final ד — which has the numerical value of four — bear in mind that God is Master in all four directions, meaning everywhere.

◆§ בָּרוּךְ שֵׁם — *Blessed is the Name.* Having proclaimed God as our King, we are grateful for the privilege of serving the One Whose kingdom is eternal and unbounded (*Etz Yosef*).

◆§ וְאָהַבְתָּ — *You shall love.* One should learn to fulfill the commandments out of love, rather than fear — and certainly not out of habit. The Mishnah (*Berachos* 9:5) explains that one should serve God with all his emotions and desires (*with all your heart*), even to the point of giving up his life for God (*with all your soul*), and even at the cost of his wealth (*with all your resources*).

◆§ וְהָיָה — *And it will come to pass.* Unlike the first paragraph of *Shema*, this one specifies the duty to perform מִצְוֹתַי, *My commandments,* and teaches that when the nation is righteous, it will be rewarded with success and prosperity. When it sins, it must expect poverty and exile.

בְּכָל־לְבַבְכֶם, וּבְכָל־נַפְשְׁכֶם, וְנָתַתִּי מְטַר־אַרְצְכֶם בְּעִתּוֹ, יוֹרֶה
וּמַלְקוֹשׁ, וְאָסַפְתָּ דְגָנֶךָ וְתִירֹשְׁךָ וְיִצְהָרֶךָ: וְנָתַתִּי | עֵשֶׂב | בְּשָׂדְךָ |
לִבְהֶמְתֶּךָ, וְאָכַלְתָּ וְשָׂבָעְתָּ: הִשָּׁמְרוּ* לָכֶם, פֶּן־יִפְתֶּה לְבַבְכֶם,
וְסַרְתֶּם וַעֲבַדְתֶּם | אֱלֹהִים | אֲחֵרִים, וְהִשְׁתַּחֲוִיתֶם לָהֶם:* וְחָרָה |
אַף־יהוה בָּכֶם, וְעָצַר | אֶת־הַשָּׁמַיִם, וְלֹא־יִהְיֶה מָטָר, וְהָאֲדָמָה לֹא
תִתֵּן אֶת־יְבוּלָהּ, וַאֲבַדְתֶּם* | מְהֵרָה מֵעַל הָאָרֶץ הַטֹּבָה | אֲשֶׁר |
יהוה נֹתֵן לָכֶם: וְשַׂמְתֶּם | אֶת־דְּבָרַי | אֵלֶּה, עַל־לְבַבְכֶם וְעַל־
נַפְשְׁכֶם, וּקְשַׁרְתֶּם | אֹתָם לְאוֹת | עַל־יֶדְכֶם, וְהָיוּ לְטוֹטָפֹת בֵּין |
עֵינֵיכֶם: וְלִמַּדְתֶּם | אֹתָם | אֶת־בְּנֵיכֶם, לְדַבֵּר בָּם, בְּשִׁבְתְּךָ* בְּבֵיתֶךָ,
וּבְלֶכְתְּךָ בַדֶּרֶךְ, וּבְשָׁכְבְּךָ וּבְקוּמֶךָ: וּכְתַבְתָּם | עַל־מְזוּזוֹת בֵּיתֶךָ,
וּבִשְׁעָרֶיךָ: לְמַעַן | יִרְבּוּ | יְמֵיכֶם וִימֵי בְנֵיכֶם, עַל הָאֲדָמָה | אֲשֶׁר
נִשְׁבַּע | יהוה לַאֲבֹתֵיכֶם לָתֵת לָהֶם, כִּימֵי הַשָּׁמַיִם | עַל־הָאָרֶץ:*

במדבר טו:לז-מא

**וַיֹּאמֶר** | יהוה* | אֶל־מֹשֶׁה לֵּאמֹר: דַּבֵּר | אֶל־בְּנֵי | יִשְׂרָאֵל,
וְאָמַרְתָּ אֲלֵהֶם, וְעָשׂוּ לָהֶם צִיצִת, עַל־כַּנְפֵי בִגְדֵיהֶם
לְדֹרֹתָם, וְנָתְנוּ | עַל־צִיצִת הַכָּנָף, פְּתִיל תְּכֵלֶת:* וְהָיָה לָכֶם לְצִיצִת,
וּרְאִיתֶם | אֹתוֹ, וּזְכַרְתֶּם | אֶת־כָּל־מִצְוֹת | יהוה, וַעֲשִׂיתֶם | אֹתָם,
וְלֹא תָתוּרוּ | אַחֲרֵי לְבַבְכֶם וְאַחֲרֵי | עֵינֵיכֶם, אֲשֶׁר־אַתֶּם זֹנִים |
אַחֲרֵיהֶם: לְמַעַן תִּזְכְּרוּ, וַעֲשִׂיתֶם | אֶת־כָּל־מִצְוֹתָי, וִהְיִיתֶם קְדֹשִׁים
לֵאלֹהֵיכֶם: אֲנִי | יהוה | אֱלֹהֵיכֶם, אֲשֶׁר
הוֹצֵאתִי | אֶתְכֶם | מֵאֶרֶץ מִצְרַיִם, לִהְיוֹת

Concentrate on fulfilling the<br>commandment to remember<br>the Exodus from Egypt.

לָכֶם לֵאלֹהִים, אֲנִי | יהוה | אֱלֹהֵיכֶם: אֱמֶת* —

Although the word אֱמֶת belongs to the next paragraph,<br>it is appended to the conclusion of the previous one.

**יהוה אֱלֹהֵיכֶם אֱמֶת.** — Chazzan repeats

---

וְאָכַלְתָּ וְשָׂבָעְתָּ. הִשָּׁמְרוּ — *And you will eat and be satisfied. Beware . . .* Prosperity is often the greatest challenge to religious devotion. People who are rich in wealth but poor in sophistication often succumb to temptation (Rashi).

יִפְתֶּה . . . וְהִשְׁתַּחֲוִיתֶם לָהֶם — *Be seduced . . . and bow to them,* i.e., to strange gods. An imperceptible, seemingly innocent surrender to temptation can be the beginning of a

course that will end in idolatry (Rashi).

וְלֹא יִהְיֶה מָטָר . . . וַאֲבַדְתֶּם — *So there will be no rain . . . And you will . . . be banished.* First will come famine. If that does not bring repentance, exile will follow (Vilna Gaon).

וְלִמַּדְתֶּם . . . בְּשִׁבְתְּךָ — *Teach them . . . while you sit.* In giving the command to educate children in the Torah, the verse speaks in the plural (וְלִמַּדְתֶּם), while the other words in the verse (בְּשִׁבְתְּךָ and so on) are in the

*to serve Him, with all your heart and with all your soul — then I will provide rain
for your land in its proper time, the early and late rains, that you may gather in
your grain, your wine, and your oil. I will provide grass in your field for your cattle
and you will eat and be satisfied. Beware\* lest your heart be seduced and you
turn astray and serve gods of others and bow to them.\* Then the wrath of
HASHEM will blaze against you. He will restrain the heaven so there will be no rain
and the ground will not yield its produce. And you will swiftly be banished\* from
the goodly land which HASHEM gives you. Place these words of Mine upon your
heart and upon your soul; bind them for a sign upon your arm and let them be
tefillin between your eyes. Teach them to your children, to discuss them, while
you sit\* in your home, while you walk on the way, when you retire and when
you arise. And write them on the doorposts of your house and upon your gates.
In order to prolong your days and the days of your children upon the ground that
HASHEM has sworn to your ancestors to give them, like the days of the heaven on
the earth.\**

Numbers 15:37-41

**וַיֹּאמֶר**  *And HASHEM said\* to Moses saying: Speak to the Children of Israel and
say to them that they are to make themselves tzitzis on the corners of
their garments, throughout their generations. And they are to place upon the
tzitzis of each corner a thread of techeiles.\* And it shall constitute tzitzis for you,
that you may see it and remember all the commandments of HASHEM and perform them; and not explore after your heart and after your eyes after which you
stray. So that you may remember and perform all My commandments; and be*
Concentrate on fulfilling the commandment  *holy to your God. I am HASHEM, your*
to remember the Exodus from Egypt.  *God, Who has removed you from the
land of Egypt to be a God to you; I am HASHEM your God — it is true\* —*

Although the word אֱמֶת, "true," belongs to the next paragraph,
it is appended to the conclusion of the previous one.

Chazzan repeats: **HASHEM, your God, is true.**

---

singular. This alludes to a *communal* re-
sponsibility to arrange for the Torah educa-
tion of children (*Iyun Tefillah*).

כִּימֵי הַשָּׁמַיִם עַל הָאָרֶץ — *Like the days of the
heaven on the earth.* Eretz Yisrael is the
eternal heritage of the Jewish people, just
as heaven will always remain above the
earth. Alternatively, just as heaven always
showers blessings upon the earth in the
form of life-giving rain, so too Israel will be
blessed in the land God has sworn to it.

וַיֹּאמֶר ה' — *And HASHEM said.* The third
paragraph of *Shema* is recited to fulfill the
commandment to recall the Exodus every
day. By freeing Israel from Egypt, God laid
claim to the nation's eternal allegiance. No

Jew is free to absolve himself of that
obligation (*Rashi*).

פְּתִיל תְּכֵלֶת — *A thread of techeiles.* Techeiles
is sky-blue wool dyed with the secretion of
an amphibian called *chilazon*. For many
centuries the identity of the animal has
been unknown. Even in the absence of the
*techeiles* thread, however, the commandment of *tzitzis* remains binding (*Menachos*
38a).

אֱמֶת — *True.* The law that one may not
interrupt between the last words of the
*Shema* and אֱמֶת is of ancient origin. The
reason is so that we declare, as did the
prophet [*Jeremiah* 10:10], וַה' אֱלֹהִים אֱמֶת,
*HASHEM, God, is true* (*Berachos* 14a).

וֶאֱמוּנָה* כָּל זֹאת, וְקַיָּם עָלֵינוּ, כִּי הוּא יהוה אֱלֹהֵינוּ וְאֵין זוּלָתוֹ,
וַאֲנַחְנוּ יִשְׂרָאֵל עַמּוֹ. הַפּוֹדֵנוּ מִיַּד מְלָכִים, מַלְכֵּנוּ
הַגּוֹאֲלֵנוּ מִכַּף כָּל הֶעָרִיצִים. הָאֵל הַנִּפְרָע לָנוּ מִצָּרֵינוּ, וְהַמְשַׁלֵּם
גְּמוּל לְכָל אֹיְבֵי נַפְשֵׁנוּ. הָעֹשֶׂה גְדֹלוֹת עַד אֵין חֵקֶר, וְנִפְלָאוֹת
עַד אֵין מִסְפָּר.¹ הַשָּׂם נַפְשֵׁנוּ בַּחַיִּים,* וְלֹא נָתַן לַמּוֹט רַגְלֵנוּ.²
הַמַּדְרִיכֵנוּ עַל בָּמוֹת אוֹיְבֵינוּ, וַיָּרֶם קַרְנֵנוּ עַל כָּל שׂנְאֵינוּ. הָעֹשֶׂה
לָנוּ נִסִּים וּנְקָמָה בְּפַרְעֹה, אוֹתוֹת וּמוֹפְתִים בְּאַדְמַת בְּנֵי חָם. הַמַּכֶּה
בְעֶבְרָתוֹ כָּל בְּכוֹרֵי מִצְרָיִם, וַיּוֹצֵא אֶת עַמּוֹ יִשְׂרָאֵל מִתּוֹכָם לְחֵרוּת
עוֹלָם. הַמַּעֲבִיר בָּנָיו בֵּין גִּזְרֵי יַם סוּף, אֶת רוֹדְפֵיהֶם וְאֶת שׂוֹנְאֵיהֶם
בִּתְהוֹמוֹת טִבַּע. וְרָאוּ בָנָיו גְּבוּרָתוֹ, שִׁבְּחוּ וְהוֹדוּ לִשְׁמוֹ.
❖ וּמַלְכוּתוֹ בְּרָצוֹן קִבְּלוּ עֲלֵיהֶם. מֹשֶׁה וּבְנֵי יִשְׂרָאֵל לְךָ עָנוּ שִׁירָה
בְּשִׂמְחָה רַבָּה, וְאָמְרוּ כֻלָּם:

מִי כָמְכָה בָּאֵלִם יהוה, מִי כָּמְכָה נֶאְדָּר בַּקֹּדֶשׁ,
נוֹרָא תְהִלֹּת,* עֹשֵׂה פֶלֶא.³

❖ מַלְכוּתְךָ רָאוּ בָנֶיךָ בּוֹקֵעַ יָם לִפְנֵי מֹשֶׁה, זֶה אֵלִי⁴ עָנוּ וְאָמְרוּ:

יהוה יִמְלֹךְ לְעֹלָם וָעֶד.⁵

❖ וְנֶאֱמַר: כִּי פָדָה יהוה אֶת יַעֲקֹב, וּגְאָלוֹ מִיַּד חָזָק מִמֶּנּוּ.⁶ בָּרוּךְ
אַתָּה יהוה, גָּאַל יִשְׂרָאֵל. (.Cong — אָמֵן.)

הַשְׁכִּיבֵנוּ* יהוה אֱלֹהֵינוּ לְשָׁלוֹם, וְהַעֲמִידֵנוּ מַלְכֵּנוּ לְחַיִּים,
וּפְרוֹשׂ עָלֵינוּ סֻכַּת שְׁלוֹמֶךָ, וְתַקְּנֵנוּ בְּעֵצָה טוֹבָה
מִלְּפָנֶיךָ, וְהוֹשִׁיעֵנוּ לְמַעַן שְׁמֶךָ. וְהָגֵן בַּעֲדֵנוּ, וְהָסֵר מֵעָלֵינוּ אוֹיֵב,
דֶּבֶר, וְחֶרֶב, וְרָעָב, וְיָגוֹן, וְהָסֵר שָׂטָן מִלְּפָנֵינוּ וּמֵאַחֲרֵינוּ, וּבְצֵל
כְּנָפֶיךָ תַּסְתִּירֵנוּ,⁷ כִּי אֵל שׁוֹמְרֵנוּ וּמַצִּילֵנוּ אָתָּה, כִּי אֵל מֶלֶךְ חַנּוּן
וְרַחוּם אָתָּה.⁸ ❖ וּשְׁמוֹר צֵאתֵנוּ וּבוֹאֵנוּ לְחַיִּים וּלְשָׁלוֹם מֵעַתָּה וְעַד
עוֹלָם.⁹ בָּרוּךְ אַתָּה יהוה, שׁוֹמֵר עַמּוֹ יִשְׂרָאֵל לָעַד. (.Cong — אָמֵן.)

---

אֱמֶת וֶאֱמוּנָה ﬞ — *True and faithful.* This
paragraph continues our fulfillment of the
obligation to recall the Exodus in the evening. The morning blessing of אֱמֶת וְיַצִּיב,
*True and certain,* concentrates on God's kindness in having redeemed us from Egypt,
while אֱמֶת וֶאֱמוּנָה, *True and faithful,* recited at
night, symbolizes exile and stresses our faith
that God will redeem us from this exile just

as He did at the time of the Exodus (*Berachos*
12a; *Rashi* and *Tosafos*).

הַשָּׂם נַפְשֵׁנוּ בַּחַיִּים —*Who set our soul in life.* A
reference to the night in Egypt when all
non-Jewish firstborn died, but Jewish souls
were preserved (*Abudraham*). This also implies God's protection from the murderous
designs of our enemies in all generations
(*Siach Yitzchak*).

**וֶאֱמוּנָה** *And faithful\* is all this, and it is firmly established for us that He is* HASHEM *our God, and there is none but Him, and we are Israel, His people. He redeems us from the power of kings, our King Who delivers us from the hand of all the cruel tyrants. He is the God Who exacts vengeance for us from our foes and Who brings just retribution upon all enemies of our soul; Who performs great deeds that are beyond comprehension, and wonders beyond number.* [1] *Who set our soul in life\* and did not allow our foot to falter.* [2] *Who led us upon the heights of our enemies and raised our pride above all who hate us; Who wrought for us miracles and vengeance upon Pharaoh; signs and wonders on the land of the offspring of Ham; Who struck with His anger all the firstborn of Egypt and removed His people Israel from their midst to eternal freedom; Who brought His children through the split parts of the Sea of Reeds while those who pursued them and hated them He caused to sink into the depths. When His children perceived His power, they lauded and gave grateful praise to His Name.* Chazzan— *And His Kingship they accepted upon themselves willingly. Moses and the Children of Israel raised their voices to You in song, with abundant gladness — and said unanimously:*

**Who is like You among the heavenly powers, HASHEM! Who is like You, mighty in holiness, too awesome for praise,\* doing wonders!** [3]

Chazzan— *Your children beheld Your majesty, as You split the sea before Moses, "This is my God!"* [4] *they exclaimed, then they said:*

**"HASHEM shall reign for all eternity!"** [5]

Chazzan— *And it is further said: "For* HASHEM *has redeemed Jacob and delivered him from a power mightier than he."* [6] *Blessed are You,* HASHEM, *Who redeemed Israel.* (Cong.— Amen.)

**הַשְׁכִּיבֵנוּ** *Lay us down\* to sleep,* HASHEM, *our God, in peace, raise us erect, our King, to life; and spread over us the shelter of Your peace. Set us aright with good counsel from before Your Presence, and save us for Your Name's sake. Shield us, remove from us foe, plague, sword, famine, and woe; and remove spiritual impediment from before us and behind us, and in the shadow of Your wings shelter us* [7] *— for God Who protects and rescues us are You; for God, the Gracious and Compassionate King, are You.* [8] Chazzan— *Safeguard our going and coming, for life and for peace from now to eternity.* [9] *Blessed are You,* HASHEM, *Who protects His people Israel forever.* (Cong.— Amen.)

---

(1) *Job* 9:10. (2) *Psalms* 66:9. (3) *Exodus* 15:11. (4) 15:2. (5) 15:18. (6) *Jeremiah* 31:10. (7) Cf. *Psalms* 17:8. (8) Cf. *Nehemiah* 9:31. (9) Cf. *Psalms* 121:8.

---

נוֹרָא תְהִלֹת — *Too awesome for praise.* We are too terrified to attempt a complete assessment of His greatness, because whatever we say is insufficient (*Rashi*).

Rambam comments that it is impossible for people to praise God adequately; the only way to laud Him is by simply recount-ing His awe-inspiring deeds. Thus he would render this phrase: [God's] *awesomeness constitutes His praises.*

הַשְׁכִּיבֵנוּ &#x96a; — *Lay us down.* The Talmud (*Berachos* 4a) describes this blessing as an extension of the previous blessing of redemption [גְּאוּלָה אֲרִיכְתָא]. Whereas the theme of

Some congregations omit the following on the conclusion of the Sabbath.
They continue with Half-*Kaddish* (below).

**בָּרוּךְ** יהוה לְעוֹלָם,* אָמֵן וְאָמֵן.¹ בָּרוּךְ יהוה מִצִּיּוֹן, שֹׁכֵן
יְרוּשָׁלָיִם, הַלְלוּיָהּ.² בָּרוּךְ יהוה אֱלֹהִים אֱלֹהֵי יִשְׂרָאֵל,
עֹשֵׂה נִפְלָאוֹת לְבַדּוֹ. וּבָרוּךְ שֵׁם כְּבוֹדוֹ לְעוֹלָם, וְיִמָּלֵא כְבוֹדוֹ אֶת
כָּל הָאָרֶץ, אָמֵן וְאָמֵן.³ יְהִי כְבוֹד יהוה לְעוֹלָם, יִשְׂמַח יהוה
בְּמַעֲשָׂיו.⁴ יְהִי שֵׁם יהוה מְבֹרָךְ, מֵעַתָּה וְעַד עוֹלָם.⁵ כִּי לֹא יִטֹּשׁ יהוה
אֶת עַמּוֹ בַּעֲבוּר שְׁמוֹ הַגָּדוֹל, כִּי הוֹאִיל יהוה לַעֲשׂוֹת אֶתְכֶם לוֹ
לְעָם.⁶ וַיַּרְא כָּל הָעָם וַיִּפְּלוּ עַל פְּנֵיהֶם, וַיֹּאמְרוּ, יהוה הוּא הָאֱלֹהִים,
יהוה הוּא הָאֱלֹהִים.⁷ וְהָיָה יהוה לְמֶלֶךְ עַל כָּל הָאָרֶץ, בַּיּוֹם הַהוּא
יִהְיֶה יהוה אֶחָד וּשְׁמוֹ אֶחָד.⁸ יְהִי חַסְדְּךָ יהוה עָלֵינוּ, כַּאֲשֶׁר יִחַלְנוּ
לָךְ.⁹ הוֹשִׁיעֵנוּ יהוה אֱלֹהֵינוּ, וְקַבְּצֵנוּ מִן הַגּוֹיִם, לְהוֹדוֹת לְשֵׁם
קָדְשֶׁךָ, לְהִשְׁתַּבֵּחַ בִּתְהִלָּתֶךָ.¹⁰ כָּל גּוֹיִם אֲשֶׁר עָשִׂיתָ יָבוֹאוּ וְיִשְׁתַּחֲווּ
לְפָנֶיךָ אֲדֹנָי, וִיכַבְּדוּ לִשְׁמֶךָ. כִּי גָדוֹל אַתָּה וְעֹשֵׂה נִפְלָאוֹת, אַתָּה
אֱלֹהִים לְבַדֶּךָ.¹¹ וַאֲנַחְנוּ עַמְּךָ וְצֹאן מַרְעִיתֶךָ, נוֹדֶה לְּךָ לְעוֹלָם,
לְדוֹר וָדֹר נְסַפֵּר תְּהִלָּתֶךָ.¹² בָּרוּךְ יהוה בַּיּוֹם. בָּרוּךְ יהוה בַּלָּיְלָה.
בָּרוּךְ יהוה בְּשָׁכְבֵנוּ. בָּרוּךְ יהוה בְּקוּמֵנוּ. כִּי בְיָדְךָ נַפְשׁוֹת הַחַיִּים
וְהַמֵּתִים. אֲשֶׁר בְּיָדוֹ נֶפֶשׁ כָּל חָי, וְרוּחַ כָּל בְּשַׂר אִישׁ.¹³ בְּיָדְךָ
אַפְקִיד רוּחִי, פָּדִיתָה אוֹתִי, יהוה אֵל אֱמֶת.¹⁴ אֱלֹהֵינוּ שֶׁבַּשָּׁמַיִם,
יַחֵד שְׁמֶךָ, וְקַיֵּם מַלְכוּתְךָ תָּמִיד, וּמְלוֹךְ עָלֵינוּ לְעוֹלָם וָעֶד.

**יִרְאוּ** עֵינֵינוּ וְיִשְׂמַח לִבֵּנוּ וְתָגֵל נַפְשֵׁנוּ בִּישׁוּעָתְךָ בֶּאֱמֶת, בֶּאֱמֹר
לְצִיּוֹן מָלַךְ אֱלֹהָיִךְ.¹⁵ יהוה מֶלֶךְ,¹⁶ יהוה מָלָךְ,¹⁷ יהוה יִמְלֹךְ
לְעֹלָם וָעֶד.¹⁸ ❖ כִּי הַמַּלְכוּת שֶׁלְּךָ הִיא, וּלְעוֹלְמֵי עַד תִּמְלוֹךְ בְּכָבוֹד,
כִּי אֵין לָנוּ מֶלֶךְ אֶלָּא אָתָּה. בָּרוּךְ אַתָּה יהוה, הַמֶּלֶךְ בִּכְבוֹדוֹ תָּמִיד
יִמְלוֹךְ עָלֵינוּ לְעוֹלָם וָעֶד, וְעַל כָּל מַעֲשָׂיו. (.אָמֵן – Cong.)

The *chazzan* recites חֲצִי קַדִּישׁ:

**יִתְגַּדַּל** וְיִתְקַדַּשׁ שְׁמֵהּ רַבָּא. (.אָמֵן – Cong.) בְּעָלְמָא דִּי בְרָא כִרְעוּתֵהּ.
וְיַמְלִיךְ מַלְכוּתֵהּ, בְּחַיֵּיכוֹן וּבְיוֹמֵיכוֹן וּבְחַיֵּי דְכָל בֵּית יִשְׂרָאֵל,
בַּעֲגָלָא וּבִזְמַן קָרִיב. וְאִמְרוּ: אָמֵן.
(.אָמֵן – Cong.) יְהֵא שְׁמֵהּ רַבָּא מְבָרַךְ לְעָלַם וּלְעָלְמֵי עָלְמַיָּא.)

---

the earlier blessing was God's redemption of
Israel from Egypt [and the allusion to the
future redemption], this one describes Him

as our Savior from the dangers and afflic-
tions associated with the terrors of night,
literally and figuratively (*Seder HaYom*).

Some congregations omit the following on the conclusion of the Sabbath.
They continue with Half-*Kaddish* (below).

בָּרוּךְ *Blessed is HASHEM forever,* \* *Amen and Amen.* [1] *Blessed is HASHEM from Zion, Who dwells in Jerusalem, Halleluyah!* [2] *Blessed is HASHEM, God, the God of Israel, Who alone does wondrous things. Blessed is His glorious Name forever, and may all the earth be filled with His glory, Amen and Amen.* [3] *May the glory of HASHEM endure forever, let HASHEM rejoice in His works.* [4] *Blessed be the Name of HASHEM from this time and forever.* [5] *For HASHEM will not cast off His people for the sake of His Great Name, for HASHEM has vowed to make you His own people.* [6] *Then the entire people saw and fell on their faces and said, "HASHEM — only He is God! HASHEM — only He is God!"* [7] *Then HASHEM will be King over all the world, on that day HASHEM will be One and His Name will be One.* [8] *May Your kindness, HASHEM, be upon us, just as we awaited You.* [9] *Save us, HASHEM, our God, gather us from the nations, to thank Your Holy Name and to glory in Your praise!* [10] *All the nations that You made will come and bow before You, My Lord, and shall glorify Your Name. For You are great and work wonders; You alone, O God.* [11] *Then we, Your people and the sheep of Your pasture, shall thank You forever; for generation after generation we will relate Your praise.* [12] *Blessed is HASHEM by day; blessed is HASHEM by night; Blessed is HASHEM when we retire; Blessed is HASHEM when we arise. For in Your hand are the souls of the living and the dead. He in Whose hand is the soul of all the living and the spirit of every human being.* [13] *In Your hand I shall entrust my spirit, You redeemed me, HASHEM, God of truth.* [14] *Our God, Who is in heaven, bring unity to Your Name; establish Your kingdom forever and reign over us for all eternity.*

יִרְאוּ *May our eyes see, our heart rejoice and our soul exult in Your salvation in truth, when Zion is told, "Your God has reigned!"* [15] *HASHEM reigns,* [16] *HASHEM has reigned,* [17] *HASHEM will reign for all eternity.* [18] Chazzan – *For the kingdom is Yours and You will reign for all eternity in glory, for we have no King but You. Blessed are You, HASHEM, the King in His glory — He shall constantly reign over us forever and ever, and over all His creatures.* (Cong.– *Amen.*)

The chazzan recites Half-*Kaddish:*

יִתְגַּדַּל *May His great Name grow exalted and sanctified* (Cong.– *Amen.*) *in the world that He created as He willed. May He give reign to His kingship in your lifetimes and in your days, and in the lifetimes of the entire Family of Israel, swiftly and soon. Now respond: Amen.*

(Cong. – *Amen. May His great Name be blessed forever and ever.*)

(1) *Psalms* 89:53. (2) 135:21. (3) 72:18-19. (4) 104:31. (5) 113:2. (6) *I Samuel* 12:22. (7) *I Kings* 18:39. (8) *Zechariah* 14:9. (9) *Psalms* 33:22. (10) 106:47. (11) 86:9-10. (12) 79:13. (13) *Job* 12:10. (14) *Psalms* 31:6. (15) Cf. *Isaiah* 52:7. (16) *Psalms* 10:16. (17) 93:1 et al. (18) *Exodus* 15:18.

בָּרוּךְ ה׳ לְעוֹלָם — *Blessed is HASHEM forever*. This collection of Scriptural verses was introduced during the Geonic era. At that time most people gathered in the fields for prayers (apparently on the way from their farms to their homes). In order to shorten the

יְהֵא שְׁמֵהּ רַבָּא מְבָרַךְ לְעָלַם וּלְעָלְמֵי עָלְמַיָּא.

יִתְבָּרַךְ וְיִשְׁתַּבַּח וְיִתְפָּאַר וְיִתְרוֹמַם וְיִתְנַשֵּׂא וְיִתְהַדָּר וְיִתְעַלֶּה
וְיִתְהַלָּל שְׁמֵהּ דְּקֻדְשָׁא בְּרִיךְ הוּא (.Cong – בְּרִיךְ הוּא) – לְעֵלָּא מִן כָּל
בִּרְכָתָא וְשִׁירָתָא תֻּשְׁבְּחָתָא וְנֶחֱמָתָא, דַּאֲמִירָן בְּעָלְמָא. וְאִמְרוּ: אָמֵן.
(אָמֵן –Cong.)

## ﴾ שְׁמוֹנֶה עֶשְׂרֵה – עֲמִידָה ﴿

Take three steps backward, then three steps forward. Remain standing with feet together
while reciting *Shemoneh Esrei*. Recite it with quiet devotion and without any interruption.
Although it should not be audible to others, one must pray loudly enough to hear himself.

אֲדֹנָי שְׂפָתַי תִּפְתָּח, וּפִי יַגִּיד תְּהִלָּתֶךָ.[1]

### אבות

Bend the knees at בָּרוּךְ; bow at אַתָּה; straighten up at ה'.

בָּרוּךְ אַתָּה יהוה אֱלֹהֵינוּ וֵאלֹהֵי אֲבוֹתֵינוּ, אֱלֹהֵי אַבְרָהָם,
אֱלֹהֵי יִצְחָק, וֵאלֹהֵי יַעֲקֹב, הָאֵל הַגָּדוֹל הַגִּבּוֹר וְהַנּוֹרָא, אֵל
עֶלְיוֹן, גּוֹמֵל חֲסָדִים טוֹבִים, וְקוֹנֵה הַכֹּל, וְזוֹכֵר חַסְדֵי אָבוֹת, וּמֵבִיא
גוֹאֵל לִבְנֵי בְנֵיהֶם, לְמַעַן שְׁמוֹ בְּאַהֲבָה. מֶלֶךְ עוֹזֵר וּמוֹשִׁיעַ וּמָגֵן.

Bend the knees at בָּרוּךְ; bow at אַתָּה; straighten up at ה'.

בָּרוּךְ אַתָּה יהוה, מָגֵן אַבְרָהָם.

### גבורות

אַתָּה גִּבּוֹר לְעוֹלָם אֲדֹנָי, מְחַיֵּה מֵתִים אַתָּה, רַב לְהוֹשִׁיעַ.
מַשִּׁיב הָרוּחַ וּמוֹרִיד הַגֶּשֶׁם [נ"א הַגָּשֶׁם]. מְכַלְכֵּל חַיִּים
בְּחֶסֶד, מְחַיֵּה מֵתִים בְּרַחֲמִים רַבִּים, סוֹמֵךְ נוֹפְלִים, וְרוֹפֵא חוֹלִים,
וּמַתִּיר אֲסוּרִים, וּמְקַיֵּם אֱמוּנָתוֹ לִישֵׁנֵי עָפָר. מִי כָמוֹךָ בַּעַל גְּבוּרוֹת,
וּמִי דוֹמֶה לָּךְ, מֶלֶךְ מֵמִית וּמְחַיֶּה וּמַצְמִיחַ יְשׁוּעָה. וְנֶאֱמָן אַתָּה
לְהַחֲיוֹת מֵתִים. בָּרוּךְ אַתָּה יהוה, מְחַיֵּה הַמֵּתִים.

### קדושת השם

אַתָּה קָדוֹשׁ וְשִׁמְךָ קָדוֹשׁ, וּקְדוֹשִׁים בְּכָל יוֹם יְהַלְלוּךָ סֶּלָה.
בָּרוּךְ אַתָּה יהוה, הָאֵל הַקָּדוֹשׁ.

### בינה

אַתָּה חוֹנֵן לְאָדָם דַּעַת, וּמְלַמֵּד לֶאֱנוֹשׁ בִּינָה.

---

service so that it could be completed before
dark, this collection of verses was substi-

tuted for *Shemoneh Esrei*, which would be
recited later by each individual in the safety

*May His great Name be blessed forever and ever.*
*Blessed, praised, glorified, exalted, extolled, mighty, upraised, and lauded be the Name of the Holy One, Blessed is He* (Cong.— *Blessed is He*) — *beyond any blessing and song, praise and consolation that are uttered in the world. Now respond: Amen.* (Cong.— *Amen.*)

## ⚜ SHEMONEH ESREI — AMIDAH ⚜

Take three steps backward, then three steps forward. Remain standing with feet together while reciting *Shemoneh Esrei*. Recite it with quiet devotion and without any interruption. Although it should not be audible to others, one must pray loudly enough to hear himself.

*My Lord, open my lips, that my mouth may declare Your praise.* [1]

### PATRIARCHS

Bend the knees at *"Blessed"*; bow at *"You"*; straighten up at *"HASHEM."*

בָּרוּךְ *Blessed are You, HASHEM, our God and the God of our forefathers, God of Abraham, God of Isaac, and God of Jacob; the great, mighty, and awesome God, the supreme God, Who bestows beneficial kindnesses and creates everything, Who recalls the kindnesses of the Patriarchs and brings a Redeemer to their children's children, for His Name's sake, with love. O King, Helper, Savior, and Shield.*

Bend the knees at *"Blessed"*; bow at *"You"*; straighten up at *"HASHEM."*
*Blessed are You, HASHEM, Shield of Abraham.*

### GOD'S MIGHT

אַתָּה *You are eternally mighty, my Lord, the Resuscitator of the dead are You; abundantly able to save, Who makes the wind blow and makes the rain descend; Who sustains the living with kindness, resuscitates the dead with abundant mercy, supports the fallen, heals the sick, releases the confined, and maintains His faith to those asleep in the dust. Who is like You, O Master of mighty deeds, and who is comparable to You, O King Who causes death and restores life and makes salvation sprout! And You are faithful to resuscitate the dead. Blessed are You, HASHEM, Who resuscitates the dead.*

### HOLINESS OF GOD'S NAME

אַתָּה *You are holy and Your Name is holy, and holy ones praise You every day, forever. Blessed are You, HASHEM, the holy God.*

### INSIGHT

אַתָּה *You graciously endow man with wisdom and teach insight to a frail mortal.*

---

(1) *Psalms* 51:17.

---

of his home. Another version has it that these verses were added in order to allow latecomers more time to catch up to the congregation. Whichever the reason, it was retained even after the practice of praying in the fields was discontinued.

At the conclusion of the Sabbath, add:

**אַתָּה** חוֹנַנְתָּנוּ לְמַדַּע תּוֹרָתֶךָ, וַתְּלַמְּדֵנוּ לַעֲשׂוֹת חֻקֵּי רְצוֹנֶךָ, וַתַּבְדֵּל יהוה אֱלֹהֵינוּ בֵּין קְדֶשׁ לְחוֹל, בֵּין אוֹר לְחֹשֶׁךָ, בֵּין יִשְׂרָאֵל לָעַמִּים, בֵּין יוֹם הַשְּׁבִיעִי לְשֵׁשֶׁת יְמֵי הַמַּעֲשֶׂה. אָבִינוּ מַלְכֵּנוּ הָחֵל עָלֵינוּ הַיָּמִים הַבָּאִים לִקְרָאתֵנוּ לְשָׁלוֹם, חֲשׂוּכִים מִכָּל חֵטְא, וּמְנֻקִּים מִכָּל עָוֹן וּמְדֻבָּקִים בְּיִרְאָתֶךָ. וְ ...

חָנֵּנוּ מֵאִתְּךָ דֵּעָה בִּינָה וְהַשְׂכֵּל. בָּרוּךְ אַתָּה יהוה, חוֹנֵן הַדָּעַת.

**תשובה**

**הֲשִׁיבֵנוּ** אָבִינוּ לְתוֹרָתֶךָ, וְקָרְבֵנוּ מַלְכֵּנוּ לַעֲבוֹדָתֶךָ, וְהַחֲזִירֵנוּ בִּתְשׁוּבָה שְׁלֵמָה לְפָנֶיךָ. בָּרוּךְ אַתָּה יהוה, הָרוֹצֶה בִּתְשׁוּבָה.

**סליחה**

Strike the left side of the chest with the right fist
while reciting the words חָטָאנוּ and פָּשָׁעְנוּ.

**סְלַח** לָנוּ אָבִינוּ כִּי חָטָאנוּ, מְחַל לָנוּ מַלְכֵּנוּ כִּי פָשָׁעְנוּ, כִּי מוֹחֵל וְסוֹלֵחַ אָתָּה. בָּרוּךְ אַתָּה יהוה, חַנּוּן הַמַּרְבֶּה לִסְלוֹחַ.

**גאולה**

**רְאֵה** בְעָנְיֵנוּ, וְרִיבָה רִיבֵנוּ, וּגְאָלֵנוּ¹ מְהֵרָה לְמַעַן שְׁמֶךָ, כִּי גּוֹאֵל חָזָק אָתָּה. בָּרוּךְ אַתָּה יהוה, גּוֹאֵל יִשְׂרָאֵל.

**רפואה**

**רְפָאֵנוּ** יהוה וְנֵרָפֵא, הוֹשִׁיעֵנוּ וְנִוָּשֵׁעָה, כִּי תְהִלָּתֵנוּ אָתָּה,² וְהַעֲלֵה רְפוּאָה שְׁלֵמָה לְכָל מַכּוֹתֵינוּ,° כִּי אֵל מֶלֶךְ רוֹפֵא נֶאֱמָן וְרַחֲמָן אָתָּה. בָּרוּךְ אַתָּה יהוה, רוֹפֵא חוֹלֵי עַמּוֹ יִשְׂרָאֵל.

**ברכת השנים**

**בָּרֵךְ** עָלֵינוּ יהוה אֱלֹהֵינוּ אֶת הַשָּׁנָה הַזֹּאת וְאֶת כָּל מִינֵי תְבוּאָתָהּ לְטוֹבָה, וְתֵן טַל וּמָטָר לִבְרָכָה עַל פְּנֵי הָאֲדָמָה, וְשַׂבְּעֵנוּ מִטּוּבֶךָ, וּבָרֵךְ שְׁנָתֵנוּ כַּשָּׁנִים הַטּוֹבוֹת. בָּרוּךְ אַתָּה יהוה, מְבָרֵךְ הַשָּׁנִים.

°At this point one may interject a prayer for one who is ill:
יְהִי רָצוֹן מִלְּפָנֶיךָ, יהוה אֱלֹהַי וֵאלֹהֵי אֲבוֹתַי,
שֶׁתִּשְׁלַח מְהֵרָה רְפוּאָה שְׁלֵמָה מִן הַשָּׁמַיִם, רְפוּאַת הַנֶּפֶשׁ וּרְפוּאַת הַגּוּף
for a male—לַחוֹלֶה (patient's name) בֶּן (mother's name) בְּתוֹךְ שְׁאָר חוֹלֵי יִשְׂרָאֵל.
for a female—לַחוֹלָה (patient's name) בַּת (mother's name) בְּתוֹךְ שְׁאָר חוֹלֵי יִשְׂרָאֵל.
Continue—כִּי אֵל ...

At the conclusion of the Sabbath, add:

**אַתָּה** You have graced us with intelligence to study Your Torah and You have taught us to perform the decrees You have willed. HASHEM, our God, You have distinguished between the sacred and the secular, between light and darkness, between Israel and the peoples, between the seventh day and the six days of labor. Our Father, our King, begin for us the days approaching us for peace, free from all sin, cleansed from all iniquity and attached to fear of You. And . . .

Endow us graciously from Yourself with wisdom, insight, and discernment. Blessed are You, HASHEM, gracious Giver of wisdom.

### REPENTANCE

**הֲשִׁיבֵנוּ** Bring us back, our Father, to Your Torah, and bring us near, our King, to Your service, and influence us to return in perfect repentance before You. Blessed are You, HASHEM, Who desires repentance.

### FORGIVENESS

Strike the left side of the chest with the right fist
while reciting the words "erred" and "sinned."

**סְלַח** Forgive us, our Father, for we have erred; pardon us, our King, for we have willfully sinned; for You pardon and forgive. Blessed are You, HASHEM, the gracious One Who pardons abundantly.

### REDEMPTION

**רְאֵה** Behold our affliction, take up our grievance, and redeem us [1] speedily for Your Name's sake, for You are a powerful Redeemer. Blessed are You, HASHEM, Redeemer of Israel.

### HEALTH AND HEALING

**רְפָאֵנוּ** Heal us, HASHEM — then we will be healed; save us — then we will be saved, for You are our praise. [2] Bring complete recovery for all our ailments, ° for You are God, King, the faithful and compassionate Healer. Blessed are You, HASHEM, Who heals the sick of His people Israel.

### YEAR OF PROSPERITY

**בָּרֵךְ** Bless on our behalf — O HASHEM, our God — this year and all its kinds of crops for the best, and give dew and rain for a blessing on the face of the earth, and satisfy us from Your bounty, and bless our year like the best years. Blessed are You, HASHEM, Who blesses the years.

°At this point one may interject a prayer for one who is ill:
May it be Your will, HASHEM, my God, and the God of my forefathers, that You quickly send a complete recovery from heaven, spiritual healing and physical healing to the patient (name) son/daughter of (mother's name) among the other patients of Israel.                                    Continue: for You are God . . .

(1) Cf. Psalms 119:153-154. (2) Cf. Jeremiah 17:14.

**קיבוץ גליות**

**תְּקַע** בְּשׁוֹפָר גָּדוֹל לְחֵרוּתֵנוּ, וְשָׂא נֵס לְקַבֵּץ גָּלֻיּוֹתֵינוּ, וְקַבְּצֵנוּ יַחַד מֵאַרְבַּע כַּנְפוֹת הָאָרֶץ.[1] בָּרוּךְ אַתָּה יהוה, מְקַבֵּץ נִדְחֵי עַמּוֹ יִשְׂרָאֵל.

**דין**

**הָשִׁיבָה** שׁוֹפְטֵינוּ כְּבָרִאשׁוֹנָה, וְיוֹעֲצֵינוּ כְּבַתְּחִלָּה,[2] וְהָסֵר מִמֶּנּוּ יָגוֹן וַאֲנָחָה, וּמְלוֹךְ עָלֵינוּ אַתָּה יהוה לְבַדְּךָ בְּחֶסֶד וּבְרַחֲמִים, וְצַדְּקֵנוּ בַּמִּשְׁפָּט. בָּרוּךְ אַתָּה יהוה, מֶלֶךְ אוֹהֵב צְדָקָה וּמִשְׁפָּט.

**ברכת המינים**

**וְלַמַּלְשִׁינִים** אַל תְּהִי תִקְוָה, וְכָל הָרִשְׁעָה כְּרֶגַע תֹּאבֵד, וְכָל אֹיְבֶיךָ מְהֵרָה יִכָּרֵתוּ, וְהַזֵּדִים מְהֵרָה תְעַקֵּר וּתְשַׁבֵּר וּתְמַגֵּר וְתַכְנִיעַ בִּמְהֵרָה בְיָמֵינוּ. בָּרוּךְ אַתָּה יהוה, שׁוֹבֵר אֹיְבִים וּמַכְנִיעַ זֵדִים.

**צדיקים**

**עַל הַצַּדִּיקִים** וְעַל הַחֲסִידִים, וְעַל זִקְנֵי עַמְּךָ בֵּית יִשְׂרָאֵל, וְעַל פְּלֵיטַת סוֹפְרֵיהֶם, וְעַל גֵּרֵי הַצֶּדֶק וְעָלֵינוּ, יֶהֱמוּ רַחֲמֶיךָ יהוה אֱלֹהֵינוּ, וְתֵן שָׂכָר טוֹב לְכָל הַבּוֹטְחִים בְּשִׁמְךָ בֶּאֱמֶת, וְשִׂים חֶלְקֵנוּ עִמָּהֶם לְעוֹלָם, וְלֹא נֵבוֹשׁ כִּי בְךָ בָּטָחְנוּ. בָּרוּךְ אַתָּה יהוה, מִשְׁעָן וּמִבְטָח לַצַּדִּיקִים.

**בנין ירושלים**

**וְלִירוּשָׁלַיִם** עִירְךָ בְּרַחֲמִים תָּשׁוּב, וְתִשְׁכּוֹן בְּתוֹכָהּ כַּאֲשֶׁר דִּבַּרְתָּ, וּבְנֵה אוֹתָהּ בְּקָרוֹב בְּיָמֵינוּ בִּנְיַן עוֹלָם, וְכִסֵּא דָוִד מְהֵרָה לְתוֹכָהּ תָּכִין. בָּרוּךְ אַתָּה יהוה, בּוֹנֵה יְרוּשָׁלָיִם.

**מלכות בית דוד**

**אֶת צֶמַח** דָּוִד עַבְדְּךָ מְהֵרָה תַצְמִיחַ, וְקַרְנוֹ תָּרוּם בִּישׁוּעָתֶךָ, כִּי לִישׁוּעָתְךָ קִוִּינוּ כָּל הַיּוֹם. בָּרוּךְ אַתָּה יהוה, מַצְמִיחַ קֶרֶן יְשׁוּעָה.

**קבלת תפלה**

**שְׁמַע קוֹלֵנוּ** יהוה אֱלֹהֵינוּ, חוּס וְרַחֵם עָלֵינוּ, וְקַבֵּל בְּרַחֲמִים וּבְרָצוֹן אֶת תְּפִלָּתֵנוּ, כִּי אֵל שׁוֹמֵעַ תְּפִלּוֹת וְתַחֲנוּנִים אָתָּה. וּמִלְּפָנֶיךָ מַלְכֵּנוּ, רֵיקָם אַל תְּשִׁיבֵנוּ,

### INGATHERING OF EXILES

תְּקַע Sound the great shofar for our freedom, raise the banner to gather our exiles and gather us together from the four corners of the earth. [1] Blessed are You, HASHEM, Who gathers in the dispersed of His people Israel.

### RESTORATION OF JUSTICE

הָשִׁיבָה Restore our judges as in earliest times and our counselors as at first; [2] remove from us sorrow and groan; and reign over us — You, HASHEM, alone — with kindness and compassion, and justify us through judgment. Blessed are You, HASHEM, the King Who loves righteousness and judgment.

### AGAINST HERETICS

וְלַמַּלְשִׁינִים And for slanderers let there be no hope; and may all wickedness perish in an instant; and may all Your enemies be cut down speedily. May You speedily uproot, smash, cast down, and humble the wanton sinners — speedily in our days. Blessed are You, HASHEM, Who breaks enemies and humbles wanton sinners.

### THE RIGHTEOUS

עַל הַצַּדִּיקִים On the righteous, on the devout, on the elders of Your people the Family of Israel, on the remnant of their scholars, on the righteous converts and on ourselves — may Your compassion be aroused, HASHEM, our God, and give goodly reward to all who sincerely believe in Your Name. Put our lot with them forever, and we will not feel ashamed, for we trust in You. Blessed are You, HASHEM, Mainstay and Assurance of the righteous.

### REBUILDING JERUSALEM

וְלִירוּשָׁלַיִם And to Jerusalem, Your city, may You return in compassion, and may You rest within it, as You have spoken. May You rebuild it soon in our days as an eternal structure, and may You speedily establish the throne of David within it. Blessed are You, HASHEM, the Builder of Jerusalem.

### DAVIDIC REIGN

אֶת צֶמַח The offspring of Your servant David may You speedily cause to flourish, and enhance his pride through Your salvation, for we hope for Your salvation all day long. Blessed are You, HASHEM, Who causes the pride of salvation to flourish.

### ACCEPTANCE OF PRAYER

שְׁמַע קוֹלֵנוּ Hear our voice, HASHEM, our God, pity and be compassionate to us, and accept — with compassion and favor — our prayer, for God Who hears prayers and supplications are You. From before Yourself, our King, turn us not away empty-handed,

---

(1) Cf. *Isaiah* 11:12. (2) Cf. 1:26.

°° כִּי אַתָּה שׁוֹמֵעַ תְּפִלַּת עַמְּךָ יִשְׂרָאֵל בְּרַחֲמִים. בָּרוּךְ אַתָּה יהוה, שׁוֹמֵעַ תְּפִלָּה.

**עבודה**

**רְצֵה** יהוה אֱלֹהֵינוּ בְּעַמְּךָ יִשְׂרָאֵל וּבִתְפִלָּתָם, וְהָשֵׁב אֶת הָעֲבוֹדָה לִדְבִיר בֵּיתֶךָ. וְאִשֵּׁי יִשְׂרָאֵל וּתְפִלָּתָם בְּאַהֲבָה תְקַבֵּל בְּרָצוֹן, וּתְהִי לְרָצוֹן תָּמִיד עֲבוֹדַת יִשְׂרָאֵל עַמֶּךָ.

**וְתֶחֱזֶינָה** עֵינֵינוּ בְּשׁוּבְךָ לְצִיּוֹן בְּרַחֲמִים. בָּרוּךְ אַתָּה יהוה, הַמַּחֲזִיר שְׁכִינָתוֹ לְצִיּוֹן.

**הודאה**

Bow at מוֹדִים; straighten up at ה'.

**מוֹדִים** אֲנַחְנוּ לָךְ, שָׁאַתָּה הוּא יהוה אֱלֹהֵינוּ וֵאלֹהֵי אֲבוֹתֵינוּ לְעוֹלָם וָעֶד. צוּר חַיֵּינוּ, מָגֵן יִשְׁעֵנוּ אַתָּה הוּא לְדוֹר וָדוֹר. נוֹדֶה לְּךָ וּנְסַפֵּר תְּהִלָּתֶךָ[1] עַל חַיֵּינוּ הַמְּסוּרִים בְּיָדֶךָ, וְעַל נִשְׁמוֹתֵינוּ הַפְּקוּדוֹת לָךְ, וְעַל נִסֶּיךָ שֶׁבְּכָל יוֹם עִמָּנוּ, וְעַל נִפְלְאוֹתֶיךָ וְטוֹבוֹתֶיךָ שֶׁבְּכָל עֵת, עֶרֶב וָבֹקֶר וְצָהֳרָיִם. הַטּוֹב כִּי לֹא כָלוּ רַחֲמֶיךָ, וְהַמְרַחֵם כִּי לֹא תַמּוּ חֲסָדֶיךָ,[2] מֵעוֹלָם קִוִּינוּ לָךְ.

**(וְ)עַל** הַנִּסִּים, וְעַל הַפֻּרְקָן, וְעַל הַגְּבוּרוֹת, וְעַל הַתְּשׁוּעוֹת, וְעַל הַמִּלְחָמוֹת, שֶׁעָשִׂיתָ לַאֲבוֹתֵינוּ בַּיָּמִים הָהֵם בַּזְּמַן הַזֶּה.

---

°°One may insert either or both of these personal prayers.

For livelihood:

**אַתָּה** הוּא יהוה הָאֱלֹהִים, הַזָּן וּמְפַרְנֵס וּמְכַלְכֵּל מִקַּרְנֵי רְאֵמִים עַד בֵּיצֵי כִנִּים. הַטְרִיפֵנִי לֶחֶם חֻקִּי, וְהַמְצֵא לִי וּלְכָל בְּנֵי בֵיתִי מְזוֹנוֹתַי קוֹדֶם שֶׁאֶצְטָרֵךְ לָהֶם, בְּנַחַת וְלֹא בְצַעַר, בְּהֶתֵּר וְלֹא בְאִסּוּר, בְּכָבוֹד וְלֹא בְבִזָּיוֹן, לְחַיִּים וּלְשָׁלוֹם, מִשֶּׁפַע בְּרָכָה וְהַצְלָחָה, וּמִשֶּׁפַע בְּרָכָה עֶלְיוֹנָה, כְּדֵי שֶׁאוּכַל לַעֲשׂוֹת רְצוֹנֶךָ וְלַעֲסוֹק בְּתוֹרָתֶךָ וּלְקַיֵּם מִצְוֹתֶיךָ. וְאַל תַּצְרִיכֵנִי לִידֵי מַתְּנַת בָּשָׂר וָדָם. וִיקֻיַּם בִּי מִקְרָא שֶׁכָּתוּב: פּוֹתֵחַ אֶת יָדֶךָ, וּמַשְׂבִּיעַ לְכָל חַי רָצוֹן.[3] וְכָתוּב: הַשְׁלֵךְ עַל יהוה יְהָבְךָ, וְהוּא יְכַלְכְּלֶךָ.[4]

For forgiveness:

**אָנָּא** יהוה, חָטָאתִי עָוִיתִי וּפָשַׁעְתִּי לְפָנֶיךָ, מִיוֹם הֱיוֹתִי עַל הָאֲדָמָה עַד הַיּוֹם הַזֶּה (וּבִפְרָט בַּחֵטְא .........). אָנָּא יהוה, עֲשֵׂה לְמַעַן שִׁמְךָ הַגָּדוֹל, וּתְכַפֶּר לִי עַל עֲוֹנִי וַחֲטָאַי וּפְשָׁעַי שֶׁחָטָאתִי וְשֶׁעָוִיתִי וְשֶׁפָּשַׁעְתִּי לְפָנֶיךָ, מִנְּעוּרַי עַד הַיּוֹם הַזֶּה. וּתְמַלֵּא כָּל הַשְּׁמוֹת שֶׁפָּגַמְתִּי בְּשִׁמְךָ הַגָּדוֹל.

Continue — כִּי אַתָּה שׁוֹמֵעַ תְּפִלַּת ... (above)

°° *for You hear the prayer of Your people Israel with compassion. Blessed are You, HASHEM, Who hears prayer.*

### TEMPLE SERVICE

רְצֵה *Be favorable, HASHEM, our God, toward Your people Israel and their prayer and restore the service to the Holy of Holies of Your Temple. The fire-offerings of Israel and their prayer accept with love and favor, and may the service of Your people Israel always be favorable to You.*

וְתֶחֱזֶינָה *May our eyes behold Your return to Zion in compassion. Blessed are You, HASHEM, Who restores His Presence to Zion.*

### THANKSGIVING [MODIM]

*Bow at "We gratefully thank You"; straighten up at "HASHEM."*

מוֹדִים *We gratefully thank You, for it is You Who are HASHEM, our God and the God of our forefathers for all eternity; Rock of our lives, Shield of our salvation are You from generation to generation. We shall thank You and relate Your praise*[1] *— for our lives, which are committed to Your power and for our souls that are entrusted to You; for Your miracles that are with us every day; and for Your wonders and favors in every season — evening, morning, and afternoon. The Beneficent One, for Your compassions were never exhausted, and the Compassionate One, for Your kindnesses never ended*[2] *— always have we put our hope in You.*

(וְ)עַל הַנִּסִים *(And) for the miracles, and for the salvation, and for the mighty deeds, and for the victories, and for the battles which You performed for our forefathers in those days, at this time.*

---

°°One may insert either or both of these personal prayers.

**For forgiveness:**

אָנָּא *Please, O HASHEM, I have erred, been iniquitous, and willfully sinned before You, from the day I have existed on earth until this very day (and especially with the sin of . . .). Please, HASHEM, act for the sake of Your Great Name and grant me atonement for my iniquities, my errors, and my willful sins through which I have erred, been iniquitous, and willfully sinned before You, from my youth until this day. And make whole all the Names that I have blemished in Your Great Name.*

**For livelihood:**

אַתָּה *It is You, HASHEM, the God Who nourishes, sustains, and supports, from the horns of re'eimim to the eggs of lice. Provide me with my allotment of bread; and bring forth for me and all members of my household, my food, before I have need for it; in contentment but not in pain, in a permissible but not a forbidden manner, in honor but not in disgrace, for life and for peace; from the flow of blessing and success and from the flow of the Heavenly spring, so that I be enabled to do Your will and engage in Your Torah and fulfill Your commandments. Make me not needful of people's largesse; and may there be fulfilled in me the verse that states, "You open Your hand and satisfy the desire of every living thing,"*[3] *and that states, "Cast your burden upon HASHEM and He will support you."*[4]

Continue: for You hear the prayer . . . (above).

---

(1) Cf. *Psalms* 79:13. (2) Cf. *Lamentations* 3:22. (3) *Psalms* 145:16. (4) 55:23.

---

⊷§ עַל הַנִּסִים / **Al HaNissim**

This declaration of thanks for the miracles of Chanukah and Purim is inserted in this section of *Shemoneh Esrei* that is likewise devoted to expressions of gratitude.

**בִּימֵי** מָרְדְּכַי וְאֶסְתֵּר בְּשׁוּשַׁן הַבִּירָה, כְּשֶׁעָמַד עֲלֵיהֶם הָמָן הָרָשָׁע, בִּקֵּשׁ לְהַשְׁמִיד לַהֲרֹג וּלְאַבֵּד אֶת כָּל הַיְּהוּדִים, מִנַּעַר וְעַד זָקֵן, טַף וְנָשִׁים בְּיוֹם אֶחָד, בִּשְׁלוֹשָׁה עָשָׂר לְחֹדֶשׁ שְׁנֵים עָשָׂר, הוּא חֹדֶשׁ אֲדָר, וּשְׁלָלָם לָבוֹז.[1] וְאַתָּה בְּרַחֲמֶיךָ הָרַבִּים הֵפַרְתָּ אֶת עֲצָתוֹ, וְקִלְקַלְתָּ אֶת מַחֲשַׁבְתּוֹ, וַהֲשֵׁבוֹתָ לּוֹ גְּמוּלוֹ בְּרֹאשׁוֹ, וְתָלוּ אוֹתוֹ וְאֶת בָּנָיו עַל הָעֵץ.

[If Al HaNissim was forgotten, do not repeat Shemoneh Esrei.]

וְעַל כֻּלָּם יִתְבָּרַךְ וְיִתְרוֹמַם שִׁמְךָ מַלְכֵּנוּ תָּמִיד לְעוֹלָם וָעֶד.

Bend the knees at בָּרוּךְ; bow at אַתָּה; straighten up at ה'.

וְכֹל הַחַיִּים יוֹדוּךָ סֶּלָה, וִיהַלְלוּ אֶת שִׁמְךָ בֶּאֱמֶת, הָאֵל יְשׁוּעָתֵנוּ וְעֶזְרָתֵנוּ סֶלָה. בָּרוּךְ אַתָּה יְהוָה, הַטּוֹב שִׁמְךָ וּלְךָ נָאֶה לְהוֹדוֹת.

### שלום

**שָׁלוֹם** רָב עַל יִשְׂרָאֵל עַמְּךָ תָּשִׂים לְעוֹלָם, כִּי אַתָּה הוּא מֶלֶךְ אָדוֹן לְכָל הַשָּׁלוֹם. וְטוֹב בְּעֵינֶיךָ לְבָרֵךְ אֶת עַמְּךָ יִשְׂרָאֵל, בְּכָל עֵת וּבְכָל שָׁעָה בִּשְׁלוֹמֶךָ. בָּרוּךְ אַתָּה יְהוָה, הַמְבָרֵךְ אֶת עַמּוֹ יִשְׂרָאֵל בַּשָּׁלוֹם.

יִהְיוּ לְרָצוֹן אִמְרֵי פִי וְהֶגְיוֹן לִבִּי לְפָנֶיךָ, יְהוָה צוּרִי וְגֹאֲלִי.[2]

**אֱלֹהַי,** נְצוֹר לְשׁוֹנִי מֵרָע, וּשְׂפָתַי מִדַּבֵּר מִרְמָה,[3] וְלִמְקַלְלַי נַפְשִׁי תִדֹּם, וְנַפְשִׁי כֶּעָפָר לַכֹּל תִּהְיֶה. פְּתַח לִבִּי בְּתוֹרָתֶךָ, וּבְמִצְוֹתֶיךָ תִּרְדּוֹף נַפְשִׁי. וְכָל הַחוֹשְׁבִים עָלַי רָעָה, מְהֵרָה הָפֵר עֲצָתָם וְקַלְקֵל מַחֲשַׁבְתָּם. עֲשֵׂה לְמַעַן שְׁמֶךָ, עֲשֵׂה לְמַעַן יְמִינֶךָ, עֲשֵׂה לְמַעַן קְדֻשָּׁתֶךָ, עֲשֵׂה לְמַעַן תּוֹרָתֶךָ. לְמַעַן יֵחָלְצוּן יְדִידֶיךָ, הוֹשִׁיעָה יְמִינְךָ וַעֲנֵנִי.[4]

Some recite verses pertaining to their names at this point.

יִהְיוּ לְרָצוֹן אִמְרֵי פִי וְהֶגְיוֹן לִבִּי לְפָנֶיךָ, יְהוָה צוּרִי וְגֹאֲלִי. עֹשֶׂה שָׁלוֹם בִּמְרוֹמָיו, הוּא יַעֲשֶׂה שָׁלוֹם עָלֵינוּ, וְעַל כָּל יִשְׂרָאֵל. וְאִמְרוּ: אָמֵן.

Bow. Take three steps back. Bow left and say . . . עֹשֶׂה; bow right and say . . . הוּא; bow forward and say . . . וְעַל כָּל.

**יְהִי רָצוֹן** מִלְּפָנֶיךָ, יְהוָה אֱלֹהֵינוּ וֵאלֹהֵי אֲבוֹתֵינוּ, שֶׁיִּבָּנֶה בֵּית הַמִּקְדָּשׁ בִּמְהֵרָה בְיָמֵינוּ, וְתֵן חֶלְקֵנוּ בְּתוֹרָתֶךָ. וְשָׁם נַעֲבָדְךָ בְּיִרְאָה, כִּימֵי עוֹלָם וּכְשָׁנִים קַדְמוֹנִיּוֹת. וְעָרְבָה לַיהוָה מִנְחַת יְהוּדָה וִירוּשָׁלָיִם, כִּימֵי עוֹלָם וּכְשָׁנִים קַדְמוֹנִיּוֹת.[5]

*SHEMONEH ESREI* ENDS HERE.
Remain standing in place for a few moments before taking three steps forward.

בִּימֵי  *In the days of Mordechai and Esther, in Shushan, the capital, when Haman, the wicked, rose up against them and sought to destroy, to slay, and to exterminate all the Jews, young and old, infants and women, on the same day, on the thirteenth of the twelfth month which is the month of Adar, and to plunder their possessions.* [1] *But You, in Your abundant mercy, nullified his counsel and frustrated his intention and caused his design to return upon his own head and they hanged him and his sons on the gallows.*

[If *Al HaNissim* was forgotten, do not repeat *Shemoneh Esrei.* ]

*For all these, may Your Name be blessed and exalted, our King, continually forever and ever.*

Bend the knees at *"Blessed";* bow at *"You";* straighten up at *"HASHEM."*

*Everything alive will gratefully acknowledge You, Selah! and praise Your Name sincerely, O God of our salvation and help, Selah! Blessed are You, HASHEM, Your Name is "The Beneficent One" and to You it is fitting to give thanks.*

**PEACE**

שָׁלוֹם  *Establish abundant peace upon Your people Israel forever, for You are King, Master of all peace. May it be good in Your eyes to bless Your people Israel at every time and at every hour, with Your peace. Blessed are You, HASHEM, Who blesses His people Israel with peace.*

*May the expressions of my mouth and the thoughts of my heart find favor before You, HASHEM, my Rock and my Redeemer.* [2]

אֱלֹהַי  *My God, guard my tongue from evil and my lips from speaking deceitfully.* [3] *To those who curse me, let my soul be silent; and let my soul be like dust to everyone. Open my heart to Your Torah, then my soul will pursue Your commandments. As for all those who design evil against me, speedily nullify their counsel and disrupt their design. Act for Your Name's sake; act for Your right hand's sake; act for Your sanctity's sake; act for Your Torah's sake. That Your beloved ones may be given rest; let Your right hand save, and respond to me.* [4]

Some recite verses pertaining to their names at this point.

*May the expressions of my mouth and the thoughts of my heart find favor*

Bow. Take three steps back. Bow left and say, *"He Who . . .";* bow right and say, *"may He . . .";* bow forward and say, *"and upon all . . ."*

*before You, HASHEM, my Rock and my Redeemer. He Who makes peace in His heights, may He make peace upon us, and upon all Israel. Now respond: Amen.*

יְהִי רָצוֹן  *May it be Your will, HASHEM, our God and the God of our forefathers, that the Holy Temple be rebuilt, speedily in our days. Grant us our share in Your Torah, and may we serve You there with reverence, as in days of old and in former years. Then the offering of Judah and Jerusalem will be pleasing to HASHEM, as in days of old and in former years.* [5]

*SHEMONEH ESREI* ENDS HERE.

Remain standing in place for a few moments before taking three steps forward.

---

(1) *Esther* 3:13. (2) *Psalms* 19:15. (3) Cf. 34:14. (4) 60:7; 108:7. (5) *Malachi* 3:4.

קדיש שלם

The *chazzan* recites קַדִּישׁ שָׁלֵם.

**יִתְגַּדַּל** וְיִתְקַדַּשׁ שְׁמֵהּ רַבָּא. (.Cong – אָמֵן.) בְּעָלְמָא דִּי בְרָא כִרְעוּתֵהּ. וְיַמְלִיךְ מַלְכוּתֵהּ, בְּחַיֵּיכוֹן וּבְיוֹמֵיכוֹן וּבְחַיֵּי דְכָל בֵּית יִשְׂרָאֵל, בַּעֲגָלָא וּבִזְמַן קָרִיב. וְאִמְרוּ: אָמֵן.

(.Cong – אָמֵן. יְהֵא שְׁמֵהּ רַבָּא מְבָרַךְ לְעָלַם וּלְעָלְמֵי עָלְמַיָּא.)

יְהֵא שְׁמֵהּ רַבָּא מְבָרַךְ לְעָלַם וּלְעָלְמֵי עָלְמַיָּא.

יִתְבָּרַךְ וְיִשְׁתַּבַּח וְיִתְפָּאַר וְיִתְרוֹמַם וְיִתְנַשֵּׂא וְיִתְהַדָּר וְיִתְעַלֶּה וְיִתְהַלָּל שְׁמֵהּ דְּקֻדְשָׁא בְּרִיךְ הוּא (.Cong – בְּרִיךְ הוּא) – לְעֵלָּא מִן כָּל בִּרְכָתָא וְשִׁירָתָא תֻּשְׁבְּחָתָא וְנֶחֱמָתָא, דַּאֲמִירָן בְּעָלְמָא. וְאִמְרוּ: אָמֵן. (.Cong – אָמֵן.)

(.Cong – קַבֵּל בְּרַחֲמִים וּבְרָצוֹן אֶת תְּפִלָּתֵנוּ.)

תִּתְקַבֵּל צְלוֹתְהוֹן וּבָעוּתְהוֹן דְּכָל (בֵּית) יִשְׂרָאֵל קֳדָם אֲבוּהוֹן דִּי בִשְׁמַיָּא. וְאִמְרוּ: אָמֵן. (.Cong – אָמֵן.)

(.Cong – יְהִי שֵׁם יהוה מְבֹרָךְ, מֵעַתָּה וְעַד עוֹלָם.[1])

יְהֵא שְׁלָמָא רַבָּא מִן שְׁמַיָּא, וְחַיִּים עָלֵינוּ וְעַל כָּל יִשְׂרָאֵל. וְאִמְרוּ: אָמֵן. (.Cong – אָמֵן.)

(.Cong – עֶזְרִי מֵעִם יהוה, עֹשֵׂה שָׁמַיִם וָאָרֶץ.[2])

Bow. Take three steps back. Bow left and say . . . עֹשֶׂה; bow right and say . . . הוּא; bow forward and say . . . וְעַל כָּל. Remain in place for a few moments, then take three steps forward.

עֹשֶׂה שָׁלוֹם בִּמְרוֹמָיו, הוּא יַעֲשֶׂה שָׁלוֹם עָלֵינוּ, וְעַל כָּל יִשְׂרָאֵל. וְאִמְרוּ: אָמֵן. (.Cong – אָמֵן.)

# ברכות לפני קריאת המגילה

Before reading *Megillas Esther* [both at night and again in the morning], the reader recites the following three blessings. The congregation should answer *Amen* only [not בָּרוּךְ הוּא וּבָרוּךְ שְׁמוֹ] after each blessing, and have in mind that they thereby fulfill the obligation of reciting the blessings themselves. During the morning reading, they should also have in mind that the third blessing applies to the other *mitzvos* of Purim — *shalach manos*, gifts to the poor, and the festive Purim meal — as well as to the *Megillah* reading.

**בָּרוּךְ** אַתָּה יהוה אֱלֹהֵינוּ מֶלֶךְ הָעוֹלָם, אֲשֶׁר קִדְּשָׁנוּ בְּמִצְוֹתָיו, וְצִוָּנוּ עַל מִקְרָא מְגִלָּה. (.Cong – אָמֵן.)

**בָּרוּךְ** אַתָּה יהוה אֱלֹהֵינוּ מֶלֶךְ הָעוֹלָם, שֶׁעָשָׂה נִסִּים לַאֲבוֹתֵינוּ, בַּיָּמִים הָהֵם, בַּזְּמַן הַזֶּה. (.Cong – אָמֵן.)

**בָּרוּךְ** אַתָּה יהוה אֱלֹהֵינוּ מֶלֶךְ הָעוֹלָם, שֶׁהֶחֱיָנוּ, וְקִיְּמָנוּ, וְהִגִּיעָנוּ לַזְּמַן הַזֶּה. (.Cong – אָמֵן.)

[THE MEGILLAH IS READ.]

### FULL KADDISH
The chazzan recites Full *Kaddish:*

יִתְגַּדַּל May His great Name grow exalted and sanctified (Cong.— Amen.) in the world that He created as He willed. May He give reign to His kingship in your lifetimes and in your days, and in the lifetimes of the entire Family of Israel, swiftly and soon. Now respond: Amen.

(Cong. — Amen. May His great Name be blessed forever and ever.)
May His great Name be blessed forever and ever.

Blessed, praised, glorified, exalted, extolled, mighty, upraised, and lauded be the Name of the Holy One, Blessed is He (Cong.— Blessed is He) — beyond any blessing and song, praise and consolation that are uttered in the world. Now respond: Amen. (Cong.— Amen.)

(Cong.— Accept our prayers with mercy and favor.)
May the prayers and supplications of the entire Family of Israel be accepted before their Father Who is in Heaven. Now respond: Amen. (Cong.— Amen.)

(Cong.— Blessed be the Name of HASHEM, from this time and forever. [1])
May there be abundant peace from Heaven, and life, upon us and upon all Israel. Now respond: Amen. (Cong.— Amen.)

(Cong.— My help is from HASHEM, Maker of heaven and earth. [2])

Bow. Take three steps back. Bow left and say, "He Who makes . . ."; bow right and say, "may He . . ."; bow forward and say, "and upon all . . ." Remain in place for a few moments, then take three steps forward.

He Who makes peace in His heights, may He make peace upon us, and upon all Israel. Now respond: Amen. (Cong.— Amen.)

## BLESSINGS BEFORE MEGILLAH READING

Before reading *Megillas Esther* [both at night and again in the morning], the reader recites the following three blessings. The congregation should answer *Amen* only [not בָּרוּךְ הוּא וּבָרוּךְ שְׁמוֹ] after each blessing, and have in mind that they thereby fulfill the obligation of reciting the blessings themselves. During the morning reading, they should also have in mind that the third blessing applies to the other *mitzvos* of Purim — *shalach manos,* gifts to the poor, and the festive Purim meal — as well as to the *Megillah* reading.

בָּרוּךְ Blessed are You, HASHEM, our God, King of the universe, Who has sanctified us with His commandments and has commanded us regarding the reading of the Megillah.       (Cong. — Amen.)

בָּרוּךְ Blessed are You, HASHEM, our God, King of the universe, Who has wrought miracles for our forefathers, in those days at this season.
(Cong. — Amen.)

בָּרוּךְ Blessed are You, HASHEM, our God, King of the universe, Who has kept us alive, sustained us and brought us to this season.
(Cong. — Amen.)

[THE MEGILLAH IS READ.]

(1) *Psalms* 113:2. (2) 121:2.

# ﴾ מגילת אסתר ﴿

א **א** וַיְהִי בִּימֵי אֲחַשְׁוֵרוֹשׁ הוּא אֲחַשְׁוֵרוֹשׁ הַמֹּלֵךְ מֵהֹדּוּ וְעַד־כּוּשׁ שֶׁבַע וְעֶשְׂרִים וּמֵאָה מְדִינָה: **ב** בַּיָּמִים הָהֵם כְּשֶׁבֶת | הַמֶּלֶךְ אֲחַשְׁוֵרוֹשׁ עַל כִּסֵּא מַלְכוּתוֹ אֲשֶׁר בְּשׁוּשַׁן הַבִּירָה: **ג** בִּשְׁנַת שָׁלוֹשׁ לְמָלְכוֹ עָשָׂה מִשְׁתֶּה לְכָל־שָׂרָיו וַעֲבָדָיו חֵיל | פָּרַס וּמָדַי הַפַּרְתְּמִים וְשָׂרֵי הַמְּדִינוֹת לְפָנָיו: **ד** בְּהַרְאֹתוֹ אֶת־עֹשֶׁר כְּבוֹד מַלְכוּתוֹ וְאֶת־יְקָר תִּפְאֶרֶת גְּדוּלָּתוֹ יָמִים רַבִּים שְׁמוֹנִים וּמְאַת יוֹם: **ה** וּבִמְלוֹאת | הַיָּמִים הָאֵלֶּה עָשָׂה הַמֶּלֶךְ לְכָל־הָעָם הַנִּמְצְאִים בְּשׁוּשַׁן הַבִּירָה לְמִגָּדוֹל וְעַד־קָטָן מִשְׁתֶּה שִׁבְעַת יָמִים בַּחֲצַר גִּנַּת בִּיתַן הַמֶּלֶךְ: **ו** חוּר | כַּרְפַּס וּתְכֵלֶת אָחוּז בְּחַבְלֵי־בוּץ וְאַרְגָּמָן עַל־גְּלִילֵי כֶסֶף וְעַמּוּדֵי שֵׁשׁ מִטּוֹת | זָהָב וָכֶסֶף עַל רִצְפַת בַּהַט־וָשֵׁשׁ וְדַר וְסֹחָרֶת: **ז** וְהַשְׁקוֹת בִּכְלֵי זָהָב וְכֵלִים מִכֵּלִים שׁוֹנִים וְיֵין מַלְכוּת רָב כְּיַד הַמֶּלֶךְ: **ח** וְהַשְּׁתִיָּה כַדָּת אֵין אֹנֵס כִּי־כֵן | יִסַּד הַמֶּלֶךְ עַל כָּל־רַב בֵּיתוֹ לַעֲשׂוֹת כִּרְצוֹן אִישׁ־וָאִישׁ: **ט** גַּם וַשְׁתִּי הַמַּלְכָּה עָשְׂתָה מִשְׁתֵּה נָשִׁים בֵּית הַמַּלְכוּת אֲשֶׁר לַמֶּלֶךְ אֲחַשְׁוֵרוֹשׁ: **י** בַּיּוֹם הַשְּׁבִיעִי כְּטוֹב לֵב־הַמֶּלֶךְ בַּיָּיִן אָמַר לִמְהוּמָן בִּזְּתָא חַרְבוֹנָא בִּגְתָא וַאֲבַגְתָא זֵתַר וְכַרְכַּס שִׁבְעַת הַסָּרִיסִים הַמְשָׁרְתִים אֶת־פְּנֵי הַמֶּלֶךְ אֲחַשְׁוֵרוֹשׁ: **יא** לְהָבִיא אֶת־וַשְׁתִּי הַמַּלְכָּה לִפְנֵי הַמֶּלֶךְ בְּכֶתֶר מַלְכוּת לְהַרְאוֹת הָעַמִּים וְהַשָּׂרִים אֶת־יָפְיָהּ כִּי־טוֹבַת מַרְאֶה הִיא: **יב** וַתְּמָאֵן הַמַּלְכָּה וַשְׁתִּי לָבוֹא בִּדְבַר הַמֶּלֶךְ אֲשֶׁר בְּיַד הַסָּרִיסִים וַיִּקְצֹף הַמֶּלֶךְ מְאֹד וַחֲמָתוֹ בָּעֲרָה בוֹ: **יג** וַיֹּאמֶר הַמֶּלֶךְ לַחֲכָמִים יֹדְעֵי הָעִתִּים כִּי־כֵן דְּבַר הַמֶּלֶךְ לִפְנֵי כָּל־יֹדְעֵי דָּת וָדִין: **יד** וְהַקָּרֹב אֵלָיו כַּרְשְׁנָא שֵׁתָר אַדְמָתָא תַרְשִׁישׁ מֶרֶס מַרְסְנָא מְמוּכָן שִׁבְעַת שָׂרֵי | פָּרַס וּמָדַי רֹאֵי פְּנֵי הַמֶּלֶךְ הַיֹּשְׁבִים רִאשֹׁנָה בַּמַּלְכוּת: **טו** כְּדָת מַה־לַּעֲשׂוֹת בַּמַּלְכָּה וַשְׁתִּי עַל | אֲשֶׁר לֹא־עָשְׂתָה אֶת־מַאֲמַר הַמֶּלֶךְ אֲחַשְׁוֵרוֹשׁ בְּיַד הַסָּרִיסִים: **טז** וַיֹּאמֶר

---

﴾ מגילת אסתר / **MEGILLAS ESTHER** ﴿

**1:1.** אֲחַשְׁוֵרוֹשׁ — *Ahasuerus* — successor to Cyrus toward the end of the seventy years of the Babylonian exile [the fourth century B.C.E.].

מֵהֹדּוּ וְעַד כּוּשׁ — *From Hodu to Cush. Hodu* and *Cush* are usually identified as India and Ethiopia, respectively.

**1:3.** בִּשְׁנַת שָׁלוֹשׁ — *In the third year:* 3395 from Creation. According to his (erroneous) calculation, the seventieth year of the Jews' exile had passed, thus belying the prophets who had foretold the exile's end after seventy years, and Ahasuerus rejoiced in this frustration of Jewish hope; he had completed the building of his magnificent throne; he was finally secure

## ⸨ MEGILLAS ESTHER ⸩

**1** **1** **A**nd it came to pass in the days of Ahasuerus — he is the Ahasuerus who reigned from Hodu to Cush, a hundred and twenty-seven provinces — ² in those days, when King Ahasuerus sat on his royal throne which was in Shushan the capital, ³ in the third year of his reign, he made a feast for all his officials and his servants; the army of Persia and Media; the nobles and officials of the provinces being present; ⁴ when he displayed the riches of his glorious kingdom and the honor of his splendrous majesty for many days, a hundred and eighty days. ⁵ And when these days were fulfilled, the king made a seven-day feast for all the people who were present in Shushan the capital, great and small alike, in the courtyard of the garden of the king's palace. ⁶ There were [hangings of] white, fine cotton, and turquoise wool, held with cords of fine linen and purple wool, upon silver rods and marble pillars; the couches of gold and silver were on a pavement of variegated marble. ⁷ The drinks were served in golden vessels — vessels of diverse form — and royal wine in abundance, in accordance with the king's wealth. ⁸ And the drinking was according to the law, there was no coercion, for so the king had established for every officer of his house to do according to each man's pleasure.

⁹ Queen Vashti also made a feast for the women in the royal house of King Ahasuerus. ¹⁰ On the seventh day, when the heart of the king was merry with wine, he told Mehuman, Bizzetha, Harbona, Bigtha and Abagtha, Zethar and Carcas, the seven chamberlains who attended King Ahasuerus, ¹¹ to bring Queen Vashti before the king [adorned] with the royal crown, to show off to the people and the officials her beauty, for she was beautiful of appearance. ¹² But Queen Vashti refused to come at the king's command [conveyed] by the hand of the chamberlains; the king therefore became very enraged and his wrath burned in him.

¹³ Then the king spoke to the wise men, those who knew the times (for such was the king's procedure [to turn] to all who knew law and judgment), ¹⁴ those closest to him — Carshena, Shethar, Admatha, Tarshish, Meres, Marsena and Memuchan, the seven officers of Persia and Media, who had access to the king, who sat first in the kingdom: ¹⁵ "By the law, what should be done to Queen Vashti for not having obeyed the bidding of the King Ahasuerus [conveyed] by the hand of the chamberlains?"

---

in his reign; he took Vashti as his queen. Thus he had many reasons for such a lavish feast (*Midrash*).

**1:6.** חוּר —*Hangings of white.* The letter ח has the numerical value of 8. In the Megillah the ח of the word חוּר, *white garments,* is enlarged to imply that on that climactic day Ahasuerus adorned himself with the eight garments of the High Priest. In punishment for this, he suffered the

multiple evils of the resulting episode with Vashti, her death, his embarrassment and subsequent depression (*Alkabetz*).

**1:9.** וַשְׁתִּי — *Vashti,* the daughter of Belshazzar, and granddaughter of Nebuchadnezzar.

**1:11.** בְּכֶתֶר מַלְכוּת — *[adorned with] the royal crown.* She was to wear *only* the royal crown, i.e., unclothed (*Midrash*).

*Vashti refused,* not because of modesty.

°מוּמְכָן [°מְמוּכָן ק'] לִפְנֵי הַמֶּלֶךְ וְהַשָּׂרִים לֹא עַל־הַמֶּלֶךְ לְבַדּוֹ
עָוְתָה וַשְׁתִּי הַמַּלְכָּה כִּי עַל־כָּל־הַשָּׂרִים וְעַל־כָּל־הָעַמִּים אֲשֶׁר
בְּכָל־מְדִינוֹת הַמֶּלֶךְ אֲחַשְׁוֵרוֹשׁ: יז כִּי־יֵצֵא דְבַר־הַמַּלְכָּה עַל־כָּל־
הַנָּשִׁים לְהַבְזוֹת בַּעְלֵיהֶן בְּעֵינֵיהֶן בְּאָמְרָם הַמֶּלֶךְ אֲחַשְׁוֵרוֹשׁ אָמַר
לְהָבִיא אֶת־וַשְׁתִּי הַמַּלְכָּה לְפָנָיו וְלֹא־בָאָה: יח וְהַיּוֹם הַזֶּה
תֹּאמַרְנָה | שָׂרוֹת פָּרַס־וּמָדַי אֲשֶׁר שָׁמְעוּ אֶת־דְּבַר הַמַּלְכָּה לְכֹל
שָׂרֵי הַמֶּלֶךְ וּכְדַי בִּזָּיוֹן וָקָצֶף: יט אִם־עַל־הַמֶּלֶךְ טוֹב יֵצֵא דְבַר־
מַלְכוּת מִלְּפָנָיו וְיִכָּתֵב בְּדָתֵי פָרַס־וּמָדַי וְלֹא יַעֲבוֹר אֲשֶׁר לֹא־
תָבוֹא וַשְׁתִּי לִפְנֵי הַמֶּלֶךְ אֲחַשְׁוֵרוֹשׁ וּמַלְכוּתָהּ יִתֵּן הַמֶּלֶךְ לִרְעוּתָהּ
הַטּוֹבָה מִמֶּנָּה: כ וְנִשְׁמַע פִּתְגָם הַמֶּלֶךְ אֲשֶׁר־יַעֲשֶׂה בְּכָל־מַלְכוּתוֹ
כִּי רַבָּה הִיא וְכָל־הַנָּשִׁים יִתְּנוּ יְקָר לְבַעְלֵיהֶן לְמִגָּדוֹל וְעַד־קָטָן:
כא וַיִּיטַב הַדָּבָר בְּעֵינֵי הַמֶּלֶךְ וְהַשָּׂרִים וַיַּעַשׂ הַמֶּלֶךְ כִּדְבַר מְמוּכָן:
כב וַיִּשְׁלַח סְפָרִים אֶל־כָּל־מְדִינוֹת הַמֶּלֶךְ אֶל־מְדִינָה וּמְדִינָה
כִּכְתָבָהּ וְאֶל־עַם וָעָם כִּלְשׁוֹנוֹ לִהְיוֹת כָּל־אִישׁ שֹׂרֵר בְּבֵיתוֹ וּמְדַבֵּר
כִּלְשׁוֹן עַמּוֹ: **ב א** אַחַר הַדְּבָרִים הָאֵלֶּה כְּשֹׁךְ חֲמַת
הַמֶּלֶךְ אֲחַשְׁוֵרוֹשׁ זָכַר אֶת־וַשְׁתִּי וְאֵת אֲשֶׁר־עָשָׂתָה וְאֵת אֲשֶׁר־
נִגְזַר עָלֶיהָ: ג וַיֹּאמְרוּ נַעֲרֵי־הַמֶּלֶךְ מְשָׁרְתָיו יְבַקְשׁוּ לַמֶּלֶךְ נְעָרוֹת
בְּתוּלוֹת טוֹבוֹת מַרְאֶה: ג וְיַפְקֵד הַמֶּלֶךְ פְּקִידִים בְּכָל־מְדִינוֹת
מַלְכוּתוֹ וְיִקְבְּצוּ אֶת־כָּל־נַעֲרָה־בְתוּלָה טוֹבַת מַרְאֶה אֶל־שׁוּשַׁן
הַבִּירָה אֶל־בֵּית הַנָּשִׁים אֶל־יַד הֵגֵא סְרִיס הַמֶּלֶךְ שֹׁמֵר הַנָּשִׁים
וְנָתוֹן תַּמְרֻקֵיהֶן: ד וְהַנַּעֲרָה אֲשֶׁר תִּיטַב בְּעֵינֵי הַמֶּלֶךְ תִּמְלֹךְ תַּחַת
וַשְׁתִּי וַיִּיטַב הַדָּבָר בְּעֵינֵי הַמֶּלֶךְ וַיַּעַשׂ כֵּן: ה **אִישׁ יְהוּדִי**
**הָיָה בְּשׁוּשַׁן הַבִּירָה וּשְׁמוֹ מָרְדֳּכַי בֶּן יָאִיר בֶּן־שִׁמְעִי בֶּן־קִישׁ אִישׁ**
**יְמִינִי:** ו אֲשֶׁר הָגְלָה מִירוּשָׁלַיִם עִם־הַגֹּלָה אֲשֶׁר הָגְלְתָה עִם יְכָנְיָה
מֶלֶךְ־יְהוּדָה אֲשֶׁר הֶגְלָה נְבוּכַדְנֶאצַּר מֶלֶךְ בָּבֶל: ז וַיְהִי אֹמֵן אֶת־
הֲדַסָּה הִיא אֶסְתֵּר בַּת־דֹּדוֹ כִּי אֵין לָהּ אָב וָאֵם וְהַנַּעֲרָה יְפַת־
תֹּאַר וְטוֹבַת מַרְאֶה וּבְמוֹת אָבִיהָ וְאִמָּהּ לְקָחָהּ מָרְדֳּכַי לוֹ לְבַת:

---

The reason for her refusal was that God caused leprosy to break out on her, and paved the way for her downfall (Midrash).

**1:16.** מְמוּכָן — Memuchan. "Memuchan is Haman. Why was he called Memuchan? Because he was destined [מוּכָן] for destruction" (Talmud).

**1:17.** כִּי יֵצֵא דְבַר הַמַּלְכָּה — For the queen's deed will come to the attention . . . When the word gets out that the queen acted contemptibly to the king, every woman will consider this as license to act likewise to her own husband (Rashi).

**1:21.** וַיִּיטַב הַדָּבָר בְּעֵינֵי הַמֶּלֶךְ — This proposal

<sup>16</sup> *Memuchan declared before the king and the officials, "Not only against the king has Queen Vashti done wrong, but against all the officials and all the people in all the provinces of King Ahasuerus.* <sup>17</sup> *For the queen's deed will come to the attention of all women, making their husbands contemptible in their eyes, when they will say, 'King Ahasuerus said to bring Queen Vashti before him, but she did not come!'* <sup>18</sup> *And this day the princesses of Persia and Media who have heard of the queen's deed will speak of it to all the king's officials, and there will be much contempt and rage.* <sup>19</sup> *If it pleases the king, let there go forth a royal edict from him, and let it be written into the laws of Persia and Media, that it not be revoked, that Vashti never again appear before King Ahasuerus; and let the king confer her royal estate upon another who is better than she.* <sup>20</sup> *Then, the king's decree which he will proclaim shall be heard throughout all his kingdom — great though it be — and all the wives will show respect to their husbands, great and small alike."* <sup>21</sup> *This proposal was favorable in the eyes of the king and the officials, and the king did according to the word of Memuchan;* <sup>22</sup> *and he sent letters into all the king's provinces, to each province in its own script, and to each people in its own language, [to the effect that] every man should rule in his own home, and speak the language of his own people.*

2 <sup>1</sup> **A**fter these things, when the wrath of King Ahasuerus subsided, he remembered Vashti, and what she had done, and what had been decreed against her. <sup>2</sup> Then the king's attendants said, "Let there be sought for the king young maidens of beautiful appearance; <sup>3</sup> and let the king appoint commissioners in all the provinces of his kingdom, that they gather together every young maiden of beautiful appearance to Shushan the capital, to the harem, under the charge of Hegai the king's chamberlain, guardian of the women; and let their cosmetics be given them. <sup>4</sup> Then, let the girl who pleases the king reign in place of Vashti." The matter pleased the king, and he did so.

<sup>5</sup> **There was a Jewish man in Shushan the capital whose name was Mordechai son of Jair son of Shimei son of Kish, a Benjamite,** <sup>6</sup> who had been exiled from Jerusalem along with the exiles who had been exiled with Jeconiah king of Judah, whom Nebuchadnezzar king of Babylon had exiled. <sup>7</sup> And he had reared Hadassah, she is Esther, his uncle's daughter; for she had neither father nor mother. The maiden was finely featured and beautiful of appearance, and when her father and mother had died, Mordechai adopted her as [his] daughter.

---

*was favorable in the eyes of the king.* "He gave the order and they brought in her head on a platter" (*Midrash*).

**2:1. Ahasuerus Seeks a New Queen**

He remembered the order he had given her to appear unclothed before him and how she refused, and how he had been wroth with her and put her to death (*Midrash*).

**2:5.** This verse is among the four verses said aloud in the synagogue by the congregation during the public reading of the Megillah.

**2:7.** הֲדַסָּה — *Hadassah.* There is a difference of opinion among the Sages whether Hadassah was her proper name and Esther was added later, or vice versa. Both names are descriptive of her virtues. Hadassah is derived from the Hebrew word הֲדַס — "myrtle"; Esther from אֶסְתַּהֵר — *Istahar,*

ח וַיְהִי בְּהִשָּׁמַע דְּבַר־הַמֶּלֶךְ וְדָתוֹ וּבְהִקָּבֵץ נְעָרוֹת רַבּוֹת אֶל־שׁוּשַׁן הַבִּירָה אֶל־יַד הֵגַי וַתִּלָּקַח אֶסְתֵּר אֶל־בֵּית הַמֶּלֶךְ אֶל־יַד הֵגַי שֹׁמֵר הַנָּשִׁים: ט וַתִּיטַב הַנַּעֲרָה בְעֵינָיו וַתִּשָּׂא חֶסֶד לְפָנָיו וַיְבַהֵל אֶת־תַּמְרוּקֶיהָ וְאֶת־מָנוֹתֶהָ לָתֵת לָהּ וְאֵת שֶׁבַע הַנְּעָרוֹת הָרְאֻיוֹת לָתֶת־לָהּ מִבֵּית הַמֶּלֶךְ וַיְשַׁנֶּהָ וְאֶת־נַעֲרוֹתֶיהָ לְטוֹב בֵּית הַנָּשִׁים: י לֹא־הִגִּידָה אֶסְתֵּר אֶת־עַמָּהּ וְאֶת־מוֹלַדְתָּהּ כִּי מָרְדֳּכַי צִוָּה עָלֶיהָ אֲשֶׁר לֹא־תַגִּיד: יא וּבְכָל־יוֹם וָיוֹם מָרְדֳּכַי מִתְהַלֵּךְ לִפְנֵי חֲצַר בֵּית־הַנָּשִׁים לָדַעַת אֶת־שְׁלוֹם אֶסְתֵּר וּמַה־יֵּעָשֶׂה בָּהּ: יב וּבְהַגִּיעַ תֹּר נַעֲרָה וְנַעֲרָה לָבוֹא ׀ אֶל־הַמֶּלֶךְ אֲחַשְׁוֵרוֹשׁ מִקֵּץ הֱיוֹת לָהּ כְּדָת הַנָּשִׁים שְׁנֵים עָשָׂר חֹדֶשׁ כִּי כֵּן יִמְלְאוּ יְמֵי מְרוּקֵיהֶן שִׁשָּׁה חֳדָשִׁים בְּשֶׁמֶן הַמֹּר וְשִׁשָּׁה חֳדָשִׁים בַּבְּשָׂמִים וּבְתַמְרוּקֵי הַנָּשִׁים: יג וּבָזֶה הַנַּעֲרָה בָּאָה אֶל־הַמֶּלֶךְ אֵת כָּל־אֲשֶׁר תֹּאמַר יִנָּתֵן לָהּ לָבוֹא עִמָּהּ מִבֵּית הַנָּשִׁים עַד־בֵּית הַמֶּלֶךְ: יד בָּעֶרֶב ׀ הִיא בָאָה וּבַבֹּקֶר הִיא שָׁבָה אֶל־בֵּית הַנָּשִׁים שֵׁנִי אֶל־יַד שַׁעֲשְׁגַז סְרִיס הַמֶּלֶךְ שֹׁמֵר הַפִּילַגְשִׁים לֹא־תָבוֹא עוֹד אֶל־הַמֶּלֶךְ כִּי אִם־חָפֵץ בָּהּ הַמֶּלֶךְ וְנִקְרְאָה בְשֵׁם: טו וּבְהַגִּיעַ תֹּר־אֶסְתֵּר בַּת־אֲבִיחַיִל ׀ דֹּד מָרְדֳּכַי אֲשֶׁר לָקַח־לוֹ לְבַת לָבוֹא אֶל־הַמֶּלֶךְ לֹא בִקְשָׁה דָּבָר כִּי אִם אֶת־אֲשֶׁר יֹאמַר הֵגַי סְרִיס־הַמֶּלֶךְ שֹׁמֵר הַנָּשִׁים וַתְּהִי אֶסְתֵּר נֹשֵׂאת חֵן בְּעֵינֵי כָּל־רֹאֶיהָ: טז וַתִּלָּקַח אֶסְתֵּר אֶל־הַמֶּלֶךְ אֲחַשְׁוֵרוֹשׁ אֶל־בֵּית מַלְכוּתוֹ בַּחֹדֶשׁ הָעֲשִׂירִי הוּא־חֹדֶשׁ טֵבֵת בִּשְׁנַת־שֶׁבַע לְמַלְכוּתוֹ: יז וַיֶּאֱהַב הַמֶּלֶךְ אֶת־אֶסְתֵּר מִכָּל־הַנָּשִׁים וַתִּשָּׂא־חֵן וָחֶסֶד לְפָנָיו מִכָּל־הַבְּתוּלוֹת וַיָּשֶׂם כֶּתֶר־מַלְכוּת בְּרֹאשָׁהּ וַיַּמְלִיכֶהָ תַּחַת וַשְׁתִּי: יח וַיַּעַשׂ הַמֶּלֶךְ מִשְׁתֶּה גָדוֹל לְכָל־שָׂרָיו וַעֲבָדָיו אֵת מִשְׁתֵּה אֶסְתֵּר וַהֲנָחָה לַמְּדִינוֹת עָשָׂה וַיִּתֵּן מַשְׂאֵת כְּיַד הַמֶּלֶךְ: יט וּבְהִקָּבֵץ בְּתוּלוֹת שֵׁנִית וּמָרְדֳּכַי יֹשֵׁב בְּשַׁעַר־הַמֶּלֶךְ: כ אֵין אֶסְתֵּר מַגֶּדֶת מוֹלַדְתָּהּ וְאֶת־עַמָּהּ כַּאֲשֶׁר צִוָּה עָלֶיהָ מָרְדֳּכָי וְאֶת־מַאֲמַר מָרְדֳּכַי אֶסְתֵּר עֹשָׂה כַּאֲשֶׁר הָיְתָה בְאָמְנָה אִתּוֹ: כא בַּיָּמִים הָהֵם וּמָרְדֳּכַי יֹשֵׁב בְּשַׁעַר־הַמֶּלֶךְ קָצַף בִּגְתָן וָתֶרֶשׁ שְׁנֵי־סָרִיסֵי הַמֶּלֶךְ מִשֹּׁמְרֵי הַסַּף

---

"as beautiful as the moon" (Talmud).

### 2:8. Esther Is Brought to the Harem

**2:10.** לֹא הִגִּידָה אֶסְתֵּר — *Esther had not told.* Esther, a descendant of King Saul, did not declare her *royal* lineage. She had hoped

the king would think that she was of humble origin and send her away (Rashi). Alternatively: She feared that had she declared her faith, she would have been forced to transgress the dictates of her religion (Ibn Ezra).

⁸ *So it came to pass, when the king's bidding and decree were announced, and when many young maidens were being brought together to Shushan the capital, under the charge of Hegai, that Esther was taken to the king's palace, under the charge of Hegai, guardian of the women.* ⁹ *The girl was pleasing in his eyes, and she found favor before him; he hurriedly prepared her cosmetics and her allowance of delicacies to present [to] her, along with the seven attendants from the king's palace, and he transferred her and her maidens to the best [quarters] in the harem.* ¹⁰ *Esther had not told of her people or her kindred, for Mordechai had instructed her not to tell.* ¹¹ *Day after day Mordechai would walk about in front of the courtyard of the harem to learn about Esther's well-being and what would become of her.*

¹² *Now when each maiden's turn arrived to come to King Ahasuerus, after having been treated according to the law prescribed for women for twelve months (for so was the prescribed length of their anointing accomplished: six months with oil of myrrh, and six months with perfumes and feminine cosmetics)* — ¹³ *and when the girl came in this manner to the king, she was given whatever she requested to accompany her from the harem to the king's palace.* ¹⁴ *In the evening she would come, and in the morning she would return to the second harem in the charge of Shaashgaz, the king's chamberlain, guardian of the concubines. She would never again come to the king unless the king desired her, and she was summoned by name.*

¹⁵ *Now when the turn came for Esther daughter of Abihail uncle of Mordechai (who had adopted her as [his] daughter) to come to the king, she requested nothing except that which Hegai, the king's chamberlain, guardian of the women, had advised. Esther would find favor in the eyes of all who saw her.* ¹⁶ *Esther was taken to King Ahasuerus into his royal palace in the tenth month, which is the month of Teves, in the seventh year of his reign.* ¹⁷ *The king loved Esther more than all the women, and she found more favor and kindness before him than all the other maidens; so that he set the royal crown upon her head, and made her queen in place of Vashti.* \* ¹⁸ *Then the king made a great banquet for all his officers and his servants — it was Esther's banquet — and he proclaimed an amnesty for the provinces, and gave gifts worthy of the king's hand.*

¹⁹ *And when the maidens were gathered together the second time, and Mordechai sat at the king's gate,* ²⁰ *Esther still told nothing of her kindred or her people as Mordechai had instructed her; for Esther continued to obey Mordechai, just as when she was reared by him.*

²¹ *In those days, while Mordechai was sitting at the king's gate, Bigthan and Teresh, two of the king's chamberlains of the guardians of the threshold,*

---

**2:14.** Having consorted with the king, it would not be proper for them to marry other men. They were required to return to the harem and remain there for the rest of their lives as concubines, to await the possibility of being crowned queen if the king found no one better.

**2:21. Mordechai Foils a Plot Against the King**

Being a member of the Sanhedrin, Mordechai was well versed in seventy languages. The plotters spoke in their native Tarsian tongue in Mordechai's presence, not expecting him to understand them (*Talmud*).

וַיְבַקְשׁוּ לִשְׁלֹחַ יָד בַּמֶּלֶךְ אֲחַשְׁוֵרֹשׁ: כב וַיִּוָּדַע הַדָּבָר לְמָרְדֳּכַי
וַיַּגֵּד לְאֶסְתֵּר הַמַּלְכָּה וַתֹּאמֶר אֶסְתֵּר לַמֶּלֶךְ בְּשֵׁם מָרְדֳּכָי:
כג וַיְבֻקַּשׁ הַדָּבָר וַיִּמָּצֵא וַיִּתָּלוּ שְׁנֵיהֶם עַל־עֵץ וַיִּכָּתֵב בְּסֵפֶר
דִּבְרֵי הַיָּמִים לִפְנֵי הַמֶּלֶךְ: ג א אַחַר ׀ הַדְּבָרִים הָאֵלֶּה גִּדַּל
הַמֶּלֶךְ אֲחַשְׁוֵרֹושׁ אֶת־הָמָן בֶּן־הַמְּדָתָא הָאֲגָגִי וַיְנַשְּׂאֵהוּ וַיָּשֶׂם אֶת־
כִּסְאוֹ מֵעַל כָּל־הַשָּׂרִים אֲשֶׁר אִתּוֹ: ב וְכָל־עַבְדֵי הַמֶּלֶךְ אֲשֶׁר־בְּשַׁעַר
הַמֶּלֶךְ כֹּרְעִים וּמִשְׁתַּחֲוִים לְהָמָן כִּי־כֵן צִוָּה־לוֹ הַמֶּלֶךְ וּמָרְדֳּכַי לֹא
יִכְרַע וְלֹא יִשְׁתַּחֲוֶה: ג וַיֹּאמְרוּ עַבְדֵי הַמֶּלֶךְ אֲשֶׁר־בְּשַׁעַר הַמֶּלֶךְ
לְמָרְדֳּכָי מַדּוּעַ אַתָּה עוֹבֵר אֵת מִצְוַת הַמֶּלֶךְ: ד וַיְהִי °בְּאָמְרָם
[°כְּאָמְרָם ק] אֵלָיו יוֹם וָיוֹם וְלֹא שָׁמַע אֲלֵיהֶם וַיַּגִּידוּ לְהָמָן לִרְאוֹת
הֲיַעַמְדוּ דִּבְרֵי מָרְדֳּכַי כִּי־הִגִּיד לָהֶם אֲשֶׁר־הוּא יְהוּדִי: ה וַיַּרְא הָמָן
כִּי־אֵין מָרְדֳּכַי כֹּרֵעַ וּמִשְׁתַּחֲוֶה לוֹ וַיִּמָּלֵא הָמָן חֵמָה: ו וַיִּבֶז בְּעֵינָיו
לִשְׁלֹחַ יָד בְּמָרְדֳּכַי לְבַדּוֹ כִּי־הִגִּידוּ לוֹ אֶת־עַם מָרְדֳּכָי וַיְבַקֵּשׁ הָמָן
לְהַשְׁמִיד אֶת־כָּל־הַיְּהוּדִים אֲשֶׁר בְּכָל־מַלְכוּת אֲחַשְׁוֵרוֹשׁ עַם
מָרְדֳּכָי: ז בַּחֹדֶשׁ הָרִאשׁוֹן הוּא־חֹדֶשׁ נִיסָן בִּשְׁנַת שְׁתֵּים עֶשְׂרֵה
לַמֶּלֶךְ אֲחַשְׁוֵרוֹשׁ הִפִּיל פּוּר הוּא הַגּוֹרָל לִפְנֵי הָמָן מִיּוֹם ׀ לְיוֹם
וּמֵחֹדֶשׁ לְחֹדֶשׁ שְׁנֵים־עָשָׂר הוּא־חֹדֶשׁ אֲדָר: ח וַיֹּאמֶר
הָמָן לַמֶּלֶךְ אֲחַשְׁוֵרֹשׁ יֶשְׁנוֹ עַם־אֶחָד מְפֻזָּר וּמְפֹרָד בֵּין הָעַמִּים
בְּכֹל מְדִינוֹת מַלְכוּתֶךָ וְדָתֵיהֶם שֹׁנוֹת מִכָּל־עָם וְאֶת־דָּתֵי הַמֶּלֶךְ
אֵינָם עֹשִׂים וְלַמֶּלֶךְ אֵין־שֹׁוֶה לְהַנִּיחָם: ט אִם־עַל־הַמֶּלֶךְ טוֹב
יִכָּתֵב לְאַבְּדָם וַעֲשֶׂרֶת אֲלָפִים כִּכַּר־כֶּסֶף אֶשְׁקוֹל עַל־יְדֵי עֹשֵׂי
הַמְּלָאכָה לְהָבִיא אֶל־גִּנְזֵי הַמֶּלֶךְ: י וַיָּסַר הַמֶּלֶךְ אֶת־טַבַּעְתּוֹ
מֵעַל יָדוֹ וַיִּתְּנָהּ לְהָמָן בֶּן־הַמְּדָתָא הָאֲגָגִי צֹרֵר הַיְּהוּדִים: יא וַיֹּאמֶר
הַמֶּלֶךְ לְהָמָן הַכֶּסֶף נָתוּן לָךְ וְהָעָם לַעֲשׂוֹת בּוֹ כַּטּוֹב בְּעֵינֶיךָ:
יב וַיִּקָּרְאוּ סֹפְרֵי הַמֶּלֶךְ בַּחֹדֶשׁ הָרִאשׁוֹן בִּשְׁלוֹשָׁה עָשָׂר יוֹם בּוֹ

---

**2:23.** סֵפֶר דִּבְרֵי הַיָּמִים — *The book of chronicles.* This is not the Scriptural Book of Chronicles; rather it is the annals of Persia and Media spoken of in 10:2.

**3:1. Haman Is Advanced**
   Haman was a descendant of Agag, king of Amalek [*I Samuel* 15:9].

**2.** To make it manifest that the homage due him was of an idolatrous character, Haman had the image of an idol fastened

to his clothes, so that whoever bowed down before him worshipped an idol at the same time. Therefore Mordechai would not bow down or prostrate himself (*Midrash*).

**6. Haman Plans the Destruction of All the Jews**
   The reaction of Haman to a personal affront is typical of the most rabid anti-Semites throughout the ages.

became enraged and sought to send [their] hand against King Ahasuerus. ²² The matter became known to Mordechai, who told it to Queen Esther, and Esther informed the king in Mordechai's name. ²³ The matter was investigated and found [to be true], and they were both hanged on a gallows. It was recorded in the book of chronicles in the king's presence.

**3** ¹ **A**fter these things King Ahasuerus promoted Haman son of Hammedatha the Agagite and elevated him; he set his seat above all the officers who were with him. ² All the king's servants at the king's gate would bow down and prostrate themselves before Haman, for so had the king commanded concerning him. But Mordechai would not bow and would not prostrate himself. ³ So the king's servants who were at the king's gate said to Mordechai, "Why do you disobey the king's command?" ⁴ Now it happened when they said this to him day after day and he did not heed them, they told Haman, to see whether Mordechai's words would prevail; for he had told them that he was a Jew. ⁵ When Haman, himself, saw that Mordechai did not bow down and prostrate himself before him, Haman was filled with wrath. ⁶ However, it seemed contemptible to him to send [his] hand against Mordechai alone, for they had told him of the people of Mordechai. So Haman sought to destroy all the Jews who were throughout the entire kingdom of Ahasuerus — the people of Mordechai. ⁷ In the first month, which is the month of Nissan, in the twelfth year of King Ahasuerus, pur (that is, the lot) was cast in the presence of Haman from day to day, and from month to month, to the twelfth month, which is the month of Adar.

⁸ Then Haman said to King Ahasuerus, "There is a certain people scattered abroad and dispersed among the peoples in all the provinces of your realm. Their laws are different from every other people's and they do not observe the king's laws; therefore it is not befitting the king to tolerate them.

⁹ If it pleases the king, let it be recorded that they be destroyed; and I will pay ten thousand silver talents into the hands of those who perform the duties, for deposit in the king's treasuries."

¹⁰ So the king removed his signet ring from his hand, and gave it to Haman son of Hammedatha the Agagite, enemy of the Jews. ¹¹ Then the king said to Haman, "The silver is given to you, the people also, to do with as you see fit."

¹² The king's scribes were summoned on the thirteenth day of the first month,

---

**3:8. Haman Slanders the Jews**

Haman said: "They eat and drink and despise the throne. For if a fly falls into a Jew's cup, he throws out the fly and drinks the wine; but if His Majesty were to merely touch his cup, he would throw it to the ground and not drink from it" (*Talmud*).

**3:9.** עֲשֶׂרֶת אֲלָפִים כִּכַּר כֶּסֶף — *Ten thousand silver talents.* The price Haman was ready to pay for the right to exterminate the Jews, 10,000 talents, was 24 million ounces, or 750 tons of silver!

**3:10. The King Consents**

The king's signet ring symbolized that Haman had full authority to act (*Rashi*).

וַיִּכָּתֵ֡ב כְּכָל־אֲשֶׁר־צִוָּ֣ה הָמָ֣ן אֶ֣ל אֲחַשְׁדַּרְפְּנֵי־הַ֠מֶּלֶךְ וְֽאֶל־הַפַּחוֹת֩
אֲשֶׁ֨ר ׀ עַל־מְדִינָ֜ה וּמְדִינָ֗ה וְאֶל־שָׂ֤רֵי עַם֙ וָעָ֔ם מְדִינָ֤ה וּמְדִינָה֙ כִּכְתָבָ֔הּ
וְעַ֥ם וָעָ֖ם כִּלְשׁוֹנ֑וֹ בְּשֵׁ֨ם הַמֶּ֤לֶךְ אֲחַשְׁוֵרֹשׁ֙ נִכְתָּ֔ב וְנֶחְתָּ֖ם בְּטַבַּ֥עַת
הַמֶּֽלֶךְ: יג וְנִשְׁל֨וֹחַ סְפָרִ֜ים בְּיַ֣ד הָרָצִים֮ אֶל־כָּל־מְדִינ֣וֹת הַמֶּלֶךְ֒
לְהַשְׁמִ֡יד לַהֲרֹ֣ג וּלְאַבֵּ֣ד אֶת־כָּל־הַ֠יְּהוּדִים מִנַּ֨עַר וְעַד־זָקֵ֜ן טַ֤ף וְנָשִׁים֙
בְּי֣וֹם אֶחָ֔ד בִּשְׁלוֹשָׁ֥ה עָשָׂ֛ר לְחֹ֥דֶשׁ שְׁנֵים־עָשָׂ֖ר הוּא־חֹ֣דֶשׁ אֲדָ֑ר
וּשְׁלָלָ֖ם לָבֽוֹז: יד פַּתְשֶׁ֣גֶן הַכְּתָ֗ב לְהִנָּ֤תֵֽן דָּת֙ בְּכָל־מְדִינָ֣ה וּמְדִינָ֔ה גָּל֖וּי
לְכָל־הָֽעַמִּ֑ים לִהְי֥וֹת עֲתִדִ֖ים לַיּ֥וֹם הַזֶּֽה: טו הָרָצִ֞ים יָֽצְא֤וּ דְחוּפִים֙
בִּדְבַ֣ר הַמֶּ֔לֶךְ וְהַדָּ֥ת נִתְּנָ֖ה בְּשׁוּשַׁ֣ן הַבִּירָ֑ה וְהַמֶּ֤לֶךְ וְהָמָן֙ יָֽשְׁב֣וּ
לִשְׁתּ֔וֹת וְהָעִ֥יר שׁוּשָׁ֖ן נָבֽוֹכָה: ד א וּמָרְדֳּכַ֗י יָדַע֙ אֶת־
כָּל־אֲשֶׁ֣ר נַעֲשָׂ֔ה וַיִּקְרַ֤ע מָרְדֳּכַי֙ אֶת־בְּגָדָ֔יו וַיִּלְבַּ֥שׁ שַׂ֖ק וָאֵ֑פֶר וַיֵּצֵא֙
בְּת֣וֹךְ הָעִ֔יר וַיִּזְעַ֛ק זְעָקָ֥ה גְדֹלָ֖ה וּמָרָֽה: ב וַיָּב֕וֹא עַ֖ד לִפְנֵ֣י שַֽׁעַר־הַמֶּ֑לֶךְ
כִּ֣י אֵ֥ין לָב֛וֹא אֶל־שַׁ֥עַר הַמֶּ֖לֶךְ בִּלְב֥וּשׁ שָֽׂק: ג וּבְכָל־מְדִינָ֣ה וּמְדִינָ֗ה
מְקוֹם֙ אֲשֶׁ֨ר דְּבַר־הַמֶּ֤לֶךְ וְדָתוֹ֙ מַגִּ֔יעַ אֵ֤בֶל גָּדוֹל֙ לַיְּהוּדִ֔ים וְצ֥וֹם וּבְכִ֖י
וּמִסְפֵּ֑ד שַׂ֣ק וָאֵ֔פֶר יֻצַּ֖ע לָֽרַבִּֽים: ד °וַתְּבוֹאֶינָה [ °וַתָּב֩וֹאנָה ק] נַעֲרוֹת֨
אֶסְתֵּ֤ר וְסָרִיסֶ֨יהָ֙ וַיַּגִּ֣ידוּ לָ֔הּ וַתִּתְחַלְחַ֥ל הַמַּלְכָּ֖ה מְאֹ֑ד וַתִּשְׁלַ֨ח בְּגָדִ֜ים
לְהַלְבִּ֣ישׁ אֶֽת־מָרְדֳּכַ֗י וּלְהָסִ֥יר שַׂקּ֛וֹ מֵעָלָ֖יו וְלֹ֥א קִבֵּֽל: ה וַתִּקְרָא֩
אֶסְתֵּ֨ר לַהֲתָ֜ךְ מִסָּרִיסֵ֤י הַמֶּ֨לֶךְ֙ אֲשֶׁ֣ר הֶעֱמִ֣יד לְפָנֶ֔יהָ וַתְּצַוֵּ֖הוּ עַֽל־
מָרְדֳּכָ֑י לָדַ֥עַת מַה־זֶּ֖ה וְעַל־מַה־זֶּֽה: ו וַיֵּצֵ֥א הֲתָ֖ךְ אֶֽל־מָרְדֳּכָ֑י אֶל־
רְח֣וֹב הָעִ֔יר אֲשֶׁ֖ר לִפְנֵ֥י שַֽׁעַר־הַמֶּֽלֶךְ: ז וַיַּגֶּד־ל֣וֹ מָרְדֳּכַ֔י אֵ֖ת כָּל־
אֲשֶׁ֣ר קָרָ֑הוּ וְאֵ֣ת ׀ פָּרָשַׁ֣ת הַכֶּ֗סֶף אֲשֶׁ֨ר אָמַ֤ר הָמָן֙ לִ֠שְׁקוֹל עַל־גִּנְזֵ֧י
הַמֶּ֛לֶךְ °בַּיְּהוּדִיים [ °בַּיְּהוּדִ֖ים ק] לְאַבְּדָֽם: ח וְאֶת־פַּתְשֶׁ֣גֶן כְּתָֽב־
הַדָּ֡ת אֲשֶׁר־נִתַּן֩ בְּשׁוּשָׁ֨ן לְהַשְׁמִידָ֜ם נָ֣תַן ל֗וֹ לְהַרְא֥וֹת אֶת־אֶסְתֵּ֖ר
וּלְהַגִּ֣יד לָ֑הּ וּלְצַוּ֣וֹת עָלֶ֗יהָ לָב֨וֹא אֶל־הַמֶּ֧לֶךְ לְהִֽתְחַנֶּן־ל֛וֹ וּלְבַקֵּ֥שׁ
מִלְּפָנָ֖יו עַל־עַמָּֽהּ: ט וַיָּב֖וֹא הֲתָ֑ךְ וַיַּגֵּ֣ד לְאֶסְתֵּ֔ר אֵ֖ת דִּבְרֵ֥י מָרְדֳּכָֽי:
י וַתֹּ֤אמֶר אֶסְתֵּר֙ לַהֲתָ֔ךְ וַתְּצַוֵּ֖הוּ אֶֽל־מָרְדֳּכָֽי: יא כָּל־עַבְדֵ֣י הַמֶּ֡לֶךְ
וְעַם־מְדִינ֨וֹת הַמֶּ֜לֶךְ יֽוֹדְעִ֗ים אֲשֶׁ֣ר כָּל־אִ֣ישׁ וְאִשָּׁ֡ה אֲשֶׁ֣ר יָבֽוֹא־אֶל־
הַמֶּ֩לֶךְ֩ אֶל־הֶחָצֵ֨ר הַפְּנִימִ֜ית אֲשֶׁ֣ר לֹֽא־יִקָּרֵ֗א אַחַ֤ת דָּתוֹ֙ לְהָמִ֔ית
לְבַ֞ד מֵאֲשֶׁ֧ר יֽוֹשִֽׁיט־ל֣וֹ הַמֶּ֗לֶךְ אֶת־שַׁרְבִ֥יט הַזָּהָ֖ב וְחָיָ֑ה וַאֲנִ֗י לֹ֤א

---

**3:14.** The strange haste in publishing a decree that would not be executed for eleven months was because Haman was afraid that the fickle king would have a change of heart. Also, he wanted to prolong the agony of the Jews throughout the kingdom by telling them of the impending massacre so far in advance.

and everything was written exactly as Haman had dictated, to the king's satraps, to the governors who were over every province, and to the officials of every people; [to] each province in its own script, and [to] each people in its own language; it was written in the name of King Ahasuerus, and it was sealed with the king's signet ring. <sup>13</sup> Letters were sent by courier to all the provinces of the king, to destroy, to slay and to exterminate all the Jews, from young to old, children and women, in one day, on the thirteenth of the twelfth month, which is the month of Adar, and to plunder their possessions. <sup>14</sup> Copies of the document were to be promulgated in every province, and be published to all peoples, for them to be prepared for that day. <sup>15</sup> The couriers went forth hurriedly by order of the king, and the edict was distributed in Shushan the capital. The king and Haman sat down to drink, but the city of Shushan was bewildered.

**4** <sup>1</sup> **M**ordechai learned of all that had been done; and Mordechai tore his clothes and donned sackcloth and ashes. He went out into the midst of the city, and cried a loud and bitter cry. <sup>2</sup> He came until the front of the king's gate for it was forbidden to enter the king's gate in a garment of sackcloth. <sup>3</sup> And in every province, any place the king's command and his decree extended, there was great mourning among the Jews, and fasting and weeping and lament; sackcloth and ashes were spread out for the masses.

<sup>4</sup> And Esther's maidens came, as well as her chamberlains, and told her about it, and the queen was greatly distressed; she sent garments to clothe Mordechai, and to remove his sackcloth from upon him, but he would not accept [them].

<sup>5</sup> Then Esther summoned Hathach, one of the king's chamberlains whom he had stationed before her, and ordered him [to go] to Mordechai, to learn what this was about and why. <sup>6</sup> So Hathach went out to Mordechai to the city square, which was in front of the king's gate. <sup>7</sup> And Mordechai told him of all that had happened to him, and about the sum of money that Haman had promised to pay to the royal treasuries for the annihilation of the Jews. <sup>8</sup> He also gave him a copy of the text of the decree that was distributed in Shushan for their destruction, so that he might show it to Esther and inform her, and bid her to go to the king, to implore of him, and to plead with him for her people.

<sup>9</sup> Hathach came and told Esther the words of Mordechai. <sup>10</sup> Then Esther told Hathach, and ordered him [to return] to Mordechai, [saying]: <sup>11</sup> "All the king's servants and the people of the king's provinces know that any man or woman who approaches the king in the inner court, who is not summoned, his law is one — to be put to death; except for the one to whom the king shall extend the gold scepter so that he may live. Now I, I have not

---

**4:1. Mordechai and the Jews Mourn**

**4:4.** Esther had not yet revealed her origins, but her interest in Mordechai — who had always inquired about her welfare — was well known throughout the palace.

**4:5.** Hasach was a great man, Esther's confidant, one who could keep secrets, and whom no one would suspect or dare to question about his mission. In the Talmud he is identified with Daniel.

**4:8.** The time had come for Esther to reveal her identity and thus gain the king's mercy (*Alshich*).

נִקְרֵאתִי לָבוֹא אֶל־הַמֶּלֶךְ זֶה שְׁלוֹשִׁים יוֹם: יב וַיַּגִּידוּ לְמָרְדֳּכָי אֵת
דִּבְרֵי אֶסְתֵּר: יג וַיֹּאמֶר מָרְדֳּכַי לְהָשִׁיב אֶל־אֶסְתֵּר אַל־תְּדַמִּי
בְנַפְשֵׁךְ לְהִמָּלֵט בֵּית־הַמֶּלֶךְ מִכָּל־הַיְּהוּדִים: יד כִּי אִם־הַחֲרֵשׁ
תַּחֲרִישִׁי בָּעֵת הַזֹּאת רֶוַח וְהַצָּלָה יַעֲמוֹד לַיְּהוּדִים מִמָּקוֹם אַחֵר
וְאַתְּ וּבֵית־אָבִיךְ תֹּאבֵדוּ וּמִי יוֹדֵעַ אִם־לְעֵת כָּזֹאת הִגַּעַתְּ לַמַּלְכוּת:
טו וַתֹּאמֶר אֶסְתֵּר לְהָשִׁיב אֶל־מָרְדֳּכָי: טז לֵךְ כְּנוֹס אֶת־כָּל־
הַיְּהוּדִים הַנִּמְצְאִים בְּשׁוּשָׁן וְצוּמוּ עָלַי וְאַל־תֹּאכְלוּ וְאַל־תִּשְׁתּוּ
שְׁלֹשֶׁת יָמִים לַיְלָה וָיוֹם גַּם־אֲנִי וְנַעֲרֹתַי אָצוּם כֵּן וּבְכֵן אָבוֹא אֶל־
הַמֶּלֶךְ אֲשֶׁר לֹא־כַדָּת וְכַאֲשֶׁר אָבַדְתִּי אָבָדְתִּי: יז וַיַּעֲבֹר מָרְדֳּכָי
וַיַּעַשׂ כְּכֹל אֲשֶׁר־צִוְּתָה עָלָיו אֶסְתֵּר: ה א וַיְהִי | בַּיּוֹם הַשְּׁלִישִׁי
וַתִּלְבַּשׁ אֶסְתֵּר מַלְכוּת וַתַּעֲמֹד בַּחֲצַר בֵּית־הַמֶּלֶךְ הַפְּנִימִית נֹכַח
בֵּית הַמֶּלֶךְ וְהַמֶּלֶךְ יוֹשֵׁב עַל־כִּסֵּא מַלְכוּתוֹ בְּבֵית הַמַּלְכוּת נֹכַח
פֶּתַח הַבָּיִת: ב וַיְהִי כִרְאוֹת הַמֶּלֶךְ אֶת־אֶסְתֵּר הַמַּלְכָּה עֹמֶדֶת
בֶּחָצֵר נָשְׂאָה חֵן בְּעֵינָיו וַיּוֹשֶׁט הַמֶּלֶךְ לְאֶסְתֵּר אֶת־שַׁרְבִיט הַזָּהָב
אֲשֶׁר בְּיָדוֹ וַתִּקְרַב אֶסְתֵּר וַתִּגַּע בְּרֹאשׁ הַשַּׁרְבִיט: ג וַיֹּאמֶר לָהּ
הַמֶּלֶךְ מַה־לָּךְ אֶסְתֵּר הַמַּלְכָּה וּמַה־בַּקָּשָׁתֵךְ עַד־חֲצִי הַמַּלְכוּת
וְיִנָּתֵן לָךְ: ד וַתֹּאמֶר אֶסְתֵּר אִם־עַל־הַמֶּלֶךְ טוֹב יָבוֹא הַמֶּלֶךְ וְהָמָן
הַיּוֹם אֶל־הַמִּשְׁתֶּה אֲשֶׁר־עָשִׂיתִי לוֹ: ה וַיֹּאמֶר הַמֶּלֶךְ מַהֲרוּ אֶת־
הָמָן לַעֲשׂוֹת אֶת־דְּבַר אֶסְתֵּר וַיָּבֹא הַמֶּלֶךְ וְהָמָן אֶל־הַמִּשְׁתֶּה אֲשֶׁר־
עָשְׂתָה אֶסְתֵּר: ו וַיֹּאמֶר הַמֶּלֶךְ לְאֶסְתֵּר בְּמִשְׁתֵּה הַיַּיִן מַה־שְּׁאֵלָתֵךְ
וְיִנָּתֵן לָךְ וּמַה־בַּקָּשָׁתֵךְ עַד־חֲצִי הַמַּלְכוּת וְתֵעָשׂ: ז וַתַּעַן אֶסְתֵּר
וַתֹּאמַר שְׁאֵלָתִי וּבַקָּשָׁתִי: ח אִם־מָצָאתִי חֵן בְּעֵינֵי הַמֶּלֶךְ וְאִם־עַל־
הַמֶּלֶךְ טוֹב לָתֵת אֶת־שְׁאֵלָתִי וְלַעֲשׂוֹת אֶת־בַּקָּשָׁתִי יָבוֹא הַמֶּלֶךְ
וְהָמָן אֶל־הַמִּשְׁתֶּה אֲשֶׁר אֶעֱשֶׂה לָהֶם וּמָחָר אֶעֱשֶׂה כִּדְבַר הַמֶּלֶךְ:
ט וַיֵּצֵא הָמָן בַּיּוֹם הַהוּא שָׂמֵחַ וְטוֹב לֵב וְכִרְאוֹת הָמָן אֶת־מָרְדֳּכַי
בְּשַׁעַר הַמֶּלֶךְ וְלֹא־קָם וְלֹא־זָע מִמֶּנּוּ וַיִּמָּלֵא הָמָן עַל־מָרְדֳּכַי חֵמָה:
י וַיִּתְאַפַּק הָמָן וַיָּבוֹא אֶל־בֵּיתוֹ וַיִּשְׁלַח וַיָּבֵא אֶת־אֹהֲבָיו וְאֶת־

---

**4:13. Mordechai Encourages Esther**
'You may, by some remote twist of fate,
manage to save your body. But how will
you save your soul?'

**4:15. Esther Agrees to Go Unsummoned
to the King**

**4:16.** הַיְּהוּדִים הַנִּמְצְאִים בְּשׁוּשָׁן — *The Jews*

*that are to be found in Shushan.* Esther
limited the assembly to the Jews in
Shushan because it would have been impossible to assemble Jews living further
away on such short notice (*Gaon of Vilna*).

**5:1. Esther Goes Before the King**
בַּיּוֹם הַשְּׁלִישִׁי — *On the third day* of the fast. It

*been summoned to come to the king for these [past] thirty days."*
[12] *They related Esther's words to Mordechai.* [13] *Then Mordechai said to reply to Esther, "Do not imagine in your soul that you will be able to escape in the king's palace any more than the rest of the Jews.* [14] *For if you persist in keeping silent at a time like this, relief and deliverance will come to the Jews from another place, while you and your father's house will perish. And who knows whether it was just for such a time as this that you attained the royal position!'"*
[15] *Then Esther said to reply to Mordechai:* [16] *"Go, assemble all the Jews that are to be found in Shushan, and fast for me; do not eat or drink for three days, night or day: And I, with my maids, will fast also. Thus I will come to the king though it is unlawful; and if I perish, I perish."* [17] *Mordechai then left and did exactly as Esther had commanded him.*

**5** [1] **N**ow *it came to pass on the third day, Esther donned royalty and stood in the inner courtyard of the king's palace facing the king's palace, while the king was sitting on his royal throne in the royal palace facing the entrance of the palace.* [2] *When the king noticed Queen Esther standing in the courtyard, she found favor in his eyes. The king extended to Esther the gold scepter that was in his hand, and Esther approached and touched the tip of the scepter.*
[3] *The king said to her, "What is it for you, O Queen Esther? And what is your petition? [Even if it be] until half the kingdom, it shall be granted you."*
[4] *Esther said, "If it please the king, let the king and Haman come today to the banquet that I have prepared for him."*
[5] *Then the king commanded, "Hasten Haman to fulfill Esther's word." So the king and Haman came to the banquet that Esther had prepared.*
[6] *The king said to Esther during the wine feast, "What is your request? It shall be granted you. And what is your petition? [Even if it be] until half the kingdom, it shall be fulfilled."*
[7] *So Esther responded and said, "My request and my petition:* [8] *If I have found favor in the king's eyes, and if it pleases the king to grant my request and to fulfill my petition, let the king and Haman come to the banquet that I shall prepare for them, and tomorrow I shall fulfill the king's word."*
[9] *That day Haman went out joyful and exuberant. But when Haman noticed Mordechai in the king's gate and that he did not stand up and did not stir before him, Haman was filled with wrath at Mordechai.* [10] *[Nevertheless,] Haman restrained himself and went home. He sent and summoned his friends and*

---

was, according to the Talmud, the first day of Passover.

**5:4. Esther Lays a Trap for Haman**
To show that God protects Israel in hidden ways, His Name is not mentioned explicitly in this Book. However, in this verse it is alluded to, since the first Hebrew letters of the words יָבֹא הַמֶּלֶךְ וְהָמָן הַיּוֹם, *let the king and Haman come today,* spell the

Holy Name of God (*Rabbeinu Bachya*). This is one of several places throughout the Megillah where God's Name is indirectly hinted (*Kad HaKemach*).

**5:8.** Esther's ruse worked. When Haman arrived at Esther's first banquet, he was apprehensive of Esther's reason for inviting him. He suspected a connection between the new edict concerning the Jews

זֶרֶשׁ אִשְׁתּוֹ: יא וַיְסַפֵּר לָהֶם הָמָן אֶת־כְּבוֹד עָשְׁרוֹ וְרֹב בָּנָיו וְאֵת כָּל־
אֲשֶׁר גִּדְּלוֹ הַמֶּלֶךְ וְאֵת אֲשֶׁר נִשְּׂאוֹ עַל־הַשָּׂרִים וְעַבְדֵי הַמֶּלֶךְ:
יב וַיֹּאמֶר הָמָן אַף לֹא־הֵבִיאָה אֶסְתֵּר הַמַּלְכָּה עִם־הַמֶּלֶךְ אֶל־
הַמִּשְׁתֶּה אֲשֶׁר־עָשָׂתָה כִּי אִם־אוֹתִי וְגַם־לְמָחָר אֲנִי קָרוּא־לָהּ עִם־
הַמֶּלֶךְ: יג וְכָל־זֶה אֵינֶנּוּ שֹׁוֶה לִי בְּכָל־עֵת אֲשֶׁר אֲנִי רֹאֶה אֶת־
מָרְדֳּכַי הַיְּהוּדִי יוֹשֵׁב בְּשַׁעַר הַמֶּלֶךְ: יד וַתֹּאמֶר לוֹ זֶרֶשׁ אִשְׁתּוֹ וְכָל־
אֹהֲבָיו יַעֲשׂוּ־עֵץ גָּבֹהַּ חֲמִשִּׁים אַמָּה וּבַבֹּקֶר ׀ אֱמֹר לַמֶּלֶךְ וְיִתְלוּ
אֶת־מָרְדֳּכַי עָלָיו וּבֹא־עִם־הַמֶּלֶךְ אֶל־הַמִּשְׁתֶּה שָׂמֵחַ וַיִּיטַב הַדָּבָר
לִפְנֵי הָמָן וַיַּעַשׂ הָעֵץ:      ו א בַּלַּיְלָה הַהוּא נָדְדָה שְׁנַת הַמֶּלֶךְ
וַיֹּאמֶר לְהָבִיא אֶת־סֵפֶר הַזִּכְרֹנוֹת דִּבְרֵי הַיָּמִים וַיִּהְיוּ נִקְרָאִים לִפְנֵי
הַמֶּלֶךְ: ב וַיִּמָּצֵא כָתוּב אֲשֶׁר הִגִּיד מָרְדֳּכַי עַל־בִּגְתָנָא וָתֶרֶשׁ שְׁנֵי
סָרִיסֵי הַמֶּלֶךְ מִשֹּׁמְרֵי הַסַּף אֲשֶׁר בִּקְשׁוּ לִשְׁלֹחַ יָד בַּמֶּלֶךְ
אֲחַשְׁוֵרוֹשׁ: ג וַיֹּאמֶר הַמֶּלֶךְ מַה־נַּעֲשָׂה יְקָר וּגְדוּלָּה לְמָרְדֳּכַי עַל־זֶה
וַיֹּאמְרוּ נַעֲרֵי הַמֶּלֶךְ מְשָׁרְתָיו לֹא־נַעֲשָׂה עִמּוֹ דָּבָר: ד וַיֹּאמֶר הַמֶּלֶךְ
מִי בֶחָצֵר וְהָמָן בָּא לַחֲצַר בֵּית־הַמֶּלֶךְ הַחִיצוֹנָה לֵאמֹר לַמֶּלֶךְ
לִתְלוֹת אֶת־מָרְדֳּכַי עַל־הָעֵץ אֲשֶׁר־הֵכִין לוֹ: ה וַיֹּאמְרוּ נַעֲרֵי הַמֶּלֶךְ
אֵלָיו הִנֵּה הָמָן עֹמֵד בֶּחָצֵר וַיֹּאמֶר הַמֶּלֶךְ יָבוֹא: ו וַיָּבוֹא הָמָן וַיֹּאמֶר
לוֹ הַמֶּלֶךְ מַה־לַּעֲשׂוֹת בָּאִישׁ אֲשֶׁר הַמֶּלֶךְ חָפֵץ בִּיקָרוֹ וַיֹּאמֶר הָמָן
בְּלִבּוֹ לְמִי יַחְפֹּץ הַמֶּלֶךְ לַעֲשׂוֹת יְקָר יוֹתֵר מִמֶּנִּי: ז וַיֹּאמֶר הָמָן אֶל־
הַמֶּלֶךְ אִישׁ אֲשֶׁר הַמֶּלֶךְ חָפֵץ בִּיקָרוֹ: ח יָבִיאוּ לְבוּשׁ מַלְכוּת אֲשֶׁר
לָבַשׁ־בּוֹ הַמֶּלֶךְ וְסוּס אֲשֶׁר רָכַב עָלָיו הַמֶּלֶךְ וַאֲשֶׁר נִתַּן כֶּתֶר מַלְכוּת
בְּרֹאשׁוֹ: ט וְנָתוֹן הַלְּבוּשׁ וְהַסּוּס עַל־יַד־אִישׁ מִשָּׂרֵי הַמֶּלֶךְ הַפַּרְתְּמִים
וְהִלְבִּישׁוּ אֶת־הָאִישׁ אֲשֶׁר הַמֶּלֶךְ חָפֵץ בִּיקָרוֹ וְהִרְכִּיבֻהוּ עַל־הַסּוּס
בִּרְחוֹב הָעִיר וְקָרְאוּ לְפָנָיו כָּכָה יֵעָשֶׂה לָאִישׁ אֲשֶׁר הַמֶּלֶךְ חָפֵץ
בִּיקָרוֹ: י וַיֹּאמֶר הַמֶּלֶךְ לְהָמָן מַהֵר קַח אֶת־הַלְּבוּשׁ וְאֶת־הַסּוּס
כַּאֲשֶׁר דִּבַּרְתָּ וַעֲשֵׂה־כֵן לְמָרְדֳּכַי הַיְּהוּדִי הַיּוֹשֵׁב בְּשַׁעַר הַמֶּלֶךְ אַל־
תַּפֵּל דָּבָר מִכֹּל אֲשֶׁר דִּבַּרְתָּ: יא וַיִּקַּח הָמָן אֶת־הַלְּבוּשׁ וְאֶת־הַסּוּס
וַיַּלְבֵּשׁ אֶת־מָרְדֳּכַי וַיַּרְכִּיבֵהוּ בִּרְחוֹב הָעִיר וַיִּקְרָא לְפָנָיו כָּכָה

---

and his invitation. Only now, having left the first party at which he was overwhelmed with flattery, was he joyous and confident. He was unprepared, therefore, for the consequences of Esther's next banquet (*Alkabetz*).

**5:13.** Notice that Haman did not mention to his wife and children that he was angry because of Mordechai's refusal to bow down to him; he thought it beneath his dignity to admit that such a minor slight could ruffle him so. Rather he claimed that

*his wife, Zeresh.* ¹¹ *Haman recounted to them the glory of his wealth and of his many sons, and all [the ways] in which the king had promoted him and elevated him above the officials and royal servants.* ¹² *Haman said, "Moreover, Queen Esther brought no one but myself to accompany the king to the banquet that she had prepared, and tomorrow, too, I am invited by her along with the king.* ¹³ *Yet all this is worth nothing to me so long as I see Mordechai the Jew sitting at the king's gate."*

¹⁴ *So his wife, Zeresh, as well as all his friends, said to him, "Let them make a gallows, fifty cubits high; and in the morning speak to the king and have them hang Mordechai on it. Then, accompany the king to the banquet in good spirits."* *This suggestion pleased Haman, and he had the gallows made.*

**6** ¹ *That night the king's sleep was disturbed so he commanded to bring the book of records, the chronicles, and that they be read before the king.* ² *And it was found written [there] that Mordechai had denounced Bigthana and Teresh, two of the king's chamberlains of the guardians of the threshold, who had sought to send [their] hand against King Ahasuerus.* ³ *The king said, "What honor or majesty has been done for Mordechai for this?"*

*The king's attendants, his ministrants, said, "Nothing has been done for him."* ⁴ *The king said, "Who is in the courtyard?" (Now Haman was [just] coming into the outer courtyard of the royal palace to speak to the king about hanging Mordechai on the gallows that he had prepared for him.)*

⁵ *So the king's attendants said to him, "Behold! Haman stands in the court-yard."*

*And the king said, "Let him enter."* ⁶ *Haman entered and the king said to him, "What should be done for the man whom the king desires to honor?"*

*Now Haman said in his heart, "Whom would the king especially want to honor more than me?"* ⁷ *So Haman said to the king, "For the man whom the king desires to honor,* ⁸ *have them bring royal attire that the king has worn and a horse upon which the king has ridden, one with a royal crown placed on his head.* ⁹ *Then let the attire and the horse be given over into the hand of one of the king's most noble officials, and let them dress the man whom the king desires to honor, and have him ride on the horse through the city square, and let them proclaim before him, 'This is what shall be done for the man whom the king desires to honor.'"*

¹⁰ *Then the king said to Haman, "Hurry, take the attire and the horse as you have said, and do all this for Mordechai the Jew, who sits at the king's gate. Do not omit a single detail of all that you have suggested!"*

¹¹ *So Haman took the garment and the horse and dressed Mordechai, and had him ride through the city square, and proclaimed before him, "This is what*

---

he was angry because *he saw "Mordechai the Jew sitting at the king's gate"* and he was totally unworthy of such a high honor (*Me'am Loez*).

**6:1. Mordechai Is Finally Rewarded**
Allegorically the *Midrash* comments that the distress of the Jews caused God's Heavenly throne to be shaken.

יֵעָשֶׂה לָאִישׁ אֲשֶׁר הַמֶּלֶךְ חָפֵץ בִּיקָרוֹ: יב וַיָּשָׁב מָרְדֳּכַי אֶל-שַׁעַר
הַמֶּלֶךְ וְהָמָן נִדְחַף אֶל-בֵּיתוֹ אָבֵל וַחֲפוּי רֹאשׁ: יג וַיְסַפֵּר הָמָן לְזֶרֶשׁ
אִשְׁתּוֹ וּלְכָל-אֹהֲבָיו אֵת כָּל-אֲשֶׁר קָרָהוּ וַיֹּאמְרוּ לוֹ חֲכָמָיו וְזֶרֶשׁ
אִשְׁתּוֹ אִם מִזֶּרַע הַיְּהוּדִים מָרְדֳּכַי אֲשֶׁר הַחִלּוֹתָ לִנְפֹּל לְפָנָיו לֹא-
תוּכַל לוֹ כִּי-נָפוֹל תִּפּוֹל לְפָנָיו: יד עוֹדָם מְדַבְּרִים עִמּוֹ וְסָרִיסֵי הַמֶּלֶךְ
הִגִּיעוּ וַיַּבְהִלוּ לְהָבִיא אֶת-הָמָן אֶל-הַמִּשְׁתֶּה אֲשֶׁר-עָשְׂתָה אֶסְתֵּר:
ז א וַיָּבֹא הַמֶּלֶךְ וְהָמָן לִשְׁתּוֹת עִם-אֶסְתֵּר הַמַּלְכָּה: ב וַיֹּאמֶר הַמֶּלֶךְ
לְאֶסְתֵּר גַּם בַּיּוֹם הַשֵּׁנִי בְּמִשְׁתֵּה הַיַּיִן מַה-שְּׁאֵלָתֵךְ אֶסְתֵּר הַמַּלְכָּה
וְתִנָּתֵן לָךְ וּמַה-בַּקָּשָׁתֵךְ עַד-חֲצִי הַמַּלְכוּת וְתֵעָשׂ: ג וַתַּעַן אֶסְתֵּר
הַמַּלְכָּה וַתֹּאמַר אִם-מָצָאתִי חֵן בְּעֵינֶיךָ הַמֶּלֶךְ וְאִם-עַל-הַמֶּלֶךְ
טוֹב תִּנָּתֶן-לִי נַפְשִׁי בִּשְׁאֵלָתִי וְעַמִּי בְּבַקָּשָׁתִי: ד כִּי נִמְכַּרְנוּ אֲנִי
וְעַמִּי לְהַשְׁמִיד לַהֲרוֹג וּלְאַבֵּד וְאִלּוּ לַעֲבָדִים וְלִשְׁפָחוֹת נִמְכַּרְנוּ
הֶחֱרַשְׁתִּי כִּי אֵין הַצָּר שֹׁוֶה בְּנֵזֶק הַמֶּלֶךְ: ה וַיֹּאמֶר הַמֶּלֶךְ
אֲחַשְׁוֵרוֹשׁ וַיֹּאמֶר לְאֶסְתֵּר הַמַּלְכָּה מִי הוּא זֶה וְאֵי-זֶה הוּא אֲשֶׁר-
מְלָאוֹ לִבּוֹ לַעֲשׂוֹת כֵּן: ו וַתֹּאמֶר אֶסְתֵּר אִישׁ צַר וְאוֹיֵב הָמָן הָרָע
הַזֶּה וְהָמָן נִבְעַת מִלִּפְנֵי הַמֶּלֶךְ וְהַמַּלְכָּה: ז וְהַמֶּלֶךְ קָם בַּחֲמָתוֹ
מִמִּשְׁתֵּה הַיַּיִן אֶל-גִּנַּת הַבִּיתָן וְהָמָן עָמַד לְבַקֵּשׁ עַל-נַפְשׁוֹ מֵאֶסְתֵּר
הַמַּלְכָּה כִּי רָאָה כִּי-כָלְתָה אֵלָיו הָרָעָה מֵאֵת הַמֶּלֶךְ: ח וְהַמֶּלֶךְ שָׁב
מִגִּנַּת הַבִּיתָן אֶל-בֵּית מִשְׁתֵּה הַיַּיִן וְהָמָן נֹפֵל עַל-הַמִּטָּה אֲשֶׁר
אֶסְתֵּר עָלֶיהָ וַיֹּאמֶר הַמֶּלֶךְ הֲגַם לִכְבּוֹשׁ אֶת-הַמַּלְכָּה עִמִּי בַּבָּיִת
הַדָּבָר יָצָא מִפִּי הַמֶּלֶךְ וּפְנֵי הָמָן חָפוּ: ט וַיֹּאמֶר חַרְבוֹנָה אֶחָד מִן-
הַסָּרִיסִים לִפְנֵי הַמֶּלֶךְ גַּם הִנֵּה-הָעֵץ אֲשֶׁר-עָשָׂה הָמָן לְמָרְדֳּכַי
אֲשֶׁר דִּבֶּר-טוֹב עַל-הַמֶּלֶךְ עֹמֵד בְּבֵית הָמָן גָּבֹהַּ חֲמִשִּׁים אַמָּה
וַיֹּאמֶר הַמֶּלֶךְ תְּלֻהוּ עָלָיו: י וַיִּתְלוּ אֶת-הָמָן עַל-הָעֵץ אֲשֶׁר-
הֵכִין לְמָרְדֳּכָי וַחֲמַת הַמֶּלֶךְ שָׁכָכָה: ח א בַּיּוֹם הַהוּא
נָתַן הַמֶּלֶךְ אֲחַשְׁוֵרוֹשׁ לְאֶסְתֵּר הַמַּלְכָּה אֶת-בֵּית הָמָן צֹרֵר
°הַיְּהוּדִיים [ הַיְּהוּדִים ק׳] וּמָרְדֳּכַי בָּא לִפְנֵי הַמֶּלֶךְ כִּי-הִגִּידָה אֶסְתֵּר

---

**6:13. Haman's Doom Is Forecast**
Zeresh and the advisers were sure the
king's command to honor Mordechai was
not coincidental; it signified the beginning
of the Jews' rise — and of Haman's downfall (*Yosef Lekach*; *Malbim*).

**7:1. Esther Presents Her Request**

It was one of God's miracles that, as
disturbed as Ahasuerus was, he came to
the feast, was cheered by the wine, and
regained his good cheer to the extent that
he was prepared to fulfill Esther's every
wish.

**7:3.** The first הַמֶּלֶךְ, *King,* is taken to refer

*shall be done for the man whom the king desires to honor."*
¹² *Mordechai returned to the king's gate; but Haman hurried home, despondent and with his head covered.* ¹³ *Haman told his wife, Zeresh, and all his friends everything that had happened to him, and his wise men and his wife, Zeresh, said to him, "If Mordechai, before whom you have begun to fall, is of Jewish descent, you will not prevail against him, but will undoubtedly fall before him."* ¹⁴ *While they were still talking with him, the king's chamberlains arrived, and they hurried to bring Haman to the banquet which Esther had prepared.*

**7** ¹ **S**o the king and Haman came to feast with Queen Esther. ² *The king asked Esther again on the second day at the wine feast, "What is your request, Queen Esther? — it shall be granted you. And what is your petition? [Even if it be] until half the kingdom, it shall be fulfilled."*

³ *So Queen Esther responded and said, "If I have found favor in your eyes, O king, and if it pleases the king, let my life be granted to me as my request and my people as my petition.* ⁴ *For we have been sold, I and my people, to be destroyed, to be slain and to be exterminated. Had we been sold as slaves and maidservants, I would have kept quiet, for the adversary is not worthy of the king's damage."*

⁵ *Thereupon, King Ahasuerus exclaimed and said to Queen Esther, "Who is this? Where is this one who dared to do so?"*

⁶ *And Esther said, "A man who is an adversary and an enemy! This wicked Haman!" Haman trembled in terror before the king and queen.*

⁷ *The king rose in his wrath from the wine feast and went into the palace garden while Haman remained to beg Queen Esther for his soul, for he saw that evil had been determined against him by the king.* ⁸ *When the king returned from the palace garden to the hall of the wine feast, Haman had fallen onto the couch upon which Esther was; so the king exclaimed, "Would he actually assault the queen while I'm in the house?" As soon as the king uttered this, they covered Haman's face.*

⁹ *Then Harbonah, one of the chamberlains [in attendance] before the king, said, "Furthermore, the gallows which Haman made for Mordechai — who spoke good for the king — is standing in Haman's house; it is fifty cubits high." And the king said, "Hang him on it."* ¹⁰ *So they hanged Haman on the gallows that he had prepared for Mordechai, and the king's anger abated.*

**8** ¹ **T**hat very day, King Ahasuerus gave the estate of Haman, the enemy of the Jews, to Queen Esther. Mordechai came before the king, for Esther had

---

to God, the second to Ahasuerus. "Esther cast her eyes heavenward and said: 'If I have found favor in Your sight, O Supreme King, and if it pleases you, O King Ahasuerus, let my life be given me, and let my people be rescued from the hands of the enemy' " (*Targum*).

**7:7.** וְהַמֶּלֶךְ קָם בַּחֲמָתוֹ — *The king rose in his wrath.* The king went out to "cool off" from

his anger, part of God's master plan, to give Haman the opportunity to incriminate himself even further in the king's absence.

**7:9. Haman Is Executed**
Our Sages ordained that one should always say חַרְבוֹנָה זָכוּר לָטוֹב — *"Charbonah of blessed memory,"* because it was Charbonah's swift advice that prevented Haman from possibly talking — or bribing

מֶה הוּא־לָהּ: ב וַיָּסַר הַמֶּלֶךְ אֶת־טַבַּעְתּוֹ אֲשֶׁר הֶעֱבִיר מֵהָמָן וַיִּתְּנָהּ
לְמָרְדֳּכָי וַתָּשֶׂם אֶסְתֵּר אֶת־מָרְדֳּכַי עַל־בֵּית הָמָן: ג וַתּוֹסֶף
אֶסְתֵּר וַתְּדַבֵּר לִפְנֵי הַמֶּלֶךְ וַתִּפֹּל לִפְנֵי רַגְלָיו וַתֵּבְךְּ וַתִּתְחַנֶּן־לוֹ
לְהַעֲבִיר אֶת־רָעַת הָמָן הָאֲגָגִי וְאֵת מַחֲשַׁבְתּוֹ אֲשֶׁר חָשַׁב עַל־
הַיְּהוּדִים: ד וַיּוֹשֶׁט הַמֶּלֶךְ לְאֶסְתֵּר אֵת שַׁרְבִט הַזָּהָב וַתָּקָם אֶסְתֵּר
וַתַּעֲמֹד לִפְנֵי הַמֶּלֶךְ: ה וַתֹּאמֶר אִם־עַל־הַמֶּלֶךְ טוֹב וְאִם־מָצָאתִי חֵן
לְפָנָיו וְכָשֵׁר הַדָּבָר לִפְנֵי הַמֶּלֶךְ וְטוֹבָה אֲנִי בְּעֵינָיו יִכָּתֵב לְהָשִׁיב
אֶת־הַסְּפָרִים מַחֲשֶׁבֶת הָמָן בֶּן־הַמְּדָתָא הָאֲגָגִי אֲשֶׁר כָּתַב לְאַבֵּד
אֶת־הַיְּהוּדִים אֲשֶׁר בְּכָל־מְדִינוֹת הַמֶּלֶךְ: ו כִּי אֵיכָכָה אוּכַל וְרָאִיתִי
בָּרָעָה אֲשֶׁר־יִמְצָא אֶת־עַמִּי וְאֵיכָכָה אוּכַל וְרָאִיתִי בְּאָבְדָן
מוֹלַדְתִּי: ז וַיֹּאמֶר הַמֶּלֶךְ אֲחַשְׁוֵרֹשׁ לְאֶסְתֵּר הַמַּלְכָּה
וּלְמָרְדֳּכַי הַיְּהוּדִי הִנֵּה בֵית־הָמָן נָתַתִּי לְאֶסְתֵּר וְאֹתוֹ תָּלוּ עַל־הָעֵץ
עַל אֲשֶׁר־שָׁלַח יָדוֹ °בַּיְּהוּדִים [°בַּיְּהוּדִיים ק]: ח וְאַתֶּם כִּתְבוּ עַל־
הַיְּהוּדִים כַּטּוֹב בְּעֵינֵיכֶם בְּשֵׁם הַמֶּלֶךְ וְחִתְמוּ בְּטַבַּעַת הַמֶּלֶךְ כִּי־
כְתָב אֲשֶׁר־נִכְתָּב בְּשֵׁם־הַמֶּלֶךְ וְנַחְתּוֹם בְּטַבַּעַת הַמֶּלֶךְ אֵין לְהָשִׁיב:
ט וַיִּקָּרְאוּ סֹפְרֵי־הַמֶּלֶךְ בָּעֵת־הַהִיא בַּחֹדֶשׁ הַשְּׁלִישִׁי הוּא־חֹדֶשׁ
סִיוָן בִּשְׁלוֹשָׁה וְעֶשְׂרִים בּוֹ וַיִּכָּתֵב כְּכָל־אֲשֶׁר־צִוָּה מָרְדֳּכַי אֶל־
הַיְּהוּדִים וְאֶל הָאֲחַשְׁדַּרְפְּנִים וְהַפַּחוֹת וְשָׂרֵי הַמְּדִינוֹת אֲשֶׁר ׀
מֵהֹדּוּ וְעַד־כּוּשׁ שֶׁבַע וְעֶשְׂרִים וּמֵאָה מְדִינָה מְדִינָה וּמְדִינָה כִּכְתָבָהּ
וְעַם וָעָם כִּלְשֹׁנוֹ וְאֶל־הַיְּהוּדִים כִּכְתָבָם וְכִלְשׁוֹנָם: י וַיִּכְתֹּב בְּשֵׁם
הַמֶּלֶךְ אֲחַשְׁוֵרֹשׁ וַיַּחְתֹּם בְּטַבַּעַת הַמֶּלֶךְ וַיִּשְׁלַח סְפָרִים בְּיַד
הָרָצִים בַּסּוּסִים רֹכְבֵי הָרֶכֶשׁ הָאֲחַשְׁתְּרָנִים בְּנֵי הָרַמָּכִים: יא אֲשֶׁר
נָתַן הַמֶּלֶךְ לַיְּהוּדִים ׀ אֲשֶׁר ׀ בְּכָל־עִיר־וָעִיר לְהִקָּהֵל וְלַעֲמֹד
עַל־נַפְשָׁם לְהַשְׁמִיד וְלַהֲרֹג וּלְאַבֵּד אֶת־כָּל־חֵיל עַם וּמְדִינָה
הַצָּרִים אֹתָם טַף וְנָשִׁים וּשְׁלָלָם לָבוֹז: יב בְּיוֹם אֶחָד בְּכָל־מְדִינוֹת
הַמֶּלֶךְ אֲחַשְׁוֵרוֹשׁ בִּשְׁלוֹשָׁה עָשָׂר לְחֹדֶשׁ שְׁנֵים־עָשָׂר הוּא־חֹדֶשׁ
אֲדָר: יג פַּתְשֶׁגֶן הַכְּתָב לְהִנָּתֵן דָּת בְּכָל־מְדִינָה וּמְדִינָה גָּלוּי
לְכָל־הָעַמִּים וְלִהְיוֹת °הַיְּהוּדִיים עֲתוּדִים [°הַיְּהוּדִים עֲתִידִים ק]
לַיּוֹם הַזֶּה לְהִנָּקֵם מֵאֹיְבֵיהֶם: יד הָרָצִים רֹכְבֵי הָרֶכֶשׁ הָאֲחַשְׁתְּרָנִים
יָצְאוּ מְבֹהָלִים וּדְחוּפִים בִּדְבַר הַמֶּלֶךְ וְהַדָּת נִתְּנָה בְּשׁוּשַׁן

— his way back into the king's good graces. **8:8.** The Holy One, Blessed is He, now performed an unprecedented miracle.

told [the king] what he was to her. ² The king removed his signet ring, which he had taken away from Haman, and gave it to Mordechai; and Esther put Mordechai in charge of Haman's estate.

³ Esther yet again spoke to the king, she fell at his feet, and wept and implored him to avert the evil [intention] of Haman the Agagite, and his scheme that he had plotted against the Jews. ⁴ The king extended the gold scepter to Esther, and Esther arose and stood before the king. ⁵ She said, "If it pleases the king, and if I have found favor before him, and the proposal seems proper before the king, and I be pleasing in his eyes, let it be written to countermand those dispatches, the scheme of Haman the son of Hammedatha the Agagite, [in] which he had written to exterminate the Jews who are in all the king's provinces. ⁶ For how can I bear to witness the disaster which will befall my people?! How can I bear to witness the extermination of my kindred?!"

⁷ Then King Ahasuerus said to Queen Esther and to Mordechai the Jew, "Behold, I have given Haman's estate to Esther, and they have hanged him on the gallows because he sent [his] hand against the Jews. ⁸ You may write concerning the Jews whatever is favorable in your eyes, in the name of the king, and seal it with the king's signet, for an edict which is written in the king's name and sealed with the king's signet may not be revoked."

⁹ So they summoned the king's scribes at that time, in the third month, which is the month of Sivan, on its twenty-third [day], and it was written as Mordechai had dictated to the Jews and to the satraps, the governors and officials of the provinces from Hodu to Cush, a hundred and twenty-seven provinces, to each province in its own script, and each people in its own language, and to the Jews in their own script and language. ¹⁰ He wrote in the name of King Ahasuerus and sealed it with the king's signet. He sent dispatches by couriers on horseback, riders of swift mules bred of mares, ¹¹ [to the effect] that the king had given [permission] to the Jews of every city to organize and to defend themselves; to destroy, to slay and to exterminate every armed force of any people or province that threaten them, [along with their] children and women, and to plunder their possessions, ¹² on one day in all the provinces of King Ahasuerus, namely, upon the thirteenth day of the twelfth month, that is, the month of Adar. ¹³ Copies of the document were to be promulgated in every province, and be published to all peoples, for the Jews to be prepared for that day to avenge themselves on their enemies. ¹⁴ The couriers, riders of swift mules, went forth in urgent haste by word of the king, and the edict was distributed in Shushan the capital.

---

Was there ever in history such a miracle that Israel should wreak vengeance on the other nations and do with their enemies as they pleased? (*Midrash*).

**8:11.** Only by organizing and unifying themselves in begging for God's assistance could the Jews be victorious despite being seriously outnumbered.

הַבִּירָה: טו **וּמָרְדֳּכַי יָצָא | מִלִּפְנֵי הַמֶּלֶךְ בִּלְבוּשׁ מַלְכוּת**
**תְּכֵלֶת וָחוּר וַעֲטֶרֶת זָהָב גְּדוֹלָה וְתַכְרִיךְ בּוּץ וְאַרְגָּמָן וְהָעִיר שׁוּשָׁן**
**צָהֲלָה וְשָׂמֵחָה:** טז **לַיְּהוּדִים הָיְתָה אוֹרָה וְשִׂמְחָה וְשָׂשֹׂן וִיקָר:**
יז וּבְכָל־מְדִינָה וּמְדִינָה וּבְכָל־עִיר וָעִיר מְקוֹם אֲשֶׁר דְּבַר־הַמֶּלֶךְ
וְדָתוֹ מַגִּיעַ שִׂמְחָה וְשָׂשׂוֹן לַיְּהוּדִים מִשְׁתֶּה וְיוֹם טוֹב וְרַבִּים מֵעַמֵּי
הָאָרֶץ מִתְיַהֲדִים כִּי־נָפַל פַּחַד־הַיְּהוּדִים עֲלֵיהֶם: ט א וּבִשְׁנֵים עָשָׂר
חֹדֶשׁ הוּא־חֹדֶשׁ אֲדָר בִּשְׁלוֹשָׁה עָשָׂר יוֹם בּוֹ אֲשֶׁר הִגִּיעַ דְּבַר־
הַמֶּלֶךְ וְדָתוֹ לְהֵעָשׂוֹת בַּיּוֹם אֲשֶׁר שִׂבְּרוּ אֹיְבֵי הַיְּהוּדִים לִשְׁלוֹט בָּהֶם
וְנַהֲפוֹךְ הוּא אֲשֶׁר יִשְׁלְטוּ הַיְּהוּדִים הֵמָּה בְּשֹׂנְאֵיהֶם: ב נִקְהֲלוּ
הַיְּהוּדִים בְּעָרֵיהֶם בְּכָל־מְדִינוֹת הַמֶּלֶךְ אֲחַשְׁוֵרוֹשׁ לִשְׁלֹחַ יָד
בִּמְבַקְשֵׁי רָעָתָם וְאִישׁ לֹא־עָמַד לִפְנֵיהֶם כִּי־נָפַל פַּחְדָּם עַל־כָּל־
הָעַמִּים: ג וְכָל־שָׂרֵי הַמְּדִינוֹת וְהָאֲחַשְׁדַּרְפְּנִים וְהַפַּחוֹת וְעֹשֵׂי
הַמְּלָאכָה אֲשֶׁר לַמֶּלֶךְ מְנַשְּׂאִים אֶת־הַיְּהוּדִים כִּי־נָפַל פַּחַד־מָרְדֳּכַי
עֲלֵיהֶם: ד כִּי־גָדוֹל מָרְדֳּכַי בְּבֵית הַמֶּלֶךְ וְשָׁמְעוֹ הוֹלֵךְ בְּכָל־הַמְּדִינוֹת
כִּי־הָאִישׁ מָרְדֳּכַי הוֹלֵךְ וְגָדוֹל: ה וַיַּכּוּ הַיְּהוּדִים בְּכָל־אֹיְבֵיהֶם מַכַּת־
חֶרֶב וְהֶרֶג וְאַבְדָן וַיַּעֲשׂוּ בְשֹׂנְאֵיהֶם כִּרְצוֹנָם: ו וּבְשׁוּשַׁן הַבִּירָה הָרְגוּ
הַיְּהוּדִים וְאַבֵּד חֲמֵשׁ מֵאוֹת אִישׁ:

| | |
|---|---|
| וְאֵת \| | ז פַּרְשַׁנְדָּתָא |
| וְאֵת \| | דַּלְפוֹן |
| וְאֵת \| | אַסְפָּתָא: |
| וְאֵת \| | ח פּוֹרָתָא |
| וְאֵת \| | אֲדַלְיָא |
| וְאֵת \| | אֲרִידָתָא: |
| וְאֵת \| | ט פַּרְמַשְׁתָּא |
| וְאֵת \| | אֲרִיסַי |
| וְאֵת \| | אֲרִדַי |
| עֲשֶׂרֶת י | וַיְזָתָא: |

בְּנֵי הָמָן בֶּן־הַמְּדָתָא צֹרֵר הַיְּהוּדִים הָרָגוּ וּבַבִּזָּה לֹא שָׁלְחוּ אֶת־

---

**8:15-16.** These are among the four verses said aloud in the synagogue by the congregation during the public reading of the Megillah.

**8:16.** 'Rav Yehudah said: אוֹרָה, *light*, refers

to Torah; שִׂמְחָה, *gladness*, refers to holiday; שָׂשֹׂן, *joy*, refers to circumcision; and יְקָר, *honor*, refers to תְּפִילִין, *tefillin*, [i.e., they were finally able to resume the study of Torah and without hindrance] the perfor-

¹⁵ **Mordechai left the king's presence clad in royal apparel of turquoise and white with a large gold crown and a robe of fine linen and purple; then the city of Shushan was cheerful and glad.** ¹⁶ **The Jews had light and gladness and joy and honor.** ¹⁷ And in every province, and in every city, every place where the king's word and his decree reached, the Jews had gladness and joy, a feast and a holiday. Moreover, many from among the people of the land professed themselves Jews, for the fear of the Jews had fallen upon them.

**9** ¹ Then, in the twelfth month, which is the month of Adar, on its thirteenth day, when the king's command and edict were about to be enforced, on the day that the enemies of the Jews expected to prevail over them, and it was turned about: The Jews prevailed over their adversaries. ² The Jews organized themselves in their cities in all the provinces of King Ahasuerus, to send forth [their] hand against those who sought their hurt; and no man could stand before them, for fear of them had fallen upon all the peoples. ³ And all the officials of the provinces, the satraps and the governors and those that conduct the king's affairs, exalted the Jews for the fear of Mordechai had fallen upon them. ⁴ For Mordechai was now pre-eminent in the royal palace and his fame was spreading throughout all the provinces, for the man Mordechai grew increasingly greater. ⁵ And the Jews struck at all their enemies with the stroke of the sword, slaughtering and annihilating; they treated their enemies as they pleased. ⁶ In Shushan the capital, the Jews slew and annihilated five hundred men.    ⁷ and

Parshandatha                                        and
Dalphon                                             and
Aspatha                                          ⁸ and
Poratha                                             and
Adalia                                              and
Aridatha                                         ⁹ and
Parmashta                                           and
Arisai                                              and
Aridai                                              and
Vaizatha                                     ¹⁰ the ten

sons of Haman son of Hammedatha, the Jews' enemy; but they did not lay their hand on the spoils.

---

mance of *mitzvos* (Talmud).

**9:1. The Turnabout: The Jews Avenge Themselves**

**9:7.** The ten sons of Haman and the word עֲשֶׂרֶת, *ten,* which follows, should be said [by one reading the Megillah on Purim] in one breath . . . to indicate that they all died together (Talmud).

**9:9.** וַיְזָתָא — *Vaizatha.* The letter ו (*vuv*) of *Vaizatha* is enlarged in the Megillah like a long pole to indicate that they were all

strung [one underneath the other] on one long pole (Talmud).

**9:10.** וּבַבִּזָּה לֹא שָׁלְחוּ אֶת יָדָם — *But they did not lay their hand on the spoils.* It was obviously most difficult for poor Jews to restrain themselves from taking spoils. In reward for their restraint, it was established that, throughout all generations, the poor — without exception and investigation as to need — will be the recipients of מַתָּנוֹת לָאֶבְיוֹנִים, *gifts to the poor* (Rebbe of Ger).

יָדָם: יא בַּיִּוֹם הַהֹוּא בָּא מִסְפַּר הַהֲרוּגֵים בְּשׁוּשַׁן הַבִּירָה לִפְנֵי הַמֶּלֶךְ: יב וַיֹּאמֶר הַמֶּלֶךְ לְאֶסְתֵּר הַמַּלְכָּה בְּשׁוּשַׁן הַבִּירָה הָרְגוּ הַיְהוּדִים וְאַבֵּד חֲמֵשׁ מֵאוֹת אִישׁ וְאֵת עֲשֶׂרֶת בְּנֵי־הָמָן בִּשְׁאָר מְדִינָוֹת הַמֶּלֶךְ מֶה עָשֹׂוּ וּמַה־שְּׁאֵלָתֵךְ וְיִנָּתֵן לָךְ וּמַה־בַּקָּשָׁתֵךְ עֶוֹד וְתֵעָשׂ: יג וַתֹּאמֶר אֶסְתֵּר אִם־עַל־הַמֶּלֶךְ טוֹב יִנָּתֵן גַּם־מָחָר לַיְּהוּדִים אֲשֶׁר בְּשׁוּשָׁן לַעֲשֹׂוֹת כְּדָת הַיֹּוֹם וְאֵת עֲשֶׂרֶת בְּנֵי־הָמָן יִתְלוּ עַל־הָעֵץ: יד וַיֹּאמֶר הַמֶּלֶךְ לְהֵעָשׂוֹת כֵּן וַתִּנָּתֵן דָּת בְּשׁוּשָׁן וְאֵת עֲשֶׂרֶת בְּנֵי־הָמָן תָּלוּ: טו וַיִּקָּהֲלוּ °הַיְהוּדִיים [°הַיְהוּדִים ק] אֲשֶׁר־בְּשׁוּשָׁן גַּם בְּיֹום אַרְבָּעָה עָשָׂר לְחֹדֶשׁ אֲדָר וַיַּהַרְגוּ בְשׁוּשָׁן שְׁלֹשׁ מֵאֹוֹת אִישׁ וּבַבִּזָּה לֹא שָׁלְחוּ אֶת־יָדָם: טז וּשְׁאָר הַיְהוּדִים אֲשֶׁר בִּמְדִינֹות הַמֶּלֶךְ נִקְהֲלוּ ו וְעָמֹד עַל־נַפְשָׁם וְנֹוֹחַ מֵאֹיְבֵיהֶם וְהָרֹוֹג בְּשַׂנְאֵיהֶם חֲמִשָּׁה וְשִׁבְעִים אֶלֶף וּבַבִּזָּה לֹא שָׁלְחוּ אֶת־יָדָם: יז בְּיֹום־שְׁלֹשָׁה עָשָׂר לְחֹדֶשׁ אֲדָר וְנֹוֹחַ בְּאַרְבָּעָה עָשָׂר בֹּוֹ וְעָשֹׂה אֹתֹוֹ יֹום מִשְׁתֶּה וְשִׂמְחָה: יח °וְהַיְהוּדִיים [°וְהַיְהוּדִים ק] אֲשֶׁר־בְּשׁוּשָׁן נִקְהֲלוּ בִּשְׁלֹשָׁה עָשָׂר בֹּוֹ וּבְאַרְבָּעָה עָשָׂר בֹּוֹ וְנֹוֹחַ בַּחֲמִשָּׁה עָשָׂר בֹּוֹ וְעָשֹׂה אֹתֹוֹ יֹום מִשְׁתֶּה וְשִׂמְחָה: יט עַל־כֵּן הַיְהוּדִים °הַפְּרוֹזִים [°הַפְּרָזִים ק] הַיְּשְׁבִים בְּעָרֵי הַפְּרָזֹוֹת עֹשִׂים אֵת יֹום אַרְבָּעָה עָשָׂר לְחֹדֶשׁ אֲדָר שִׂמְחָה וּמִשְׁתֶּה וְיֹום טֹוֹב וּמִשְׁלֹוֹחַ מָנֹוֹת אִישׁ לְרֵעֵהוּ: כ וַיִּכְתֹּב מָרְדֳּכַי אֶת־הַדְּבָרִים הָאֵלֶּה וַיִּשְׁלַח סְפָרִים אֶל־כָּל־הַיְּהוּדִים אֲשֶׁר בְּכָל־מְדִינֹות הַמֶּלֶךְ אֲחַשְׁוֵרֹושׁ הַקְּרוֹבִים וְהָרְחֹוֹקִים: כא לְקַיֵּם עֲלֵיהֶם לִהְיֹוֹת עֹשִׂים אֵת יֹום אַרְבָּעָה עָשָׂר לְחֹדֶשׁ אֲדָר וְאֵת יֹום־חֲמִשָּׁה עָשָׂר בֹּוֹ בְּכָל־שָׁנָה וְשָׁנָה: כב כַּיָּמִים אֲשֶׁר־נָחוּ בָהֶם הַיְּהוּדִים מֵאֹיְבֵיהֶם וְהַחֹדֶשׁ אֲשֶׁר נֶהְפַּךְ לָהֶם מִיָּגֹוֹן לְשִׂמְחָה וּמֵאֵבֶל לְיֹום טֹוֹב לַעֲשֹׂוֹת אוֹתָם יְמֵי מִשְׁתֶּה וְשִׂמְחָה וּמִשְׁלֹחַ מָנֹוֹת אִישׁ לְרֵעֵהוּ וּמַתָּנֹוֹת לָאֶבְיוֹנִים: כג וְקִבֵּל הַיְּהוּדִים אֵת אֲשֶׁר־הֵחֵלּוּ לַעֲשֹׂוֹת וְאֵת אֲשֶׁר־כָּתַב מָרְדֳּכַי אֲלֵיהֶם: כד כִּי הָמָן בֶּן־הַמְּדָתָא הָאֲגָגִי צֹרֵר כָּל־הַיְּהוּדִים חָשַׁב עַל־הַיְּהוּדִים לְאַבְּדָם וְהִפִּל פּוּר הוּא הַגֹּוֹרָל לְהֻמָּם וּלְאַבְּדָם: כה וּבְבֹאָהּ לִפְנֵי הַמֶּלֶךְ אָמַר עִם־הַסֵּפֶר יָשֹׁוּב מַחֲשַׁבְתֹּוֹ הָרָעָה אֲשֶׁר־חָשַׁב עַל־הַיְּהוּדִים עַל־רֹאשֹׁוֹ וְתָלוּ אֹתֹוֹ וְאֶת־בָּנָיו עַל־

---

**9:19.** The law of "Shushan Purim" — celebrating Purim on the 15th day of Adar in walled cities in commemoration of the victory in Shushan — is not specifically stated in the Megillah. It is implied in verses 19 and 21 and so established by the Rabbis.

[11] *That same day the number of those killed in Shushan the capital was reported to the king.* [12] *The king said to Queen Esther, "In Shushan the capital the Jews have slain and annihilated five hundred men, as well as the ten sons of Haman; what have they done in the rest of the king's provinces?! What is your request now? It shall be granted you. What is your petition further? It shall be fulfilled."*

[13] *Esther replied, "If it pleases the king, let tomorrow also be given to the Jews who are in Shushan to act as they did today, and let Haman's ten sons be hanged on the gallows."* [14] *The king ordered that this be done, and a decree was distributed in Shushan; and they hanged Haman's ten sons.* [15] *The Jews that were in Shushan assembled again on the fourteenth day of the month of Adar and slew three hundred men in Shushan; but they did not lay their hand on the spoils.*

[16] *The rest of the Jews that were in the king's provinces assembled and defended themselves gaining relief from their foes, slaying seventy-five thousand of their enemies, but they did not lay their hand on the spoils,* [17] *on the thirteenth day of the month of Adar. And they gained relief on its fourteenth [day], making it a day of feasting and gladness.* [18] *But the Jews that were in Shushan assembled on both its thirteenth [day] and its fourteenth, and they gained relief on its fifteenth, making it a day of feasting and gladness.* [19] *Therefore, Jewish villagers who live in unwalled towns celebrate the fourteenth day of the month of Adar as an occasion of gladness, feasting and festival, and for sending delicacies to one another.*

[20] *Mordechai recorded these events and sent letters to all the Jews who were in all the provinces of King Ahasuerus, the near ones and the distant ones,* [21] *[charging them] to observe annually the fourteenth day of the month of Adar and its fifteenth day,* [22] *as the days on which the Jews gained relief from their enemies, and the month which had been turned about for them from one of sorrow to gladness, and from mourning to festival; to observe them as days of feasting and gladness, and sending delicacies to one another, and gifts to the poor.* [23] *The Jews undertook [to continue] that which they had begun, just as Mordechai had prescribed to them.*

[24] *For Haman son of Hammedatha the Agagite, enemy of all the Jews, had plotted to annihilate the Jews and had cast a pur (that is, the lot) to terrify and to annihilate them.* [25] *But when she appeared before the king, he commanded by means of letters that [Haman's] wicked scheme, which he had devised against the Jews, should recoil on his own head; and they hanged him and his sons on*

---

**9:20.** וַיִּכְתֹּב מָרְדֳּכַי אֶת הַדְּבָרִים הָאֵלֶּה — *Mordechai recorded these events.* He wrote this Megillah exactly as it appears in its present text.

**9:22.** יְמֵי מִשְׁתֶּה וְשִׂמְחָה — *Days of feasting and gladness.* Eating and drinking and merry-making was instituted on Purim because the miracles occurred through feasting: the royal feast that led to the

death of Vashti; the feast of Esther's coronation; and Esther's two feasts that led to Haman's downfall.

וּמִשְׁלֹחַ מָנוֹת אִישׁ לְרֵעֵהוּ — *Sending delicacies to one another* — at least two *delicacies*, i.e., ready-to-eat foods [מָנוֹת being plural] to one man.

וּמַתָּנוֹת לָאֶבְיוֹנִים — *And gifts to the poor* — this means two gifts to two men [one gift to

הָעֵץ: כו עַל־כֵּן קָרְאוּ לַיָּמִים הָאֵלֶּה פוּרִים עַל־שֵׁם הַפּוּר עַל־כֵּן
עַל־כָּל־דִּבְרֵי הָאִגֶּרֶת הַזֹּאת וּמָה־רָאוּ עַל־כָּכָה וּמָה הִגִּיעַ אֲלֵיהֶם:
כז קִיְּמוּ °וּקִבֵּל [°וְקִבְּלוּ ק] הַיְּהוּדִים ׀ עֲלֵיהֶם ׀ וְעַל־זַרְעָם וְעַל
כָּל־הַנִּלְוִים עֲלֵיהֶם וְלֹא יַעֲבוֹר לִהְיוֹת עֹשִׂים אֵת־שְׁנֵי הַיָּמִים
הָאֵלֶּה כִּכְתָבָם וְכִזְמַנָּם בְּכָל־שָׁנָה וְשָׁנָה: כח וְהַיָּמִים הָאֵלֶּה נִזְכָּרִים
וְנַעֲשִׂים בְּכָל־דּוֹר וָדוֹר מִשְׁפָּחָה וּמִשְׁפָּחָה מְדִינָה וּמְדִינָה וְעִיר
וָעִיר וִימֵי הַפּוּרִים הָאֵלֶּה לֹא יַעַבְרוּ מִתּוֹךְ הַיְּהוּדִים וְזִכְרָם לֹא־
יָסוּף מִזַּרְעָם: כט וַתִּכְתֹּב אֶסְתֵּר הַמַּלְכָּה בַת־אֲבִיחַיִל וּמָרְדֳּכַי
הַיְּהוּדִי אֶת־כָּל־תֹּקֶף לְקַיֵּם אֵת אִגֶּרֶת הַפֻּרִים הַזֹּאת הַשֵּׁנִית:
י וַיִּשְׁלַח סְפָרִים אֶל־כָּל־הַיְּהוּדִים אֶל־שֶׁבַע וְעֶשְׂרִים וּמֵאָה מְדִינָה
מַלְכוּת אֲחַשְׁוֵרוֹשׁ דִּבְרֵי שָׁלוֹם וֶאֱמֶת: לא לְקַיֵּם אֶת־יְמֵי הַפֻּרִים
הָאֵלֶּה בִּזְמַנֵּיהֶם כַּאֲשֶׁר קִיַּם עֲלֵיהֶם מָרְדֳּכַי הַיְּהוּדִי וְאֶסְתֵּר הַמַּלְכָּה
וְכַאֲשֶׁר קִיְּמוּ עַל־נַפְשָׁם וְעַל־זַרְעָם דִּבְרֵי הַצֹּמוֹת וְזַעֲקָתָם:
לב וּמַאֲמַר אֶסְתֵּר קִיַּם דִּבְרֵי הַפֻּרִים הָאֵלֶּה וְנִכְתָּב בַּסֵּפֶר: א וַיָּשֶׂם
הַמֶּלֶךְ °אחשרש [°אֲחַשְׁוֵרוֹשׁ ק] ׀ מַס עַל־הָאָרֶץ וְאִיֵּי הַיָּם: ב וְכָל־
מַעֲשֵׂה תָקְפוֹ וּגְבוּרָתוֹ וּפָרָשַׁת גְּדֻלַּת מָרְדֳּכַי אֲשֶׁר גִּדְּלוֹ הַמֶּלֶךְ
הֲלוֹא־הֵם כְּתוּבִים עַל־סֵפֶר דִּבְרֵי הַיָּמִים לְמַלְכֵי מָדַי וּפָרָס: ג כִּי ׀
**מָרְדֳּכַי הַיְּהוּדִי מִשְׁנֶה לַמֶּלֶךְ אֲחַשְׁוֵרוֹשׁ וְגָדוֹל לַיְּהוּדִים וְרָצוּי לְרֹב
אֶחָיו דֹּרֵשׁ טוֹב לְעַמּוֹ וְדֹבֵר שָׁלוֹם לְכָל־זַרְעוֹ:**

After the *Megillah* reading, each member of the congregation
recites the following blessing.
[This blessing is not recited unless a *minyan* is present for the reading.]

**בָּרוּךְ** אַתָּה יהוה אֱלֹהֵינוּ מֶלֶךְ הָעוֹלָם, (הָאֵל) הָרָב אֶת רִיבֵנוּ,
וְהַדָּן אֶת דִּינֵנוּ, וְהַנּוֹקֵם אֶת נִקְמָתֵנוּ, וְהַמְשַׁלֵּם גְּמוּל לְכָל
אֹיְבֵי נַפְשֵׁנוּ, וְהַנִּפְרָע לָנוּ מִצָּרֵינוּ. בָּרוּךְ אַתָּה יהוה, הַנִּפְרָע לְעַמּוֹ
יִשְׂרָאֵל מִכָּל צָרֵיהֶם, הָאֵל הַמּוֹשִׁיעַ.

---

each of the two, the minimum number of
the plural אֶבְיוֹנִים, *poor*, being two] (*Talmud*).

**9:27.** קִיְּמוּ וְקִבְּלוּ — *Confirmed and undertook* — i.e., they confirmed what they
had undertaken long before at Sinai (*Talmud*).

**9:28.** "Even if all the festivals should be

annulled, Purim will never be annulled"
(*Midrash*).

**9:29.** וַתִּכְתֹּב — *Wrote.* The letter ת in this
word is enlarged to indicate that just as the
ת is the last letter of the Hebrew alphabet,
so is the story of Esther the end of all the
miracles to be included in the Bible (*Talmud*).

the gallows. <sup>26</sup> Therefore, they called these days "Purim" from the word "pur."
Therefore, because of all that was written in this letter, and because of what they
had seen concerning this, and what has happened to them, <sup>27</sup> the Jews confirmed and undertook upon themselves, and their posterity, and upon all who
might join them, without fail, to observe these two days, in their prescribed
manner, and in their proper time each year. <sup>28</sup> And these days should be
remembered and celebrated by every generation, every family, every province,
and every city; and these days of Purim should never cease among the Jews, nor
shall their remembrance perish from their descendants.

<sup>29</sup> Then Queen Esther daughter of Abihail wrote, along with Mordechai
the Jew, with full authority to ratify this second letter of Purim. <sup>30</sup> Dispatches
were sent to all the Jews, to the hundred and twenty-seven provinces of the
kingdom of Ahasuerus — [with] words of peace and truth — <sup>31</sup> to establish
these days of Purim on their [proper] dates just as Mordechai the Jew and
Queen Esther had enjoined them, and as they had confirmed upon themselves and their posterity the matter of the fasts and their lamentations.
<sup>32</sup> Esther's ordinance confirmed these regulations for Purim; and it was recorded
in the book.

**10** <sup>1</sup> K ing Ahasuerus levied a tax on the mainland and the islands of the sea.
<sup>2</sup> All his mighty and powerful acts, and the account of the greatness of
Mordechai, whom the king had promoted, are recorded in the book of chronicles
of the kings of Media and Persia. <sup>3</sup> **For Mordechai the Jew was viceroy to King
Ahasuerus; he was a great man among the Jews, and found favor with the
multitude of his brethren; he sought the good of his people and spoke for the
welfare of all his seed.**

After the *Megillah* reading, each member of the congregation
recites the following blessing.
[This blessing is not recited unless a *minyan* is present for the reading.]

בָּרוּךְ  Blessed are You, HASHEM, our God, King of the universe, (the God)
Who takes up our grievance, judges our claim, avenges our
wrong; Who brings just retribution upon all enemies of our soul and exacts
vengeance for us from our foes. Blessed are You, HASHEM, Who exacts
vengeance for His people Israel from all their foes, the God Who brings
salvation.

---

**10:1. Epilogue**
With the salvation of the Jews, affairs of
state returned to normal. Under Mordechai, the empire grew stronger.
**10:3.** With the mention of שָׁלוֹם, *welfare*
[literally *peace*], and a picture of the
stature and security of the Jews under
Mordechai, the Megillah closes.

The last verse of the Megillah is among
the four verses read aloud by the congregation during the reading of the Megillah
in the synagogue. Among the reasons
offered for this widespread custom are: to
popularize the miracle [פִּירְסוּמֵי נִיסָא]; these
verses express the essence of the miracle
through Mordechai; and to keep the chil-

After the nighttime *Megillah* reading, the following is recited.
After the daytime reading, continue with שׁוֹשַׁנַּת יַעֲקֹב (below).

אֲשֶׁר הֵנִיא עֲצַת גּוֹיִם, וַיָּפֶר מַחְשְׁבוֹת עֲרוּמִים.

בְּקוּם עָלֵינוּ אָדָם רָשָׁע, נֵצֶר זָדוֹן, מִזֶּרַע עֲמָלֵק.

גָּאָה בְעָשְׁרוֹ, וְכָרָה לוֹ בּוֹר, וּגְדֻלָּתוֹ יָקְשָׁה לּוֹ לָכֶד.

דִּמָּה בְנַפְשׁוֹ לִלְכֹּד, וְנִלְכַּד, בִּקֵּשׁ לְהַשְׁמִיד, וְנִשְׁמַד מְהֵרָה.

הָמָן הוֹדִיעַ אֵיבַת אֲבוֹתָיו, וְעוֹרֵר שִׂנְאַת אַחִים לַבָּנִים.

וְלֹא זָכַר רַחֲמֵי שָׁאוּל, כִּי בְחֶמְלָתוֹ עַל אֲגָג נוֹלַד אוֹיֵב.

זָמַם רָשָׁע לְהַכְרִית צַדִּיק, וְנִלְכַּד טָמֵא, בִּידֵי טָהוֹר.

חֶסֶד גָּבַר עַל שִׁגְגַת אָב, וְרָשָׁע הוֹסִיף חֵטְא עַל חֲטָאָיו.

טָמַן בְּלִבּוֹ מַחְשְׁבוֹת עֲרוּמָיו, וַיִּתְמַכֵּר לַעֲשׂוֹת רָעָה.

יָדוֹ שָׁלַח בִּקְדוֹשֵׁי אֵל, כַּסְפּוֹ נָתַן לְהַכְרִית זִכְרָם.

כִּרְאוֹת מָרְדְּכַי, כִּי יָצָא קֶצֶף, וְדָתֵי הָמָן נִתְּנוּ בְשׁוּשָׁן.

לָבַשׁ שַׂק וְקָשַׁר מִסְפֵּד, וְגָזַר צוֹם, וַיֵּשֶׁב עַל הָאֵפֶר.

מִי זֶה יַעֲמֹד לְכַפֵּר שְׁגָגָה, וְלִמְחֹל חַטַּאת עֲוֹן אֲבוֹתֵינוּ.

נֵץ פָּרַח מִלּוּלָב, הֵן הֲדַסָּה עָמְדָה לְעוֹרֵר יְשֵׁנִים.

סָרִיסֶיהָ הִבְהִילוּ לְהָמָן, לְהַשְׁקוֹתוֹ יֵין חֲמַת תַּנִּינִים.

עָמַד בְּעָשְׁרוֹ, וְנָפַל בְּרִשְׁעוֹ, עָשָׂה לוֹ עֵץ, וְנִתְלָה עָלָיו.

פִּיהֶם פָּתְחוּ, כָּל יוֹשְׁבֵי תֵבֵל, כִּי פוּר הָמָן נֶהְפַּךְ לְפוּרֵנוּ.

צַדִּיק נֶחֱלַץ מִיַּד רָשָׁע, אוֹיֵב נִתַּן תַּחַת נַפְשׁוֹ.

קִיְּמוּ עֲלֵיהֶם, לַעֲשׂוֹת פּוּרִים, וְלִשְׂמֹחַ בְּכָל שָׁנָה וְשָׁנָה.

רָאִיתָ אֶת תְּפִלַּת מָרְדְּכַי וְאֶסְתֵּר, הָמָן וּבָנָיו עַל הָעֵץ תָּלִיתָ.

The following is recited after both *Megillah* readings.

שׁוֹשַׁנַּת יַעֲקֹב צָהֲלָה וְשָׂמֵחָה, בִּרְאוֹתָם יַחַד תְּכֵלֶת מָרְדְּכָי.

תְּשׁוּעָתָם הָיִיתָ לָנֶצַח, וְתִקְוָתָם בְּכָל דּוֹר וָדוֹר.

לְהוֹדִיעַ, שֶׁכָּל קֹוֶיךָ לֹא יֵבֹשׁוּ, וְלֹא יִכָּלְמוּ לָנֶצַח כָּל הַחוֹסִים בָּךְ.

אָרוּר הָמָן, אֲשֶׁר בִּקֵּשׁ לְאַבְּדִי, בָּרוּךְ מָרְדְּכַי הַיְּהוּדִי.

אֲרוּרָה זֶרֶשׁ, אֵשֶׁת מַפְחִידִי, בְּרוּכָה אֶסְתֵּר בַּעֲדִי,

וְגַם חַרְבוֹנָה זָכוּר לַטּוֹב.

dren alert and prevent them from dozing off. The congregation recites the verses loudly as an expression of the joy of the day. The reader then repeats the verses because each verse must be read from the Megillah.

After the nighttime *Megillah* reading, the following is recited.
After the daytime reading, continue with שׁוֹשַׁנַּת יַעֲקֹב (below).

א *Who balked the counsel of the nations
and annulled the designs of the cunning,*

ב *When a wicked man stood up against us,
a wantonly evil branch of Amalek's offspring.*

ג *Haughty with his wealth he dug himself a grave,
and his very greatness snared him in a trap.*

ד *Fancying to trap, he became entrapped;
attempting to destroy, he was swiftly destroyed.*

ה *Haman showed his forebears' enmity, and aroused
the brotherly hate of Esau on the children.*

ו *He would not remember Saul's compassion,
that through his pity on Agag the foe was born.*

ז *The wicked one conspired to cut away the righteous,
but the impure was trapped in the pure one's hands.*

ח *Kindness overcame the father's error, and the wicked one piled sin on sins.*

ט *In his heart he hid his cunning thoughts, and devoted himself to evildoing.*

י *He stretched his hand against God's holy ones,
he spent his silver to destroy their memory.*

כ *When Mordechai saw the wrath commence,
and Haman's decrees be issued in Shushan,*

ל *He put on sackcloth and bound himself in mourning,
decreed a fast and sat on ashes:*

מ *"Who would arise to atone for error, to gain forgiveness for our ancestors' sins?'*

נ *A blossom bloomed from a lulav branch — behold!
Hadassah stood up to arouse the sleeping.*

ס *His servants hastened Haman, to serve him wine of serpent's poison.*

ע *He stood tall through his wealth and toppled through his evil —
he built the gallows on which he was hung.*

פ *The earth's inhabitants opened their mouths, for Haman's lot became our Purim,*

צ *The righteous man was saved from the wicked's hand;
the foe was substituted for him.*

ק *They undertook to establish Purim, to rejoice in every single year.*

ר *You noted the prayer of Mordechai and Esther;
Haman and his sons You hung on the gallows.*

The following is recited after both *Megillah* readings.

ש *The rose of Jacob was cheerful and glad,
when they jointly saw Mordechai robed in royal blue.*

ת *You have been their eternal salvation, and their hope throughout generations. To
make known that all who hope in You will not be shamed; nor ever be humiliated,
those taking refuge in You. Accursed be Haman who sought to destroy me,
blessed be Mordechai the Yehudi. Accursed be Zeresh the wife of my terrorizer,
blessed be Esther [who sacrificed] for me — and Charvonah, too, be remembered for good.*

## AT THE CONCLUSION OF THE SABBATH, ADD:

**וִיהִי** נֹעַם אֲדֹנָי אֱלֹהֵינוּ עָלֵינוּ, וּמַעֲשֵׂה יָדֵינוּ כּוֹנְנָה עָלֵינוּ, וּמַעֲשֵׂה יָדֵינוּ כּוֹנְנֵהוּ.¹

תהלים צא

**יֹשֵׁב** בְּסֵתֶר עֶלְיוֹן, בְּצֵל שַׁדַּי יִתְלוֹנָן. אֹמַר לַיהוה, מַחְסִי וּמְצוּדָתִי, אֱלֹהַי אֶבְטַח בּוֹ. כִּי הוּא יַצִּילְךָ מִפַּח יָקוּשׁ, מִדֶּבֶר הַוּוֹת. בְּאֶבְרָתוֹ יֶסֶךְ לָךְ, וְתַחַת כְּנָפָיו תֶּחְסֶה, צִנָּה וְסֹחֵרָה אֲמִתּוֹ. לֹא תִירָא מִפַּחַד לָיְלָה, מֵחֵץ יָעוּף יוֹמָם. מִדֶּבֶר בָּאֹפֶל יַהֲלֹךְ, מִקֶּטֶב יָשׁוּד צָהֳרָיִם. יִפֹּל מִצִּדְּךָ אֶלֶף, וּרְבָבָה מִימִינֶךָ, אֵלֶיךָ לֹא יִגָּשׁ. רַק בְּעֵינֶיךָ תַבִּיט, וְשִׁלֻּמַת רְשָׁעִים תִּרְאֶה. כִּי אַתָּה יהוה מַחְסִי, עֶלְיוֹן שַׂמְתָּ מְעוֹנֶךָ. לֹא תְאֻנֶּה אֵלֶיךָ רָעָה, וְנֶגַע לֹא יִקְרַב בְּאָהֳלֶךָ. כִּי מַלְאָכָיו יְצַוֶּה לָּךְ, לִשְׁמָרְךָ בְּכָל דְּרָכֶיךָ. עַל כַּפַּיִם יִשָּׂאוּנְךָ, פֶּן תִּגֹּף בָּאֶבֶן רַגְלֶךָ. עַל שַׁחַל וָפֶתֶן תִּדְרֹךְ, תִּרְמֹס כְּפִיר וְתַנִּין. כִּי בִי חָשַׁק וַאֲפַלְּטֵהוּ, אֲשַׂגְּבֵהוּ כִּי יָדַע שְׁמִי. יִקְרָאֵנִי וְאֶעֱנֵהוּ, עִמּוֹ אָנֹכִי בְצָרָה, אֲחַלְּצֵהוּ וַאֲכַבְּדֵהוּ. ✧ אֹרֶךְ יָמִים אַשְׂבִּיעֵהוּ, וְאַרְאֵהוּ בִּישׁוּעָתִי. אֹרֶךְ יָמִים אַשְׂבִּיעֵהוּ, וְאַרְאֵהוּ בִּישׁוּעָתִי.

The verses in bold type are the *Kedushah* of the angels.
It is preferable that the congregation recite them aloud and in unison.

**וְאַתָּה קָדוֹשׁ** יוֹשֵׁב תְּהִלּוֹת יִשְׂרָאֵל.² וְקָרָא זֶה אֶל זֶה וְאָמַר: **קָדוֹשׁ, קָדוֹשׁ, קָדוֹשׁ, יהוה צְבָאוֹת, מְלֹא כָל הָאָרֶץ כְּבוֹדוֹ.**³ וּמְקַבְּלִין דֵּין מִן דֵּין וְאָמְרִין: קַדִּישׁ בִּשְׁמֵי מְרוֹמָא עִלָּאָה בֵּית שְׁכִינְתֵּהּ, קַדִּישׁ עַל אַרְעָא עוֹבַד גְּבוּרְתֵּהּ, קַדִּישׁ לְעָלַם וּלְעָלְמֵי עָלְמַיָּא, יהוה צְבָאוֹת, מַלְיָא כָל אַרְעָא זִיו יְקָרֵהּ.⁴ ✧ וַתִּשָּׂאֵנִי רוּחַ, וָאֶשְׁמַע אַחֲרַי קוֹל רַעַשׁ גָּדוֹל: **בָּרוּךְ כְּבוֹד יהוה מִמְּקוֹמוֹ.**⁵ וּנְטָלַתְנִי רוּחָא, וְשִׁמְעֵת בַּתְרַי קָל זִיעַ סַגִּיא דִּמְשַׁבְּחִין וְאָמְרִין: בְּרִיךְ יְקָרָא דַיהוה מֵאֲתַר בֵּית שְׁכִינְתֵּהּ.⁶ **יהוה יִמְלֹךְ לְעֹלָם וָעֶד.**⁷ יהוה מַלְכוּתֵהּ קָאֵם לְעָלַם וּלְעָלְמֵי עָלְמַיָּא.⁸

יהוה אֱלֹהֵי אַבְרָהָם יִצְחָק וְיִשְׂרָאֵל אֲבֹתֵינוּ, שָׁמְרָה זֹּאת לְעוֹלָם, לְיֵצֶר מַחְשְׁבוֹת לְבַב עַמֶּךָ, וְהָכֵן לְבָבָם אֵלֶיךָ.⁹ וְהוּא רַחוּם, יְכַפֵּר עָוֹן וְלֹא יַשְׁחִית, וְהִרְבָּה לְהָשִׁיב אַפּוֹ, וְלֹא יָעִיר כָּל חֲמָתוֹ.¹⁰ כִּי אַתָּה אֲדֹנָי טוֹב וְסַלָּח, וְרַב חֶסֶד לְכָל קֹרְאֶיךָ.¹¹ צִדְקָתְךָ צֶדֶק לְעוֹלָם, וְתוֹרָתְךָ אֱמֶת.¹² תִּתֵּן אֱמֶת לְיַעֲקֹב, חֶסֶד לְאַבְרָהָם, אֲשֶׁר נִשְׁבַּעְתָּ לַאֲבֹתֵינוּ מִימֵי קֶדֶם.¹³ בָּרוּךְ אֲדֹנָי יוֹם יוֹם יַעֲמָס

---

**AT THE CONCLUSION OF THE SABBATH, ADD:**

**וִיהִי** *May the pleasantness of my Lord, our God, be upon us — may He establish our handiwork for us; our handiwork, may He establish.* [1]

*Psalm 91*

**יֹשֵׁב** *Whoever sits in the refuge of the Most High, he shall dwell in the shadow of the Almighty. I will say of HASHEM, "He is my refuge and my fortress, my God, I will trust in Him." For He will deliver you from the ensnaring trap, from devastating pestilence. With His pinion He will cover you, and beneath His wings you will be protected; shield and armor is His truth. You shall not fear the terror of night; nor the arrow that flies by day; nor the pestilence that walks in gloom; nor the destroyer who lays waste at noon. Let a thousand encamp at your side and a myriad at your right hand, but to you they shall not approach. You will merely peer with your eyes and you will see the retribution of the wicked. Because [you said,] "You, HASHEM, are my refuge," you have made the Most High your dwelling place. No evil will befall you, nor will any plague come near your tent. He will charge His angels for you, to protect you in all your ways. On your palms they will carry you, lest you strike your foot against a stone. Upon the lion and the viper you will tread; you will trample the young lion and the serpent. For he has yearned for Me and I will deliver him; I will elevate him because he knows My Name. He will call upon Me and I will answer him, I am with him in distress, I will release him and I will honor him. Chazzan— With long life will I satisfy him, and I will show him My salvation. With long life will I satisfy him, and I will show him My salvation.*

**וְאַתָּה קָדוֹשׁ** *You are the Holy One, enthroned upon the praises of Israel.* [2] *And one [angel] will call another and say:* **"Holy, holy, holy is HASHEM, Master of Legions, the whole world is filled with His glory."** [3] *And they receive permission from one another and say: "Holy in the most exalted heaven, the abode of His Presence; holy on earth, product of His strength; holy forever and ever is HASHEM, Master of Legions — the entire world is filled with the radiance of His glory."* [4] *Chazzan— And a wind lifted me; and I heard behind me the sound of a great noise:* **"Blessed is the glory of HASHEM from His place."** [5] *And a wind lifted me and I heard behind me the sound of the powerful movement of those who praised saying: "Blessed is the honor of HASHEM from the place of the abode of His Presence."* [6] **HASHEM shall reign for all eternity.** [7] *HASHEM — His kingdom is established forever and ever.* [8]

*HASHEM, God of Abraham, Isaac, and Israel, our forefathers, may You preserve this forever as the realization of the thoughts in Your people's heart, and may You direct their heart to You.* [9] *He, the Merciful One, is forgiving of iniquity and does not destroy; frequently He withdraws His anger, not arousing His entire rage.* [10] *For You, my Lord, are good and forgiving, and abundantly kind to all who call upon You.* [11] *Your righteousness remains righteous forever, and Your Torah is truth.* [12] *Grant truth to Jacob, kindness to Abraham, as You swore to our forefathers from ancient times.* [13] *Blessed is my Lord for every single day, He burdens*

---

(1) *Psalms* 90:17. (2) 22:4. (3) *Isaiah* 6:3. (4) *Targum Yonasan.* (5) *Ezekiel* 3:12.
(6) *Targum Yonasan.* (7) *Exodus* 15:18. (8) *Targum Onkelos.* (9) *I Chronicles* 29:18.
(10) *Psalms* 78:38. (11) 86:5. (12) 119:142. (13) *Micah* 7:20.

לָנוּ, הָאֵל יְשׁוּעָתֵנוּ סֶלָה.[1] יהוה צְבָאוֹת עִמָּנוּ, מִשְׂגָּב לָנוּ אֱלֹהֵי
יַעֲקֹב סֶלָה.[2] יהוה צְבָאוֹת, אַשְׁרֵי אָדָם בֹּטֵחַ בָּךְ.[3] יהוה הוֹשִׁיעָה,
הַמֶּלֶךְ יַעֲנֵנוּ בְיוֹם קָרְאֵנוּ.[4] בָּרוּךְ הוּא אֱלֹהֵינוּ שֶׁבְּרָאָנוּ לִכְבוֹדוֹ,
וְהִבְדִּילָנוּ מִן הַתּוֹעִים, וְנָתַן לָנוּ תּוֹרַת אֱמֶת, וְחַיֵּי עוֹלָם נָטַע בְּתוֹכֵנוּ.
הוּא יִפְתַּח לִבֵּנוּ בְּתוֹרָתוֹ, וְיָשֵׂם בְּלִבֵּנוּ אַהֲבָתוֹ וְיִרְאָתוֹ וְלַעֲשׂוֹת
רְצוֹנוֹ וּלְעָבְדוֹ בְּלֵבָב שָׁלֵם, לְמַעַן לֹא נִיגַע לָרִיק, וְלֹא נֵלֵד לַבֶּהָלָה.[5]
יְהִי רָצוֹן מִלְּפָנֶיךָ, יהוה אֱלֹהֵינוּ וֵאלֹהֵי אֲבוֹתֵינוּ, שֶׁנִּשְׁמֹר חֻקֶּיךָ
בָּעוֹלָם הַזֶּה, וְנִזְכֶּה וְנִחְיֶה וְנִרְאֶה וְנִירַשׁ טוֹבָה וּבְרָכָה לִשְׁנֵי יְמוֹת
הַמָּשִׁיחַ וּלְחַיֵּי הָעוֹלָם הַבָּא. לְמַעַן יְזַמֶּרְךָ כָבוֹד וְלֹא יִדֹּם, יהוה
אֱלֹהַי לְעוֹלָם אוֹדֶךָ.[6] בָּרוּךְ הַגֶּבֶר אֲשֶׁר יִבְטַח בַּיהוה, וְהָיָה יהוה
מִבְטַחוֹ.[7] בִּטְחוּ בַיהוה עֲדֵי עַד, כִּי בְּיָהּ יהוה צוּר עוֹלָמִים.[8]
❖ וְיִבְטְחוּ בְךָ יוֹדְעֵי שְׁמֶךָ, כִּי לֹא עָזַבְתָּ דֹרְשֶׁיךָ, יהוה.[9] יהוה חָפֵץ
לְמַעַן צִדְקוֹ, יַגְדִּיל תּוֹרָה וְיַאְדִּיר.[10]

קַדִּישׁ שָׁלֵם. The chazzan recites

**יִתְגַּדַּל** וְיִתְקַדַּשׁ שְׁמֵהּ רַבָּא. (.Cong – אָמֵן) בְּעָלְמָא דִּי בְרָא
כִרְעוּתֵהּ. וְיַמְלִיךְ מַלְכוּתֵהּ, בְּחַיֵּיכוֹן וּבְיוֹמֵיכוֹן וּבְחַיֵּי דְכָל
בֵּית יִשְׂרָאֵל, בַּעֲגָלָא וּבִזְמַן קָרִיב. וְאִמְרוּ: אָמֵן.
(.Cong – אָמֵן. יְהֵא שְׁמֵהּ רַבָּא מְבָרַךְ לְעָלַם וּלְעָלְמֵי עָלְמַיָּא.)
יְהֵא שְׁמֵהּ רַבָּא מְבָרַךְ לְעָלַם וּלְעָלְמֵי עָלְמַיָּא.
יִתְבָּרַךְ וְיִשְׁתַּבַּח וְיִתְפָּאַר וְיִתְרוֹמַם וְיִתְנַשֵּׂא וְיִתְהַדָּר וְיִתְעַלֶּה
וְיִתְהַלָּל שְׁמֵהּ דְּקֻדְשָׁא בְּרִיךְ הוּא (.Cong – בְּרִיךְ הוּא) – לְעֵלָּא מִן כָּל
בִּרְכָתָא וְשִׁירָתָא תֻּשְׁבְּחָתָא וְנֶחֱמָתָא, דַּאֲמִירָן בְּעָלְמָא. וְאִמְרוּ: אָמֵן.
(.Cong – אָמֵן)
(.Cong– קַבֵּל בְּרַחֲמִים וּבְרָצוֹן אֶת תְּפִלָּתֵנוּ.)
תִּתְקַבֵּל צְלוֹתְהוֹן וּבָעוּתְהוֹן דְּכָל (בֵּית) יִשְׂרָאֵל קֳדָם אֲבוּהוֹן דִּי
בִשְׁמַיָּא. וְאִמְרוּ: אָמֵן. (.Cong – אָמֵן)
(.Cong– יְהִי שֵׁם יהוה מְבֹרָךְ, מֵעַתָּה וְעַד עוֹלָם.[11])
יְהֵא שְׁלָמָא רַבָּא מִן שְׁמַיָּא, וְחַיִּים עָלֵינוּ וְעַל כָּל יִשְׂרָאֵל. וְאִמְרוּ:
אָמֵן. (.Cong – אָמֵן)
(.Cong– עֶזְרִי מֵעִם יהוה, עֹשֵׂה שָׁמַיִם וָאָרֶץ.[12])

Bow. Take three steps back. Bow left and say . . . עֹשֶׂה; bow right and say . . . הוּא; bow forward
and say . . . וְעַל כָּל. Remain in place for a few moments, then take three steps forward.

עֹשֶׂה שָׁלוֹם בִּמְרוֹמָיו, הוּא יַעֲשֶׂה שָׁלוֹם עָלֵינוּ, וְעַל כָּל יִשְׂרָאֵל.
וְאִמְרוּ: אָמֵן. (.Cong– אָמֵן)

us with blessings, the God of our salvation, Selah. [1] HASHEM, Master of Legions, is with us, a stronghold for us is the God of Jacob, Selah. [2] HASHEM, Master of Legions, praiseworthy is the man who trusts in You. [3] HASHEM, save! May the King answer us on the day we call. [4] Blessed is He, our God, Who created us for His glory, separated us from those who stray, gave us the Torah of truth and implanted eternal life within us. May He open our heart through His Torah and imbue our heart with love and awe of Him and that we may do His will and serve Him wholeheartedly, so that we do not struggle in vain nor produce for futility. [5]

May it be Your will, HASHEM, our God and the God of our forefathers, that we observe Your decrees in This World, and merit that we live and see and inherit goodness and blessing in the years of Messianic times and for the life of the World to Come. So that my soul might sing to You and not be stilled, HASHEM, my God, forever will I thank You. [6] Blessed is the man who trusts in HASHEM, then HASHEM will be his security. [7] Trust in HASHEM forever, for in God, HASHEM, is the strength of the worlds. [8] Chazzan — Those knowing Your Name will trust in You, and You forsake not those Who seek You, HASHEM. [9] HASHEM desired, for the sake of its [Israel's] righteousness, that the Torah be made great and glorious. [10]

The chazzan recites Full Kaddish:

**יִתְגַּדַּל** May His great Name grow exalted and sanctified (Cong.— Amen.) in the world that He created as He willed. May He give reign to His kingship in your lifetimes and in your days, and in the lifetimes of the entire Family of Israel, swiftly and soon. Now respond: Amen.

(Cong. — Amen. May His great Name be blessed forever and ever.)
May His great Name be blessed forever and ever.

Blessed, praised, glorified, exalted, extolled, mighty, upraised, and lauded be the Name of the Holy One, Blessed is He (Cong.— Blessed is He) — beyond any blessing and song, praise and consolation that are uttered in the world. Now respond: Amen. (Cong.— Amen.)

(Cong.— Accept our prayers with mercy and favor.)
May the prayers and supplications of the entire Family of Israel be accepted before their Father Who is in Heaven. Now respond: Amen. (Cong.— Amen.)

(Cong.— Blessed be the Name of HASHEM, from this time and forever. [11])
May there be abundant peace from Heaven, and life, upon us and upon all Israel. Now respond: Amen. (Cong.— Amen.)

(Cong.— My help is from HASHEM, Maker of heaven and earth. [12])

Bow. Take three steps back. Bow left and say, "He Who makes . . .";
bow right and say, "may He . . ."; bow forward and say, "and upon all . . ."
Remain in place for a few moments, then take three steps forward.

He Who makes peace in His heights, may He make peace upon us, and upon all Israel. Now respond: Amen. (Cong.— Amen.)

---

(1) Psalms 68:20. (2) 46:8. (3) 84:13. (4) 20:10. (5) Cf. Isaiah 65:23.
(6) Psalms 30:13. (7) Jeremiah 17:7. (8) Isaiah 26:4.
(9) Psalms 9:11. (10) Isaiah 42:21. (11) Psalms 113:2. (12) 121:2.

ON A WEEKNIGHT TURN TO PAGE 92

AT THE CONCLUSION OF THE SABBATH CONTINUE BELOW.

פסוקי ברכה

וְיִתֶּן לְךָ הָאֱלֹהִים מִטַּל הַשָּׁמַיִם וּמִשְׁמַנֵּי הָאָרֶץ, וְרֹב דָּגָן וְתִירֹשׁ. יַעַבְדוּךָ עַמִּים, וְיִשְׁתַּחֲווּ לְךָ לְאֻמִּים, הֱוֵה גְבִיר לְאַחֶיךָ, וְיִשְׁתַּחֲווּ לְךָ בְּנֵי אִמֶּךָ, אֹרְרֶיךָ אָרוּר, וּמְבָרְכֶיךָ בָּרוּךְ.¹ וְאֵל שַׁדַּי יְבָרֵךְ אֹתְךָ וְיַפְרְךָ וְיַרְבֶּךָ, וְהָיִיתָ לִקְהַל עַמִּים. וְיִתֶּן לְךָ אֶת בִּרְכַּת אַבְרָהָם, לְךָ וּלְזַרְעֲךָ אִתָּךְ, לְרִשְׁתְּךָ אֶת אֶרֶץ מְגֻרֶיךָ, אֲשֶׁר נָתַן אֱלֹהִים לְאַבְרָהָם.² מֵאֵל אָבִיךָ וְיַעְזְרֶךָּ, וְאֵת שַׁדַּי וִיבָרְכֶךָּ, בִּרְכֹת שָׁמַיִם מֵעָל, בִּרְכֹת תְּהוֹם רֹבֶצֶת תָּחַת, בִּרְכֹת שָׁדַיִם וָרָחַם. בִּרְכֹת אָבִיךָ גָּבְרוּ עַל בִּרְכֹת הוֹרַי, עַד תַּאֲוַת גִּבְעֹת עוֹלָם, תִּהְיֶיןָ לְרֹאשׁ יוֹסֵף, וּלְקָדְקֹד נְזִיר אֶחָיו.³ וַאֲהֵבְךָ וּבֵרַכְךָ וְהִרְבֶּךָ, וּבֵרַךְ פְּרִי בִטְנְךָ וּפְרִי אַדְמָתֶךָ, דְּגָנְךָ וְתִירֹשְׁךָ וְיִצְהָרֶךָ, שְׁגַר אֲלָפֶיךָ וְעַשְׁתְּרֹת צֹאנֶךָ, עַל הָאֲדָמָה אֲשֶׁר נִשְׁבַּע לַאֲבֹתֶיךָ לָתֶת לָךְ. בָּרוּךְ תִּהְיֶה מִכָּל הָעַמִּים, לֹא יִהְיֶה בְךָ עָקָר וַעֲקָרָה, וּבִבְהֶמְתֶּךָ. וְהֵסִיר יהוה מִמְּךָ כָּל חֹלִי, וְכָל מַדְוֵי מִצְרַיִם הָרָעִים אֲשֶׁר יָדַעְתָּ, לֹא יְשִׂימָם בָּךְ, וּנְתָנָם בְּכָל שֹׂנְאֶיךָ.⁴

הַמַּלְאָךְ הַגֹּאֵל אֹתִי מִכָּל רָע יְבָרֵךְ אֶת הַנְּעָרִים וְיִקָּרֵא בָהֶם שְׁמִי, וְשֵׁם אֲבֹתַי אַבְרָהָם וְיִצְחָק, וְיִדְגּוּ לָרֹב בְּקֶרֶב הָאָרֶץ.⁵ יהוה אֱלֹהֵיכֶם הִרְבָּה אֶתְכֶם, וְהִנְּכֶם הַיּוֹם כְּכוֹכְבֵי הַשָּׁמַיִם לָרֹב. יהוה אֱלֹהֵי אֲבוֹתֵכֶם יֹסֵף עֲלֵיכֶם כָּכֶם אֶלֶף פְּעָמִים, וִיבָרֵךְ אֶתְכֶם כַּאֲשֶׁר דִּבֶּר לָכֶם.⁶

בָּרוּךְ אַתָּה בָּעִיר, וּבָרוּךְ אַתָּה בַּשָּׂדֶה. בָּרוּךְ אַתָּה בְּבֹאֶךָ, וּבָרוּךְ אַתָּה בְּצֵאתֶךָ. בָּרוּךְ טַנְאֲךָ וּמִשְׁאַרְתֶּךָ. בָּרוּךְ פְּרִי בִטְנְךָ וּפְרִי אַדְמָתְךָ וּפְרִי בְהֶמְתֶּךָ, שְׁגַר אֲלָפֶיךָ וְעַשְׁתְּרוֹת צֹאנֶךָ.⁷ יְצַו יהוה אִתְּךָ אֶת הַבְּרָכָה בַּאֲסָמֶיךָ וּבְכֹל מִשְׁלַח יָדֶךָ, וּבֵרַכְךָ בָּאָרֶץ אֲשֶׁר יהוה אֱלֹהֶיךָ נֹתֵן לָךְ. יִפְתַּח יהוה לְךָ אֶת אוֹצָרוֹ הַטּוֹב, אֶת הַשָּׁמַיִם, לָתֶת מְטַר אַרְצְךָ בְּעִתּוֹ, וּלְבָרֵךְ אֵת כָּל מַעֲשֵׂה יָדֶךָ, וְהִלְוִיתָ גּוֹיִם רַבִּים, וְאַתָּה לֹא תִלְוֶה.⁸ כִּי יהוה אֱלֹהֶיךָ בֵּרַכְךָ כַּאֲשֶׁר דִּבֶּר לָךְ, וְהַעֲבַטְתָּ גּוֹיִם רַבִּים, וְאַתָּה לֹא תַעֲבֹט, וּמָשַׁלְתָּ בְּגוֹיִם רַבִּים, וּבְךָ לֹא יִמְשֹׁלוּ.⁹ אַשְׁרֶיךָ יִשְׂרָאֵל, מִי כָמוֹךָ, עַם נוֹשַׁע בַּיהוה, מָגֵן עֶזְרֶךָ, וַאֲשֶׁר חֶרֶב גַּאֲוָתֶךָ, וְיִכָּחֲשׁוּ אֹיְבֶיךָ לָךְ, וְאַתָּה עַל בָּמוֹתֵימוֹ תִדְרֹךְ.¹⁰

(1) Genesis 27:28-29. (2) 28:3-4. (3) 49:25-26. (4) Deuteronomy 7:13-15. (5) Genesis 48:16. (6) Deuteronomy 1:10-11. (7) 28:3,6,5,4. (8) 28:8,12. (9) 15:6. (10) 33:29.

ON A WEEKNIGHT TURN TO PAGE 92

AT THE CONCLUSION OF THE SABBATH CONTINUE BELOW.

### VERSES OF BLESSING

וְיִתֶּן And may God give you of the dew of the heavens and of the fatness of
the earth, and abundant grain and wine. Peoples will serve you, and
regimes will prostrate themselves to you; be a lord to your kinsmen, and your
mother's sons will prostrate themselves to you; they who curse you are cursed,
and they who bless you are blessed.[1] And may El Shaddai bless you, make you
fruitful and make you numerous, and may you be a congregation of peoples.
May He grant you the blessing of Abraham, to you and to your offspring with
you, that you may possess the land of your sojourns which God gave to
Abraham.[2] It is from the God of your father and He will help you, and with
Shaddai and He will bless you — blessings of heaven from above, blessings of the
deep crouching below, blessings of the bosom and womb. The blessings of your
father surpassed the blessings of my fathers, to the endless bounds of the world's
hills; let them be upon Joseph's head and upon the head of the one separated
from his brothers.[3] And He shall love you, and He shall bless you, and He shall
make you numerous; may He bless the fruit of your womb and the fruit of your
land, your grain, your wine, and your oil, the offspring of your cattle and the
flocks of your sheep, on the land that He swore to your forefathers to give to you.
Blessed shall you be above all peoples; there shall not be among you a barren
man or woman, nor among your cattle. HASHEM shall remove from you all illness;
and all the evil sufferings of Egypt that you knew, He will not place upon you, but
He will set them upon all your enemies.[4]

הַמַּלְאָךְ May the angel who redeems me from all evil bless the lads, and may
my name be declared upon them — and the names of my forefathers
Abraham and Isaac — and may they proliferate abundantly like fish within the
land.[5] HASHEM, your God, has made you numerous, and behold! you are today
like the stars of heaven in abundance. May HASHEM, the God of your forefathers,
increase you a thousandfold and bless you as He spoke to you.[6]

בָּרוּךְ Blessed are you in the city; blessed are you in the field. Blessed are you
upon your arrival; blessed are you upon your departure. Blessed is your
fruit basket and your kneading trough. Blessed is the fruit of your womb, the fruit
of your land, and the fruit of your animal, the offspring of your cattle and the
flocks of your sheep.[7] May HASHEM command that the blessing accompany you
in your storehouse and wherever you set your hand, and may He bless you in the
land that HASHEM, your God, gives you. May HASHEM open for you His good
treasury, the heaven, to give you rain for your land in its time and to bless your
every handiwork; and may you lend many nations, but may you not borrow.[8]
For HASHEM, your God, will have blessed you as He spoke to you; and may you
make many nations indebted to you, but may you not become indebted; and you
will dominate many nations, but they will not dominate you.[9] Praiseworthy are
you, O Israel, who is like you! — a people saved by God, Who is the Shield of your
help, and Who is the Sword of your majesty. Your enemies will be false with you,
but you will tread upon their heights.[10]

גאולה

**מָחִיתִי** כָעָב פְּשָׁעֶיךָ וְכֶעָנָן חַטֹּאותֶיךָ, שׁוּבָה אֵלַי כִּי גְאַלְתִּיךָ. רָנּוּ שָׁמַיִם, כִּי עָשָׂה יהוה, הָרִיעוּ תַּחְתִּיּוֹת אָרֶץ, פִּצְחוּ הָרִים רִנָּה, יַעַר וְכָל עֵץ בּוֹ, כִּי גָאַל יהוה יַעֲקֹב וּבְיִשְׂרָאֵל יִתְפָּאָר.[1] גֹּאֲלֵנוּ יהוה צְבָאוֹת שְׁמוֹ, קְדוֹשׁ יִשְׂרָאֵל.[2]

ישועה

**יִשְׂרָאֵל** נוֹשַׁע בַּיהוה תְּשׁוּעַת עוֹלָמִים, לֹא תֵבֹשׁוּ וְלֹא תִכָּלְמוּ עַד עוֹלְמֵי עַד.[3] וַאֲכַלְתֶּם אָכוֹל וְשָׂבוֹעַ, וְהִלַּלְתֶּם אֶת שֵׁם יהוה אֱלֹהֵיכֶם אֲשֶׁר עָשָׂה עִמָּכֶם לְהַפְלִיא, וְלֹא יֵבֹשׁוּ עַמִּי לְעוֹלָם. וִידַעְתֶּם כִּי בְקֶרֶב יִשְׂרָאֵל אָנִי, וַאֲנִי יהוה אֱלֹהֵיכֶם, וְאֵין עוֹד, וְלֹא יֵבֹשׁוּ עַמִּי לְעוֹלָם.[4] כִּי בְשִׂמְחָה תֵצֵאוּ וּבְשָׁלוֹם תּוּבָלוּן, הֶהָרִים וְהַגְּבָעוֹת יִפְצְחוּ לִפְנֵיכֶם רִנָּה, וְכָל עֲצֵי הַשָּׂדֶה יִמְחֲאוּ כָף.[5] הִנֵּה אֵל יְשׁוּעָתִי, אֶבְטַח וְלֹא אֶפְחָד, כִּי עָזִּי וְזִמְרָת יָהּ יהוה וַיְהִי לִי לִישׁוּעָה. וּשְׁאַבְתֶּם מַיִם בְּשָׂשׂוֹן, מִמַּעַיְנֵי הַיְשׁוּעָה. וַאֲמַרְתֶּם בַּיּוֹם הַהוּא, הוֹדוּ לַיהוה קִרְאוּ בִשְׁמוֹ, הוֹדִיעוּ בָעַמִּים עֲלִילֹתָיו, הַזְכִּירוּ כִּי נִשְׂגָּב שְׁמוֹ. זַמְּרוּ יהוה כִּי גֵאוּת עָשָׂה, מוּדַעַת זֹאת בְּכָל הָאָרֶץ. צַהֲלִי וָרֹנִּי יוֹשֶׁבֶת צִיּוֹן, כִּי גָדוֹל בְּקִרְבֵּךְ קְדוֹשׁ יִשְׂרָאֵל.[6] וְאָמַר בַּיּוֹם הַהוּא, הִנֵּה אֱלֹהֵינוּ זֶה, קִוִּינוּ לוֹ וְיוֹשִׁיעֵנוּ, זֶה יהוה קִוִּינוּ לוֹ, נָגִילָה וְנִשְׂמְחָה בִּישׁוּעָתוֹ.[7]

דעת ה'

**בֵּית** יַעֲקֹב, לְכוּ וְנֵלְכָה בְּאוֹר יהוה.[8] וְהָיָה אֱמוּנַת עִתֶּיךָ חֹסֶן יְשׁוּעֹת חָכְמַת וָדָעַת, יִרְאַת יהוה הִיא אוֹצָרוֹ.[9] וַיְהִי דָוִד לְכָל דְּרָכָיו מַשְׂכִּיל, וַיהוה עִמּוֹ.[10]

פדיום

**פָּדָה** בְשָׁלוֹם נַפְשִׁי מִקְּרָב לִי, כִּי בְרַבִּים הָיוּ עִמָּדִי.[11] וַיֹּאמֶר הָעָם אֶל שָׁאוּל, הֲיוֹנָתָן יָמוּת אֲשֶׁר עָשָׂה הַיְשׁוּעָה הַגְּדוֹלָה הַזֹּאת בְּיִשְׂרָאֵל, חָלִילָה, חַי יהוה, אִם יִפֹּל מִשַּׂעֲרַת רֹאשׁוֹ אַרְצָה, כִּי עִם אֱלֹהִים עָשָׂה הַיּוֹם הַזֶּה, וַיִּפְדּוּ הָעָם אֶת יוֹנָתָן וְלֹא מֵת.[12] וּפְדוּיֵי יהוה יְשֻׁבוּן, וּבָאוּ צִיּוֹן בְּרִנָּה, וְשִׂמְחַת עוֹלָם עַל רֹאשָׁם, שָׂשׂוֹן וְשִׂמְחָה יַשִּׂיגוּ וְנָסוּ יָגוֹן וַאֲנָחָה.[13]

הפוך צרה

**הָפַכְתָּ** מִסְפְּדִי לְמָחוֹל לִי, פִּתַּחְתָּ שַׂקִּי, וַתְּאַזְּרֵנִי שִׂמְחָה.[14] וְלֹא אָבָה יהוה אֱלֹהֶיךָ לִשְׁמֹעַ אֶל בִּלְעָם, וַיַּהֲפֹךְ יהוה אֱלֹהֶיךָ לְךָ אֶת הַקְּלָלָה לִבְרָכָה, כִּי אֲהֵבְךָ יהוה אֱלֹהֶיךָ.[15] אָז תִּשְׂמַח בְּתוּלָה

### REDEMPTION

**מָחִיתִי** *I have blotted out your willful sins like a thick mist and your errors like a cloud — return to Me for I have redeemed you. Sing gladly, O heaven, for HASHEM has done so; exult, O depths of the earth; break out, O mountains, in glad song, forest and every tree within it, for HASHEM has redeemed Jacob and will take pride in Israel.[1] Our Redeemer — HASHEM, Master of Legions, is His Name — is the Holy One of Israel.[2]*

### SALVATION

**יִשְׂרָאֵל** *Israel is saved by God in an everlasting salvation; they will not be shamed nor humiliated forever and ever.[3] You shall eat food and be satisfied, and you shall praise the Name of HASHEM, your God, Who has done wondrously with you, and My people shall not be shamed forever. And you shall know that in the midst of Israel am I, and I am HASHEM, your God — there is none other; and My people shall not be shamed forever.[4] For in gladness shall you go out and in peace shall you arrive; the mountains and the hills will break out before you in glad song and all the trees of the field will clap hands.[5] Behold! God is my help, I shall trust and not fear — for God is my might and my praise — HASHEM — and He was a salvation to me. You can draw water in joy, from the springs of salvation. And you shall say on that day, "Give thanks to HASHEM, declare His name, make His acts known among the peoples"; remind one another, for His Name is powerful. Make music to HASHEM for He has established grandeur — this is known throughout the earth. Exult and sing for joy, O inhabitant of Zion, for the Holy One of Israel has done greatly among you.[6] And he shall say on that day, "Behold! this is our God, we have hoped for Him, that He would save us — this is HASHEM, we have hoped for Him, we shall rejoice and be glad at His salvation."[7]*

### KNOWLEDGE OF GOD

**בֵּית** *O House of Jacob — come let us go by the light of HASHEM.[8] The stability of your times, the strength of your salvations shall be through knowledge and wisdom, fear of God — that is one's treasure.[9] And David was successful in all his ways, and HASHEM was with him.[10]*

### RESCUE

**פָּדָה** *He redeemed my soul in peace from the battles that were upon me, for the sake of the multitudes who were with me.[11] And the people said to Saul, "Shall Jonathan die, who performed this great salvation for Israel? A sacrilege! — as HASHEM lives, if a hair of his head falls to the ground, for with HASHEM has he acted this day!" And the people redeemed Jonathan and he did not die.[12] Those redeemed by God will return and arrive at Zion with glad song and eternal gladness on their heads; joy and gladness shall they attain, and sorrow and groan shall flee.[13]*

### TRANSFORMATION OF DISTRESS TO RELIEF

**הָפַכְתָּ** *You have changed for me my lament into dancing; You undid my sack-cloth and girded me with gladness.[14] HASHEM, your God, did not wish to pay heed to Balaam, and HASHEM, your God, transformed for you the curse to blessing, for HASHEM, your God, loves you.[15] Then the maiden shall rejoice*

---

(1) *Isaiah* 44:22-23. (2) 47:4. (3) 45:17. (4) *Joel* 2:26-27. (5) *Isaiah* 55:12. (6) 12:2-6. (7) 25:9. (8) 2:5. (9) 33:6. (10) *I Samuel* 18:14. (11) *Psalms* 55:19. (12) *I Samuel* 14:45. (13) *Isaiah* 35:10. (14) *Psalms* 30:12. (15) *Deuteronomy* 23:6.

בְּמָחוֹל, וּבַחֻרִים וּזְקֵנִים יַחְדָּו, וְהָפַכְתִּי אֶבְלָם לְשָׂשׂוֹן, וְנִחַמְתִּים וְשִׂמַּחְתִּים מִיגוֹנָם.¹

שלום

**בּוֹרֵא** נִיב שְׂפָתָיִם, שָׁלוֹם שָׁלוֹם לָרָחוֹק וְלַקָּרוֹב, אָמַר יהוה וּרְפָאתִיו.² וְרוּחַ לָבְשָׁה אֶת עֲמָשַׂי, רֹאשׁ הַשָּׁלִישִׁים, לְךָ דָוִיד וְעִמְּךָ בֶן יִשַׁי שָׁלוֹם, שָׁלוֹם לְךָ, וְשָׁלוֹם לְעֹזְרֶךָ כִּי עֲזָרְךָ אֱלֹהֶיךָ וַיְקַבְּלֵם דָוִיד וַיִּתְּנֵם בְּרָאשֵׁי הַגְּדוּד.³ וַאֲמַרְתֶּם, כֹּה לֶחָי, וְאַתָּה שָׁלוֹם וּבֵיתְךָ שָׁלוֹם וְכֹל אֲשֶׁר לְךָ שָׁלוֹם.⁴ יהוה עֹז לְעַמּוֹ יִתֵּן יהוה יְבָרֵךְ אֶת עַמּוֹ בַשָּׁלוֹם.⁵

מסכת מגילה לא

**אָמַר** רַבִּי יוֹחָנָן: בְּכָל מָקוֹם שֶׁאַתָּה מוֹצֵא גְדֻלָּתוֹ שֶׁל הַקָּדוֹשׁ בָּרוּךְ הוּא, שָׁם אַתָּה מוֹצֵא עַנְוְתָנוּתוֹ. דָּבָר זֶה כָּתוּב בַּתּוֹרָה, וְשָׁנוּי בַּנְּבִיאִים, וּמְשֻׁלָּשׁ בַּכְּתוּבִים. כָּתוּב בַּתּוֹרָה: כִּי יהוה אֱלֹהֵיכֶם הוּא אֱלֹהֵי הָאֱלֹהִים וַאֲדֹנֵי הָאֲדֹנִים, הָאֵל הַגָּדֹל הַגִּבֹּר וְהַנּוֹרָא אֲשֶׁר לֹא יִשָּׂא פָנִים וְלֹא יִקַּח שֹׁחַד.⁶ וּכְתִיב בַּתְרֵהּ: עֹשֶׂה מִשְׁפַּט יָתוֹם וְאַלְמָנָה, וְאֹהֵב גֵּר לָתֶת לוֹ לֶחֶם וְשִׂמְלָה.⁷ שָׁנוּי בַּנְּבִיאִים, דִּכְתִיב: כִּי כֹה אָמַר רָם וְנִשָּׂא שֹׁכֵן עַד וְקָדוֹשׁ שְׁמוֹ, מָרוֹם וְקָדוֹשׁ אֶשְׁכּוֹן, וְאֶת דַּכָּא וּשְׁפַל רוּחַ, לְהַחֲיוֹת רוּחַ שְׁפָלִים וּלְהַחֲיוֹת לֵב נִדְכָּאִים.⁸ מְשֻׁלָּשׁ בַּכְּתוּבִים, דִּכְתִיב: שִׁירוּ לֵאלֹהִים, זַמְּרוּ שְׁמוֹ, סֹלּוּ לָרֹכֵב בָּעֲרָבוֹת, בְּיָהּ שְׁמוֹ, וְעִלְזוּ לְפָנָיו.⁹ וּכְתִיב בַּתְרֵהּ: אֲבִי יְתוֹמִים וְדַיַּן אַלְמָנוֹת, אֱלֹהִים בִּמְעוֹן קָדְשׁוֹ.¹⁰

יְהִי יהוה אֱלֹהֵינוּ עִמָּנוּ כַּאֲשֶׁר הָיָה עִם אֲבֹתֵינוּ, אַל יַעַזְבֵנוּ וְאַל יִטְּשֵׁנוּ.¹¹ וְאַתֶּם הַדְּבֵקִים בַּיהוה אֱלֹהֵיכֶם חַיִּים כֻּלְּכֶם הַיּוֹם.¹² כִּי נִחַם יהוה צִיּוֹן, נִחַם כָּל חָרְבֹתֶיהָ, וַיָּשֶׂם מִדְבָּרָהּ כְּעֵדֶן וְעַרְבָתָהּ כְּגַן יהוה, שָׂשׂוֹן וְשִׂמְחָה יִמָּצֵא בָהּ, תּוֹדָה וְקוֹל זִמְרָה.¹³ יהוה חָפֵץ לְמַעַן צִדְקוֹ, יַגְדִּיל תּוֹרָה וְיַאְדִּיר.¹⁴

תהלים קכח

**שִׁיר הַמַּעֲלוֹת** אַשְׁרֵי כָּל יְרֵא יהוה, הַהֹלֵךְ בִּדְרָכָיו. יְגִיעַ כַּפֶּיךָ כִּי תֹאכֵל, אַשְׁרֶיךָ וְטוֹב לָךְ. אֶשְׁתְּךָ כְּגֶפֶן פֹּרִיָּה בְּיַרְכְּתֵי בֵיתֶךָ, בָּנֶיךָ כִּשְׁתִלֵי זֵיתִים, סָבִיב לְשֻׁלְחָנֶךָ. הִנֵּה כִי כֵן יְבֹרַךְ גֶּבֶר יְרֵא יהוה. יְבָרֶכְךָ יהוה מִצִּיּוֹן וּרְאֵה בְּטוּב יְרוּשָׁלָיִם, כֹּל יְמֵי חַיֶּיךָ. וּרְאֵה בָנִים לְבָנֶיךָ, שָׁלוֹם עַל יִשְׂרָאֵל.

In some congregations mourners recite the Mourner's Kaddish (p. 32) at this point.

(1) Jeremiah 31:12. (2) Isaiah 57:19. (3) I Chronicles 12:19. (4) I Samuel 25:6.
(5) Psalms 29:11. (7) Deuteronomy 10:17. (7) 10:18. (8) Isaiah 57:15. (9) Psalms 68:5.
(10) 68:6. (11) I Kings 8:57. (12) Deuteronomy 4:4. (13) Isaiah 51:3. (14) 42:21.

*in a dance, and lads and elders together; and I shall change their mourning to joy, and I shall console them and gladden them from their sorrow.[1]*

### PEACE

**בּוֹרֵא** *I create fruit of the lips: "Peace, peace, for far and near," says HASHEM, "and I shall heal him."[2] A spirit clothed Amasai, head of the officers, "For your sake, David, and to be with you, son of Jesse; peace, peace to you, and peace to him who helps you, for your God has helped you." David accepted them and appointed them heads of the band.[3] And you shall say: "So may it be as long as you live; peace for you, peace for your household, and peace for all that is with you."[4] HASHEM will give might to His people, HASHEM will bless His people with peace.[5]*

### Talmud, Tractate Megillah 31a

**אָמַר** *Rabbi Yochanan said: Wherever you find the greatness of the Holy One, Blessed is He, there you find His humility. This phenomenon is written in the Torah, repeated in the Prophets, and stated a third time in the Writings. It is written in the Torah: "For HASHEM, your God, He is the God of heavenly forces and the Master of masters, the great, mighty, and awesome God, Who shows no favoritism and accepts no bribe."[6] Afterwards it is written: "He performs justice for orphan and widow, and loves the stranger, to give him food and clothing."[7] It is repeated in the Prophets, as it is written: "For so says the exalted and uplifted One, Who abides forever, and Whose Name is holy, 'I abide in exaltedness and holiness — but am with the contrite and lowly of spirit, to revive the spirit of the lowly and to revive the heart of the contrite.' "[8] And it is stated a third time in the Writings, as it is written: "Sing to God, make music for His Name, extol Him Who rides in the highest heaven, with His Name — God — and exult before Him."[9] Afterwards it is written: "Father of orphans and Judge of widows, God in the habitation of His holiness."[10]*

*May HASHEM, our God, be with us as He was with our forefathers, may He not forsake us nor cast us off.[11] You who cling to HASHEM, our God, are all alive today.[12] For HASHEM comforts Zion, He comforts all her ruins, He will make her wilderness like Eden and her wastes like a garden of HASHEM — joy and gladness will be found there, thanksgiving and the sound of music.[13] HASHEM desired, for the sake of its [Israel's] righteousness, that the Torah be made great and glorious.[14]*

### Psalm 128

**שִׁיר הַמַּעֲלוֹת** *A song of ascents. Praiseworthy is each person who fears HASHEM, who walks in His paths. When you eat the labor of your hands, you are praiseworthy, and it is well with you. Your wife shall be like a fruitful vine in the inner chambers of your home; your children shall be like olive shoots surrounding your table. Behold! For so is blessed the man who fears HASHEM. May HASHEM bless you from Zion, and may you gaze upon the goodness of Jerusalem, all the days of your life. And may you see children born to children, peace upon Israel.*

In some congregations mourners recite the Mourner's *Kaddish* (p. 32) at this point.

IN MANY CONGREGATIONS *CHAZZAN* RECITES *HAVDALAH* AT THE CONCLUSION OF THE SABBATH.

סָבְרִי מָרָנָן וְרַבָּנָן וְרַבּוֹתַי:

**בָּרוּךְ** אַתָּה יהוה אֱלֹהֵינוּ מֶלֶךְ הָעוֹלָם, בּוֹרֵא פְּרִי הַגָּפֶן. (Cong.–אָמֵן.)

After the following blessing smell the spices.

**בָּרוּךְ** אַתָּה יהוה אֱלֹהֵינוּ מֶלֶךְ הָעוֹלָם, בּוֹרֵא מִינֵי בְשָׂמִים. (Cong.–אָמֵן.)

After the following blessing hold fingers up to the flame to see the reflected light:

**בָּרוּךְ** אַתָּה יהוה אֱלֹהֵינוּ מֶלֶךְ הָעוֹלָם, בּוֹרֵא מְאוֹרֵי הָאֵשׁ. (Cong.–אָמֵן.)

**בָּרוּךְ** אַתָּה יהוה אֱלֹהֵינוּ מֶלֶךְ הָעוֹלָם, הַמַּבְדִּיל בֵּין קֹדֶשׁ לְחוֹל, בֵּין אוֹר לְחֹשֶׁךְ, בֵּין יִשְׂרָאֵל לָעַמִּים, בֵּין יוֹם הַשְּׁבִיעִי לְשֵׁשֶׁת יְמֵי הַמַּעֲשֶׂה. בָּרוּךְ אַתָּה יהוה, הַמַּבְדִּיל בֵּין קֹדֶשׁ לְחוֹל. (Cong.–אָמֵן.)

*Chazzan* or someone else present for *Havdalah* drinks most of the cup.

Stand while reciting עָלֵינוּ.

**עָלֵינוּ** לְשַׁבֵּחַ לַאֲדוֹן הַכֹּל, לָתֵת גְּדֻלָּה לְיוֹצֵר בְּרֵאשִׁית, שֶׁלֹּא עָשָׂנוּ כְּגוֹיֵי הָאֲרָצוֹת, וְלֹא שָׂמָנוּ כְּמִשְׁפְּחוֹת הָאֲדָמָה. שֶׁלֹּא שָׂם חֶלְקֵנוּ כָּהֶם, וְגוֹרָלֵנוּ כְּכָל הֲמוֹנָם. (שֶׁהֵם מִשְׁתַּחֲוִים לְהֶבֶל וָרִיק, וּמִתְפַּלְלִים אֶל אֵל לֹא יוֹשִׁיעַ.[1]) וַאֲנַחְנוּ כּוֹרְעִים

Bow while reciting וַאֲנַחְנוּ כּוֹרְעִים וּמִשְׁתַּחֲוִים

וּמִשְׁתַּחֲוִים וּמוֹדִים, לִפְנֵי מֶלֶךְ מַלְכֵי הַמְּלָכִים הַקָּדוֹשׁ בָּרוּךְ הוּא. שֶׁהוּא נוֹטֶה שָׁמַיִם וְיֹסֵד אָרֶץ,[2] וּמוֹשַׁב יְקָרוֹ בַּשָּׁמַיִם מִמַּעַל, וּשְׁכִינַת עֻזּוֹ בְּגָבְהֵי מְרוֹמִים. הוּא אֱלֹהֵינוּ, אֵין עוֹד. אֱמֶת מַלְכֵּנוּ, אֶפֶס זוּלָתוֹ, כַּכָּתוּב בְּתוֹרָתוֹ: וְיָדַעְתָּ הַיּוֹם וַהֲשֵׁבֹתָ אֶל לְבָבֶךָ, כִּי יהוה הוּא הָאֱלֹהִים בַּשָּׁמַיִם מִמַּעַל וְעַל הָאָרֶץ מִתָּחַת, אֵין עוֹד.[3]

**עַל כֵּן** נְקַוֶּה לְּךָ, יהוה אֱלֹהֵינוּ, לִרְאוֹת מְהֵרָה בְּתִפְאֶרֶת עֻזֶּךָ, לְהַעֲבִיר גִּלּוּלִים מִן הָאָרֶץ, וְהָאֱלִילִים כָּרוֹת יִכָּרֵתוּן, לְתַקֵּן עוֹלָם בְּמַלְכוּת שַׁדַּי. וְכָל בְּנֵי בָשָׂר יִקְרְאוּ בִשְׁמֶךָ, לְהַפְנוֹת אֵלֶיךָ כָּל רִשְׁעֵי אָרֶץ. יַכִּירוּ וְיֵדְעוּ כָּל יוֹשְׁבֵי תֵבֵל, כִּי לְךָ תִּכְרַע כָּל בֶּרֶךְ, תִּשָּׁבַע כָּל לָשׁוֹן.[4] לְפָנֶיךָ יהוה אֱלֹהֵינוּ יִכְרְעוּ וְיִפֹּלוּ, וְלִכְבוֹד שִׁמְךָ יְקָר יִתֵּנוּ. וִיקַבְּלוּ כֻלָּם אֶת עוֹל מַלְכוּתֶךָ, וְתִמְלֹךְ עֲלֵיהֶם מְהֵרָה לְעוֹלָם וָעֶד. כִּי הַמַּלְכוּת שֶׁלְּךָ הִיא וּלְעוֹלְמֵי עַד תִּמְלוֹךְ בְּכָבוֹד, כַּכָּתוּב בְּתוֹרָתֶךָ: יהוה יִמְלֹךְ לְעֹלָם וָעֶד.[5] ❖ וְנֶאֱמַר: וְהָיָה יהוה לְמֶלֶךְ עַל כָּל הָאָרֶץ, בַּיּוֹם הַהוּא יִהְיֶה יהוה אֶחָד וּשְׁמוֹ אֶחָד.[6]

**אַל תִּירָא** מִפַּחַד פִּתְאֹם, וּמִשֹּׁאַת רְשָׁעִים כִּי תָבֹא.[7] עֻצוּ עֵצָה וְתֻפָר, דַּבְּרוּ דָבָר וְלֹא יָקוּם, כִּי עִמָּנוּ אֵל.[8] וְעַד זִקְנָה אֲנִי הוּא, וְעַד שֵׂיבָה אֲנִי אֶסְבֹּל, אֲנִי עָשִׂיתִי וַאֲנִי אֶשָּׂא, וַאֲנִי אֶסְבֹּל וַאֲמַלֵּט.[9]

In the presence of a *minyan*, mourners recite קַדִּישׁ יָתוֹם, the Mourner's *Kaddish* (p. 32).

IN MANY CONGREGATIONS *CHAZZAN* RECITES *HAVDALAH* AT THE CONCLUSION OF THE SABBATH.

By your leave, my masters and teachers:

בָּרוּךְ Blessed are You, HASHEM, our God, King of the universe, Who creates the fruit of the vine. *(Cong. — Amen.)*

After the following blessing smell the spices.

בָּרוּךְ Blessed are You, HASHEM, our God, King of the universe, Who creates species of fragrance. *(Cong. — Amen.)*

After the following blessing hold fingers up to the flame to see the reflected light:

בָּרוּךְ Blessed are You, HASHEM, our God, King of the universe, Who creates the illuminations of the fire. *(Cong. — Amen.)*

בָּרוּךְ Blessed are You, HASHEM, our God, King of the universe, Who separates between holy and secular, between light and darkness, between Israel and the nations, between the seventh day and the six days of labor. Blessed are You, HASHEM, Who separates between holy and secular. *(Cong. — Amen.)*

*Chazzan* or someone else present for *Havdalah* drinks most of the cup.

Stand while reciting עָלֵינוּ, "It is our duty . . ."

**עָלֵינוּ** It is our duty to praise the Master of all, to ascribe greatness to the Molder of primeval creation, for He has not made us like the nations of the lands and has not emplaced us like the families of the earth; for He has not assigned our portion like theirs nor our lot like all their multitudes. *(For they bow to vanity and emptiness*

Bow while reciting "But we bend our knees." *and pray to a god which helps not.* [1]*) But we bend our knees, bow, and acknowledge our thanks before the King Who reigns over kings, the Holy One, Blessed is He. He stretches out heaven and establishes earth's foundation,* [2] *the seat of His homage is in the heavens above and His powerful Presence is in the loftiest heights. He is our God and there is none other. True is our King, there is nothing beside Him, as it is written in His Torah: "You are to know this day and take to your heart that HASHEM is the only God — in heaven above and on the earth below — there is none other."* [3]

**עַל כֵּן** Therefore we put our hope in You, HASHEM, our God, that we may soon see Your mighty splendor, to remove detestable idolatry from the earth, and false gods will be utterly cut off, to perfect the universe through the Almighty's sovereignty. Then all humanity will call upon Your Name, to turn all the earth's wicked toward You. All the world's inhabitants will recognize and know that to You every knee should bend, every tongue should swear. [4] Before You, HASHEM, our God, they will bend every knee and cast themselves down, and to the glory of Your Name they will render homage, and they will all accept upon themselves the yoke of Your kingship that You may reign over them soon and eternally. For the kingdom is Yours and You will reign for all eternity in glory, as it is written in Your Torah: HASHEM shall reign for all eternity. [5] *Chazzan —* And it is said: HASHEM will be King over all the world — on that day HASHEM will be One and His Name will be One. [6]

**אַל תִּירָא** Do not fear sudden terror, or the holocaust of the wicked when it comes. [7] Plan a conspiracy and it will be annulled; speak your piece and it shall not stand, for God is with us. [8] Even till your seniority, I remain unchanged; and even till your ripe old age, I shall endure. I created you and I shall bear you; I shall endure and rescue. [9]

In the presence of a *minyan*, mourners recite the Mourner's *Kaddish* (p. 32).

---

(1) *Isaiah* 45:20. (2) 51:13. (3) *Deuteronomy* 4:39. (4) Cf. *Isaiah* 45:23. (5) *Exodus* 15:18. (6) *Zechariah* 14:9. (7) *Proverbs* 3:25. (8) *Isaiah* 8:10. (9) 46:4.

MW00649646

This volume is part of
THE ARTSCROLL SERIES®
an ongoing project of
translations, commentaries and expositions
on Scripture, Mishnah, Talmud, Halachah,
liturgy, history, the classic Rabbinic writings,
biographies and thought.

For a brochure of current publications
visit your local Hebrew bookseller
or contact the publisher:

## Mesorah Publications, ltd

4401 Second Avenue
Brooklyn, New York 11232
(718) 921-9000
www.artscroll.com